Callaghan's Journey to Downing Street

Callaghan's Journey to Downing Street

Paul J. Deveney

First published 2010 by
PALGRAVE MACMILLAN

Palgrave Macmillan in the UK is an imprint of Macmillan Publishers Limited,
registered in England, company number 785998, of Houndmills, Basingstoke,
Hampshire RG21 6XS.

Palgrave Macmillan in the US is a division of St Martin's Press LLC,
175 Fifth Avenue, New York, NY 10010.

Palgrave Macmillan is the global academic imprint of the above companies
and has companies and representatives throughout the world.

Palgrave® and Macmillan® are registered trademarks in the United States,
the United Kingdom, Europe and other countries.

ISBN-13: 978-0-230-57958-3 hardback

This book is printed on paper suitable for recycling and made from fully
managed and sustained forest sources. Logging, pulping and manufacturing
processes are expected to conform to the environmental regulations of the
country of origin.

A catalogue record for this book is available from the British Library.

Library of Congress Cataloging-in-Publication Data
Deveney, Paul J.,
    Callaghan's journey to Downing Street / Paul J. Deveney.
        p. cm.
    Includes bibliographical references and index.
    ISBN 978-0-230-57958-3
    1. Callaghan, James, 1912-2005. 2. Great Britain—Politics and
government—1945– 3. Labour Party (Great Britain)—History—
20th century 4. Prime ministers—Great Britain—Biography.
    5. Finance ministers—Great Britain—Biography. 6. Politicians—Great
Britain—Biography. I. Title.
DA591.C34D48 2010
941.085'7092—dc22
    [B]   2010023752

10   9   8   7   6   5   4   3   2   1
19 18 17 16 15 14 13 12 11 10

Printed and bound in Great Britain by
CPI Antony Rowe, Chippenham and Eastbourne

For Ed, the artist, and Eleanor, the poet

Contents

Preface

Downing Street is one of the most famous dead-end streets in the world. In October 1964, James Callaghan began his ministerial career at No. 11, the home and office of the Chancellor of the Exchequer, then the second most powerful post in the British government. After he was forced to resign in November 1967, amid a string of policy failures that led to the devaluation of the pound, he held other great offices of state. But it took him nearly a decade to return home to Downing Street, and when he did he would be ensconced next door at No. 10, the home and office of Britain's Prime Minister. This is the episodic story of that journey which begins and ends in Downing Street.

Paul J. Deveney

Acknowledgements

This project owes a debt of gratitude to those archivists and institutions that granted me permission to access their collections. They include the British Library of Political & Economic Science, the Bodleian Library at Oxford University, the John Rylands Library at the University of Manchester, the British Library, the Public Records Office at the National Archives of the United Kingdom, the National Archives of Ireland, the Labour History Archive and Study Centre, the archives of Churchill College at Cambridge University, the Institute of Historical Research, the Guardian News & Media Archive, the BBC Written Archives, and the Library of Congress. It should be gratefully noted that some of the work in Dublin was assisted by a grant from the University of London's Central Research Fund and that additional funding for later research work at Cambridge University was provided by the University of Pennsylvania.

I am also appreciative to the former Cabinet ministers, Members of Parliament, senior civil servants, trade union officials, journalists and others who agreed to be interviewed for this project. They are noted in the bibliography. Some have been quoted in the text, but all provided insights and understanding on an important period in post-war history. Thanks is extended as well to those who provided invaluable suggestions after reading parts or all of the manuscript, in particular Professor David Edgerton of Imperial College, Professor John Young of the University of Nottingham, and two anonymous readers commissioned by the publisher, Palgrave Macmillan. All of their comments were taken into consideration, although the opinions expressed throughout are mine. Parts of the manuscript were also read by two individuals with no connection to the academy but whose good sense and advice I value. They are Bill McIlwain and Thomas E. Joseph.

Since this manuscript had to be completed amid my teaching responsibilities, a word of thanks must be extended to my colleagues at the Center for Programs in Contemporary Writing at the University of Pennsylvania. Their understanding and patience, particularly in the final stages of this project, was greatly appreciated. As was the help of several individuals at Palgrave Macmillan, including the two commissioning editors Amy Lankester-Owen and Alison Howson and their associate Liz Blackmore. I am also grateful for the wit and wisdom of Antonio Silverio, whose travel advice, information technology skills and encouragement helped bring this project to fruition.

In closing, I must note that this book is a work deeply rooted in my relationship with the London School of Economics, an institution with historical ties to the Labour Party and hence an ideal environment from which to pursue such an endeavour. I am indebted to two individuals in particular at the LSE: the late Professor Gordon Smith, who was my tutor and a great inspiration to me when I studied for a master's degree in the Government Department in the 1980s. He read and commented on much of the material. As has Dr Alan Sked, of the International History Department, who gave me wise counsel then and, more recently, served as my doctoral adviser. Without Alan's support this project would not have been possible.

Cast of Characters

Philip Allen was a senior civil servant who, as the permanent secretary at the Home Office from 1966 to 1972, worked closely with Roy Jenkins and Callaghan. When Callaghan became Prime Minister, he made Allen a life peer.

George Brown placed second to Harold Wilson in the 1963 leadership contest. He was the first head of the Department of Economic Affairs, a ministry set up by Wilson to rival Callaghan and the Treasury, and became Foreign Secretary in 1966. A struggle with alcoholism led him to impulsive behaviour and triggered one too many threats to resign. He left the government in 1968 and lost his seat in Parliament in 1970.

James Callaghan held all the great offices of state: Chancellor of the Exchequer, Home Secretary, Foreign Secretary and Prime Minister. He was a member of Parliament from Cardiff constituencies from 1945 to 1987, when he was made a life peer.

Barbara Castle served first as Transport Minister and then as Secretary of Employment and Productivity, where she became the chief architect of *In Place of Strife*, the plan to reform the trade unions. She and Callaghan were often at odds during the Wilson years; one of Callaghan's first acts as Prime Minister was to request her resignation from the Cabinet.

John Cole, as the trusted No. 2 man at the *Guardian*, shaped much of the newspaper's editorial stance on the big issues of the day, including trade union reform and Northern Ireland.

Tony Crosland wrote *The Future of Socialism*, and was the Labour Party's intellectual. He was a close friend of Jenkins from their days at Oxford, but that relationship was strained by their rivalry in the Cabinet. Crosland always had a good relationship with Callaghan, whom he had supported in the 1963 leadership fight. When Callaghan became Prime Minister, he selected Crosland to be his Foreign Secretary.

Richard Crossman served as Lord President and Leader of the House of Commons, among other posts. He was a close ally of Wilson and had utter disdain for Callaghan in his early days at the Home Office, but came to admire his resiliency. Crossman's *Diaries of a Cabinet Minister* became a bestseller and gave the public a window into the day-to-day workings of the Cabinet.

Joe Haines, a former reporter for the *Sun* newspaper, was Wilson's press secretary and an influential adviser to the Prime Minister.

Denis Healey was the only major office holder in the Labour Cabinets of the 1960s and the 1970s to have remained at a ministry throughout an entire government. He was Secretary of Defence from 1964 to 1970 and, along with Callaghan, was a key figure when the Troubles erupted in Northern Ireland. When Labour was returned to power in 1974, Healey became Chancellor of the Exchequer and remained there until 1979.

Alastair Hetherington, the unassuming editor of the *Guardian* newspaper, had considerable influence, albeit in an indirect way, in Labour Party politics. He had many meetings with Wilson, Callaghan and other political figures in the 1960s and 1970s.

Douglas Houghton chaired the Parliamentary Labour Party from 1967 to 1970. He was a mentor to Callaghan in the 1930s, when Houghton was the general secretary of the Inland Revenue staff federation and Callaghan an official in that union.

Roy Jenkins played an important role in reforming the laws on censorship, abortion and homosexuality when he was Home Secretary in the 1960s. When Callaghan was forced to resign as Chancellor in 1967 over devaluation, Wilson had Callaghan and Jenkins swap jobs. As Jenkins's influence grew, the rivalry between him and Callaghan grew as well.

Jack Lynch was Prime Minister of the Republic of Ireland during the outbreak of the Troubles in 1969.

Tom McCaffrey, a career civil servant, was one of Callaghan's closest advisers. He was Callaghan's press secretary at the Home Office, the Foreign Office and at No. 10 Downing Street.

Harry Nicholas, a trade union official, became the general secretary of the Labour Party in 1968, after he defeated Anthony Greenwood, Wilson's candidate for the job. He and Callaghan became particularly close during the debate over *In Place of Strife*.

Michael Stewart was a utility player in the Wilson governments of the 1960s where he held a variety of Cabinet posts. He was Foreign Secretary twice, once from 1965 to 1966 and again from 1968 to 1970.

Marcia Williams became a power in her own right at Downing Street. She was Harold Wilson's personal secretary, but, earlier in her career, had actually worked briefly for Callaghan.

Harold Wilson led the Labour Party to victory in the general election in 1964 and again in 1966 before losing the premiership in an upset in 1970. He became Prime Minister again in 1974, and a year and a half later unexpectedly resigned.

1
Introduction

James Callaghan's greatest accomplishment was not what he achieved at No. 10 Downing Street, but how he had managed to get there in the first place. After all, his three years as Prime Minister in the late 1970s were marked by an unbroken series of economic problems. His premiership, the last the Labour Party would see for nearly a generation, was overshadowed by that of Margaret Thatcher, whose early success was built, in part, on being everything that her predecessor was not. Callaghan had the distinction of being the only premier of the twentieth century to have arrived at Downing Street having held all the great offices of state. But after he resigned as Chancellor of the Exchequer in 1967 over devaluation – swapping jobs with the then Home Secretary Roy Jenkins – most observers would agree that it was the youthful, Oxford-educated Jenkins, not Callaghan, who turned out to be the far better Chancellor. Few would disagree either that it was Jenkins, not Callaghan, who proved to be the better Home Secretary. So how was it that Callaghan, a former official for a white-collar civil service union, managed to become Prime Minister at all?

That is a question that has not been given proper attention by historians. Despite Callaghan's political recovery, there are surprisingly few serious works that focus entirely on Callaghan and even fewer that deal with the critical period leading up to his premiership. Those that do, often place greater emphasis on his policies than his political strategies. In that sense an important piece of the puzzle has been missing, particularly since Callaghan's genius had much more to do with political manoeuvring than any profound struggle over matters of policy. Therefore this book, in analysing his comeback, makes a contribution, however humble, to the works on Callaghan and the British Labour Party in two distinct ways: first, by examining an important area of

1

British history that at best has been misunderstood and at worst has been neglected, and, secondly, by responding to the evidence in this case in such a way as to give greater weight to Callaghan's politics over his policies.

Some of the events documented in these pages are addressed in Callaghan's "official" biography, his autobiography and in other works of history. I invite readers to revisit those earlier projects, which in most cases present a very different interpretation of the events leading to his political recovery. Ultimately, it is for the reader to weigh the evidence and make the final judgement. Obviously, not all political figures can be studied in the same way. While the private papers of one politician can be revelatory, even when the material is inaccurate or intentionally altered, the papers of another politician can be less helpful. The material that Callaghan left behind falls into that second category, at least for the events covered in these pages. As such, he is a difficult figure to understand – and probably intentionally so. Yet it is in the public and private papers and documents from a vast range of other sources held at London, Oxford, Manchester, Dublin and elsewhere that a credible – and, I think, a convincing – case can be made to explain the political recovery that emerged between his resignation from the Treasury in 1967 and his election as party leader nearly a decade later.

There are numerous examples of politicians who rise to the challenge after attaining the highest office in the land and manage to elevate themselves to statesmen. Was Callaghan such a politician? Possibly, but such an evaluation goes beyond the focus of this study. One thing is certain: Callaghan in his journey to Downing Street was a great political tactician. His skill as a political operator was in knowing when to take advantage of a developing crisis. He had an uncanny ability to see each crisis – whether the anti-Vietnam war protests in Grosvenor Square, trade union reform, the Troubles in Northern Ireland or Britain remaining in the European Economic Community – as an opportunity to move up the next rung of the ladder and to use that crisis to further consolidate his power and, in so doing, curb the influence of his rivals.

Unlike Richard Crossman, Jenkins, Barbara Castle, Tony Benn, Denis Healey, Tony Crosland and others in the Wilson governments, Callaghan was neither a writer, nor a historian, nor an economist, nor a political philosopher. Harold Wilson and most of the others represented a new breed of Labour MP that shaped their political views in the common rooms of Oxford colleges rather than in the shipyards of Liverpool or the coal mines of South Wales. While Jenkins, Crosland and Healey spent their formative years debating politics and economic theory at Oxford, Callaghan as a young man had a secondary education and worked as a tax clerk for the Board of Inland Revenue. He was not part of the Oxbridge crowd. And, despite a life-long identification with the trade unions, he was not fully embraced by trade union leaders either; they had been manual workers who had risen to prominent positions in powerful unions, while his ties to the movement had been as a white-collar worker who became an assistant secretary in a clerical union.[1]

Callaghan was first elected to Parliament in 1945, when the Labour Party surprised the world and itself by soundly defeating the Conservatives only a few months after the end of the war in Europe. With Winston Churchill gone and Clement Attlee in, Callaghan was able to secure junior ministerial posts at the Ministry of Transport and then the Admiralty. When Labour was defeated in 1951, he continued to ally himself with the trade unions and steadily rose through the party ranks to become an increasingly important figure in the opposition, first as shadow Colonial Secretary and later as shadow Chancellor of the Exchequer, a post to which he was appointed by his mentor, Labour Party leader Hugh Gaitskell. After Gaitskell's untimely death in 1963, Callaghan entered the race to be Gaitskell's successor, coming in third after Wilson and George Brown.

How Callaghan managed to eventually make it to No. 10 Downing Street after the biggest political setback of his career is a story that has been lost in the advent of New Labour and the general feeling that Callaghan's years as Prime Minister, which were plagued by the IMF crisis and the "Winter of Discontent", were an unsuccessful chapter in Labour Party history. Yet the political recovery that he made after having to resign as Chancellor was remarkable. So why has it been neglected for so long by historians?[2] For one thing, interest in Callaghan, after his troubled premiership, quickly faded. Thatcher was perceived as a much

---

[1] *Northern Echo*, 13 May 1983. Callaghan said that the books that shaped his political thinking in the 1930s included the short stories of Rudyard Kipling, Harold Laski's *Grammar of Politics* and the prefaces to the plays of Bernard Shaw, which Callaghan saw as "challenging notions and new ideas for a young man without a university education".

[2] The topic was addressed by two British journalists Peter Kellner and Christopher Hitchens in their book *Callaghan: The Road to Number 10* (London, 1976). The book was published at the start of Callaghan's premiership and makes some interesting observations about Callaghan's methods, but obviously the authors did not have the perspective that time provides nor the access to documents that have since become available.

stronger leader who was willing to challenge the post-war consensus to secure economic recovery, and as such attracted greater attention from a generation of historians. As for Callaghan's recovery, much of the saga escaped the attention of his colleagues and the press because it was effected behind the scenes amid multifaceted issues that were well suited to manoeuvrability.

After he left the Treasury in 1967, some observers attribute Callaghan's political comeback, which began at the Home Office, to his success in dealing with a single event, such as the anti-Vietnam war protests at Grosvenor Square in 1968, or a single issue, such as Northern Ireland. But it was more complex than that. It went through many stages and took place over many years and there was a thread that kept it together. Secondly, although no politician – as clever as he or she might be – can stand apart from the issues or the actions of those around them, Callaghan was better than most at taking advantage of the situation in which he found himself. That greatly aided him in his efforts to recast his political fortunes and put him in the position of being the only logical successor when Wilson surprised the nation by resigning the premiership in March 1976, a mere year and a half after the government had been re-elected. Finally, Callaghan, from the time he left the Treasury in November 1967 until the time, when as Foreign Secretary, he reached the end of his rehabilitation in 1975, demonstrated a profound understanding of the mechanics of the political system – hence the emphasis here on politics rather than policy.

However, this is not a book about one politician scheming his way to the top. Rather, it is a book that by studying a single politician provides important insights into a singular politician's relationship with the British Labour Party, in principle one of more democratic, innovative political organisations in the world. To this day, the Labour Party is evolving, and any comprehensive understanding of it must take into consideration a part of its history that until now has not been told. Gaining a more realistic view of such a formidable figure within the party – albeit a secondary figure as long as Wilson was in office – sheds light not only on the role of the political party, which as an institution is far more all-encompassing in the United Kingdom than the United States, but the Westminster model of government itself. Therefore, the story of Callaghan's political recovery is a story abundant in its insights into party, politics, Parliament, Cabinet, the press, the trade unions, and even the uncomfortable role that Britain found itself in when dealing with its former colonies.

Callaghan's private secretary said in May 2003 that despite my "repeated request for an interview with Lord Callaghan himself on the subject...he really does feel that he has covered the period very thoroughly in print already".[3] Although Kenneth Morgan, Callaghan's biographer, acknowledged in March 2004 that Callaghan's mind was still sharp, he agreed that an interview with the former Prime Minister for this book was not necessary,[4] "What he thought is sort of in my book and in my notes in my book and I don't think there will be anything much more really."[5] Morgan might have been right. Callaghan's unwillingness either to agree to an interview or to ease the way for the provision of at least some of his private papers for this study prior to their public release seemed at first to be a considerable obstacle. But as the findings from various areas of the research converged, the lack of candour on Callaghan's part became understandable.[6]

Of course, the interviews conducted for this book have to be viewed with the understanding that time and distance often mellow old adversaries or create new ones. Also, in any oral history, individual interpretations of events are likely to lose some significance as details fade from memory. With that in mind, none of the interviews conducted for this book was based on unnamed sources. As far as possible, the questioning of individuals was made with careful consideration of the need to corroborate the responses with other interviewees and other primary sources. However, that should never stand in the way of a researcher keeping an open mind, even when faced with what might seem to be an outrageous comment. As many historians have discovered, statements that at first seem deeply partisan and less reliable can gain validity, or at least provide hints, as the pieces of the puzzle begin to fall in place. One of the earliest interviews conducted for this project

---

[3] Letter to the author from Gina Page, private secretary to Lord Callaghan, 29 May 2003.

[4] Callaghan died in March 2005.

[5] Interview with Lord Morgan, 30 March 2004. Morgan had "many, many, many" interviews with Callaghan over an extended period, but no recording devices were used. "I did start with one. Jim was immediately ill at ease, so I just switched it off. I thought it was better to have a conversation and like you take notes and if he said anything particularly striking – which he quite often did – I tried to have it verbatim." Neither Morgan nor anyone else formally interviewed for this project raised any objection to the conversation being recorded.

[6] Callaghan was helpful in providing some limited insights in correspondence with the author. Also, it should be mentioned that while refusing to be interviewed, he did suggest that the author speak with his former press secretary, Tom McCaffrey, and the former permanent secretary at Home Office, Philip Allen. That suggestion was taken and interviews were conducted with both of those individuals, in the case of Allen a follow-up meeting was held two months later.

was with the former Labour MP Leo Abse, who was especially harsh in his criticism of the former Prime Minister, and whose comments seemed blatantly unfair, particularly when compared with the remembrances of others who knew Callaghan as well or better. It was only after this project was well under way that the *tone* of some of Abse's comments was fully appreciated for providing valuable insight into Callaghan's political fluidity.

Although Callaghan denied repeated requests for interviews, family members were more cooperative. Peter Jay, his former son-in-law who was Britain's ambassador to the United States during Callaghan's premiership, did agree to a meeting, as did Callaghan's daughter Margaret Jay, the former leader of the Labour Party in the House of Lords. In her case, however, it is not clear that she ever intended to give the interview, which had been arranged through a personal assistant; when the appointed hour came, it was clear that she had expected to be giving an interview to a different person on a different subject. When the other party did not arrive, she graciously agreed to go ahead with the interview despite what was obviously a bureaucratic mix-up. In the case of Margaret Jay, her reluctance to be interviewed about her father might be explained by her disdain for politics, which she feels is "extremely destructive of the rest of your life. And if you are engaged in it for 50 years or so you can have enormous success and fulfilment in your professional life but it doesn't leave you a lot of time for a lot of other things."[7]

While nearly all the former Labour Cabinet ministers who were approached – Healey, Merlyn Rees, Tony Benn, Roy Hattersley, Richard Marsh, Dick Taverne and William Rodgers – agreed to talk about Callaghan, one of the more significant figures from that period who did not was Michael Foot. A leading figure on the left in the Labour Party, who eventually won the leadership and led Labour into the 1983 general election, Foot was close not only to Callaghan but to Castle, a Cabinet minister who became one of Callaghan's staunchest rivals. Foot apologised, saying that he had "taken on rather too many commitments at the moment",[8] one of which apparently involved Morgan, who at the time was writing an "official" biography of Foot similar to the book undertaken about Callaghan. Obviously, Foot would have been a valuable resource, given his frankness and genuine reputation for veracity,

---

[7] Interview with Lady Jay, 3 March 2004.
[8] Letter to the author from Michael Foot, 20 May 2002. A follow-up request for an interview went unanswered.

although he is also known to be reluctant to criticise Callaghan,[9] whom he had served faithfully during Callaghan's premiership.

On the other hand, a few years before his death in April 2009, Jack Jones, the former general secretary of the Transport and General Workers' Union (TGWU), agreed to meet at Transport House, the trade union's headquarters in central London, at three important stages in the project. Those interviews were invaluable because, at one level, Jones was an insider with intimate knowledge of Callaghan and the Labour governments while, at another level, he was an outsider looking in. Unfortunately, Roy Jenkins died just as this project was conceived and, of course, Crosland had died a quarter of a century earlier. But both their wives, Jennifer Jenkins and Susan Barnes Crosland, agreed to be interviewed[10] at their homes in London and conveyed a sense of their husbands' passion for politics and the depth of their husbands' relationships with Callaghan.

It is important to mention that this period of British history was also enriched by the preponderance of titles available from Fleet Street. Publications like the *Daily Mirror*, a popular newspaper that sold five million copies a day and was passionately pro-Labour, the *Daily Mail*, *The Times*, the *Guardian*, the *Daily Telegraph*, the *Sun*, and the *Daily Express* were still closely read. That was true as well for the Sunday papers, which included *The Sunday Times* and the *Observer*, the serious-minded broadsheet owned by Roy Jenkins's friend David Astor.[11] Although the BBC and independent television were certainly changing the way the nation's affairs were being conducted, the newspaper industry remained feisty in the late 1960s and early 1970s and was still highly influential in political discourse, particularly quality newspapers like *The Times* on the centre right and the *Guardian* on the centre left. The newspaper archival material, much of which came from collections at the University of London, the Library of Congress in the United States and the archives of the

---

[9] Interview with Paul Foot, 23 April 2004. The maverick journalist Paul Foot, Michael Foot's nephew, said that he and his uncle often sharply disagreed over Callaghan, whom Paul Foot felt was a politician whose dealings were not always above board. Paul Foot, who was on the staff of *Private Eye*, died a short time after that interview.

[10] Susan Crosland provided the author with access to diaries that had not been previously available. The material is held in the archives of the British Library of Political & Economic Science, with the rest of her husband's private papers.

[11] In addition to the mainstream press, *Tribune* had a very special and influential role in Labour Party politics during this period.

city library in Dublin,[12] was valuable in framing the debate and helped to put much of the voluminous material from government and private collections into context. The same is true, although more selectively, for the written archival material of the BBC, held at Caversham, near Reading.

Although Callaghan was the exception to the rule, one of the advantages in studying the politics of this period, which covers 1967 to 1975, is a vast and spirited collection of first-person accounts that emanate from a colourful cast of characters the likes of which Britain will never see assembled around a Cabinet table again. At the ministerial level, the published diaries of Crossman, Benn and Castle are a wonderful glimpse of history. It is really the first time in any British government where you have three keen observers, all of whom are involved in the most intimate workings of the government, recording day-by-day the same events from different perspectives. For the purposes of this research, the material of the three diarists, two of whom had a background in journalism,[13] is particularly valuable because Callaghan is so often a central character in each of the voluminous accounts.

In addition, there are many ministerial memoirs – beginning with those written by Wilson, Jenkins, Healey, George Brown and Michael Stewart, and ending with figures who turned out to be less consequential, like Marsh – and they all add a powerful dimension to the story. Callaghan features quite prominently in all of them. The richness of these volumes, along with the memoirs of prominent backbenchers, is that they, too, provide great insight into the political intrigues of the time and they are incredibly valuable in that many of these people can no longer be interviewed. Also, what makes them so profoundly interesting is the fact that in some cases they are not merely the reflections of senior statesman at the end of their days, but the riveting accounts of ambitious politicians who were still central to the national debate.

---

[12] The Dublin archive made available original copies of the major Irish newspapers for the late 1960s and early 1970s, when the Troubles in Northern Ireland were at a critical point.
[13] Crossman had a long association with the *New Statesman*, and became its editor when Labour was defeated in the 1970 general election; Castle joined the staff of the *Daily Mirror* in 1944.

2
The Swap: From Treasury to Home Office

From the time that Labour won the October 1964 general election, it was confronted with the possibility of devaluation. The preceding Tory administration had left the state of Britain's finances in disarray. It was clear to the incoming Labour government that devaluation had to be seriously considered if British products were to remain competitive globally. But the narrowness of Labour's victory, with a mere four-seat overall majority in Parliament, led Harold Wilson, the Prime Minister, James Callaghan, the Chancellor of the Exchequer, and George Brown, the Secretary of State for Economic Affairs, to agree not to tackle the problem head on; although had they done so, the necessity to devalue could have been blamed on the Conservatives. Britain had devalued twice before under a Labour Prime Minister in the twentieth century; once in 1931 during the Depression under Ramsay MacDonald and again in 1949, when post-war economic turmoil left the Attlee government no alternative but to undertake a deep devaluation of sterling.

The Wilson government, in its first three years in office, did everything it could to avoid devaluation, including "adopting import surcharges, deflationary measures and borrowing from the International Monetary Fund".[1] Yet none of these moves addressed the worsening underlying problems. The government finally had no choice but to give up the fight. It devalued the currency by 14.8 per cent on 18 November 1967. That devaluation was much less than the previous one in 1949. Even so, the fact that a Labour government had been forced

---

[1] Stephen Broadberry, "Economy Policy" in *Britain Since 1945*, edited by Jonathan Hollowell (Oxford, 2003), p. 361.

to devalue after promising not to do so shook confidence on world markets. It also meant that Callaghan's days as Chancellor were numbered and that there was the possibility he would leave the government altogether.

But in the dark days immediately after devaluation the beleaguered Chancellor had a political lifeline tossed to him from an unusual quarter. It came from a newspaper column in *The Times*, one of the leading quality newspapers in the United Kingdom. The author of that column, Peter Jay, was the newspaper's economics editor and a rising star in Fleet Street. He was also Callaghan's son-in-law. Jay used his column on 23 November to minimise Callaghan's role in the debacle by vigorously challenging the Prime Minister's contention that he and the Chancellor had been *equal* partners in the failed policies that had left the government with no choice but to devalue.

Jay had been a civil servant in the Treasury before he left government service to join *The Times* in April 1967. In the column, Jay reported that Wilson ignored the advice of his economic team in 1965 and again a year later. He wrote that the Prime Minister had been so fearful that the Labour Party would be brandished the party of devaluation, after its earlier actions in 1931 and 1949, that Wilson had ordered the destruction in 1966 of all copies but one of a damning internal memorandum on government monetary policy. Jay wrote that Wilson had refused to allow any discussion among his Cabinet ministers about devaluing the pound, leaving Callaghan, his loyal Chancellor, "naked to mine enemies".[2] The column headlined "Devaluation – Who Was to Blame?" and the continuing coverage of it in *The Times* and elsewhere in the news media seriously undermined the official version of events being put out by Downing Street. The column struck at the soft underbelly of an already weakened administration and it came at an opportune moment for Callaghan, a man whose appointment as Chancellor in 1964 had more to do with his influence in the party rather than any knowledge or interest in monetary or economic policy.

Callaghan denied being the source of that column. And his son-in-law, in an appearance on the *Frost Programme* on the evening of the day the article appeared, denied that as well. Jay, whose father, Douglas Jay, had a few months earlier been sacked by Wilson from the Cabinet post of President of the Board of Trade, told the programme's host, David Frost, that there had been "absolutely no collusion or foreknowledge on

---

[2] *The Times*, 23 November 1967, p. 24.

[Callaghan's] part at all"[3] regarding the column. Such a ploy on the part of Callaghan to rehabilitate himself after the government's decision to devalue seemed so unlikely that Frost readily concurred with Jay's statement. Frost told his television audience: "I think a good politician would feel it was a bit obvious to choose his son-in-law. Just fractionally."

The Labour MP Michael Foot was also a guest on the programme. Foot, who had advocated devaluation for years, agreed with Frost on two points: he did not feel that Jay had been less than honourable in reporting the facts, nor that Callaghan had been in any way involved in the disclosures that appeared in *The Times*.[4] But Foot, the long-time editor of *Tribune*, the weekly newspaper of the Labour Party left, questioned the premise of the column, saying that Jay might have unintentionally "misled his readers" by having suggested that Callaghan was any less fervent in his opposition to devaluation than the Prime Minister. "That is the reason for bringing in Shakespeare at the end," Foot said. He added that Jay had played into the hands of a small minority in the party who were eager to take advantage of Wilson's troubles. Foot was referring to those of his fellow Labour MPs who saw the crisis over devaluation, oddly enough, as an opportunity to replace Wilson with Callaghan.

Although it is not possible to establish any involvement on Callaghan's part in the article that appeared in *The Times*, the documents from an internal Whitehall investigation[5] indicate that senior civil servants were not entirely convinced that Jay obtained the information in the way that he had said he had, that is in his "normal journalistic work" after he had resigned from the Civil Service.[6] Nor had they been convinced of Jay's statement that the disclosures in his column had "nothing whatever to do with the fact" that he had been a civil servant.[7] In the days immediately after devaluation, there were two major news stories that restored some credibility to Callaghan's standing as Chancellor and might have prevented Wilson from moving him

---

[3] PRO, PREM 13/2931. Transcript of *Frost Programme*, Rediffusion Television, 23 November 1967. In the copy of the transcript delivered to the Prime Minister, the references to the comments concerning Callaghan had been underlined for Wilson's attention.

[4] PRO, PREM 13/2931. Transcript of *Frost Programme*, Rediffusion Television, 23 November 1967.

[5] PRO, PREM 13/2931, behind Folio 7. Note for the record from Sir Laurence Helsby, 14 December 1967.

[6] PRO, PREM 13/2931. Transcript of *Frost Programme*, Rediffusion Television, 23 November 1967.

[7] Ibid.

to the backbenches. The first was the Prime Minister's Sunday evening broadcast to the nation, the day after sterling was devalued, in which he assured an anxious British public that "the pound here in Britain, in your pocket or purse"[8] will be worth the same as it had been before devaluation. Wilson, an economist, tried to put the best possible face on the crisis. But he should have known better; he undermined his own stature by the rather preposterous suggestion that the devaluation, which the government had avoided for so long, had been simply to placate international markets and would not affect the economy at home. Wilson's speech indirectly benefited Callaghan, who had handled Parliament and the press in a more skilful manner.

The other major news development in the wake of devaluation was Peter Jay's column in *The Times* which appeared later that week; a column that Barbara Castle, then Transport Minister, called an "aston-ishing" defence of "poor innocent Jim".[9] The column was reported upon by the rest of the news media in Britain and became, as Frost noted, "the main political story of the day".[10] It helped Callaghan distance himself in a credible way from an unpopular policy while publicly presenting himself as a man of principle who was taking full responsibility for his actions. While it has never been established that Callaghan was a source for that news story, the facts suggest that Jay went beyond the scope of his responsibilities as a journalist and used that column as an early attempt to rehabilitate the reputation of his father-in-law. The column raises several concerns in that regard.

First, why had Jay – the Chancellor's son-in-law, the son of a recently sacked economics minister, and a former civil servant attached to the Treasury – made those disclosures in a heavily opinionated column in the first place? The editor of *The Times*, William Rees-Mogg, told Laurence Helsby, the head of the Home Civil Service, that if Jay had asked to excuse himself from the debate, given his previous ties to the Civil Service, he would have understood and assented.[11] That sug-gests that the newspaper had been aware of a possible conflict of interest. What is puzzling is that Jay's attitude about such matters, whether as a civil servant or a journalist, had changed considerably since

[8] *Guardian*, 20 November 1967, p. 1.
[9] Barbara Castle, *The Castle Diaries, 1964–70* (London, 1984), pp. 328–329.
[10] PRO, PREM 13/2931. Transcript of *Frost Programme*, Rediffusion Television, 23 November 1967.
[11] PRO, PREM 13/2931, behind Folio 7. Note for the record from Sir Laurence Helsby, 14 December 1967.

the early days of the Labour government. Then, in deference to the fact that his father-in-law had become Chancellor, he had gone so far as to request and receive a transfer to a job in one of the Treasury's management services divisions, so as to avoid any appearance of a conflict of interest. In doing so, he had left a far more influential post in the private office of William Armstrong, who as permanent secretary was the senior civil servant who oversaw the Treasury.

Secondly, the column, while providing strong evidence to demonstrate Wilson's recalcitrant attitude towards devaluation, provided no such compelling evidence for shifting the blame for the inevitable devaluation away from Callaghan.[12] Jay wrote only that when it came to devaluation "no one will perhaps ever know what in his heart Mr. Callaghan's real attitude was, if indeed he had one".[13] While Callaghan might have had his occasional doubts about the wisdom of maintaining parity, there is little to support the idea that Callaghan's opposition to devaluation was unknown to Jay or anyone else.[14] What is closer to the truth was Foot's contention that many within the party knew that Callaghan had been "advocating the maintenance of the old parity just as Harold Wilson was".[15] What is troubling is that Jay's premise served to elevate his father-in-law above the petty politics of the debate and helped to support the column's main argument, which was that "first, last and throughout, the Prime Minister and the Prime Minister alone was the prime mover in the insistence that devaluation was out and that the parity of the pound should be maintained".[16]

The assertion in the column – around which Jay constructed his argument, implying that Callaghan somehow was less culpable and had been dragged into agreeing with a policy for which he was not enthusiastic – also conflicts with the recollections of Jay's former wife, Margaret, a political journalist herself. She recalls that her then husband and her father were often at odds over devaluation, suggesting that the Chancellor's view on the matter was anything but ambiguous and that

[12] British Library of Political & Economic Science (BLPES), Dalton I/52, Folio 7. Hugh Dalton, a close friend of Callaghan's and himself a former Chancellor, was concerned in 1960 because some people felt that "J.C.'s [*sic*] intellectual grip [was not] tightening, as it should be."

[13] *The Times*, 23 November 1967, p. 24.

[14] Roy Jenkins, *A Life at the Center* (New York, 1991), p. 185.

[15] PRO, PREM 13/2931. Transcript of *Frost Programme*, Rediffusion Television, 23 November 1967.

[16] *The Times*, 24 November 1967, p. 1.

he had been as much of a die-hard opponent of devaluation as Wilson.[17] Margaret Jay says that she and her then husband "had taken the whole opposite position on all of this" from the one held by her father and that "there was a degree of estrangement...because Peter and I were on the other side".[18] Also, when interviewed, Peter Jay raises no question of there having been a grey area concerning Callaghan's view on the subject, flatly saying that his father-in-law "knew my opinion and I knew his".[19]

Thirdly, through the column Jay placed himself at the centre of an ever-widening controversy that indirectly benefited Callaghan at one of the lowest points in his political career. At the time, Jay said that he had not spoken with his father-in-law for "two or three weeks".[20] Yet the column appeared the morning after Callaghan gave a fiery speech attacking a panel of industrialists, who had been called in to help the government with its current economic crisis, as "potentially sinister" and a threat to the democratic process.[21] Callaghan's speech deflected criticism from devaluation and was seen as a "bid for the leadership".[22] Although the timing might have been a coincidence, the fact that the column appeared on the same day as news reports of that speech gave momentum to Callaghan's resurgence and, as Castle noted, gave "weight" to the talk of "a take-over bid for Harold's job by Jim".[23] There had been no letting up; two days later the coverage in *The Sunday Times* included a well coordinated special investigation by the newspaper's Insight team, which expanded on the points disclosed by Jay in his column.[24] Wilson's "appalling press"[25] that weekend, which included news reports that Wilson had barred Jay from being included on a TV panel interviewing him about devaluation, reached such a crescendo

---

[17] James Callaghan, *Time and Chance* (London, 1987), pp. 210–215. Callaghan makes it clear in his autobiography that his view and the view of the Prime Minister had been one and the same on the issue of devaluation.

[18] Interview with Lady Jay, 3 March 2004.

[19] Interview with Peter Jay, 11 December 2003.

[20] PRO, PREM 13/2931. Transcript of *Frost Programme*, Rediffusion Television, 23 November 1967.

[21] *Sun*, 23 November 1967, p. 1. Callaghan had beaten the Prime Minister to the punch in taking responsibility for devaluation. But, at the same time, he cleverly deflected criticism by attacking the industrialists.

[22] *Guardian*, 24 November 1967, p. 1.

[23] Castle, *Diaries, 1964–70*, p. 328.

[24] *The Sunday Times*, 26 November 1967, pp. 11–12.

[25] Roy Jenkins, *A Life at the Center* (New York, 1991), p. 204.

that Roy Jenkins, one of the early advocates for devaluation, later said that it had thrown into uncertainty Wilson's ability to remain as Prime Minister.[26] Finally, the column is troubling because Jay continued to conceal his knowledge for several days after sterling was devalued and apparently had done so without the knowledge of the newspaper's editor. The editor, Rees-Mogg, in a discussion with Helsby, who had been conducting the government inquiry along with Armstrong into whether the disclosures in *The Times* violated the Official Secrets Act, said that Jay had "assured him" that he had not obtained the information until after devaluation had taken place on Saturday, 18 November.[27] If that had been the case, the delay in publication would have made sense. But Jay actually acquired that knowledge at least several months and possibly even a year or more beforehand.[28]

Shortly before Robert Neild left government service earlier that year, he had dined with Peter and Margaret Jay. At that encounter in the spring of 1967, Neild, a passionate and early proponent of devaluation, who had been a close adviser to the Chancellor, discussed the parity of the pound.[29] Neild said that at that point Callaghan's son-in-law had either joined or was about to join *The Times*, and that he told Jay "very plainly that there could of course be no question whatever of publishing anything that was said".[30] Nevertheless, Neild said he viewed Jay as someone who could be trusted and as someone "who also had a family

---

[26] Ibid.
[27] PRO, PREM 13/2931, behind Folio 7. Note for the record from Sir Laurence Helsby, 14 December 1967.
[28] PRO, PREM 13/2931. Note for the record from A.M. Bailey, 27 November 1967. In the summer of 1965, Jay had been temporarily moved back to Armstrong's office to fill in for a vacationing senior civil servant, and at that point would have been able to view some of the highly classified material, the contents of which formed the basis for that column.
[29] At a 1988 symposium sponsored by the Institute of Contemporary British History, Jay said that the source of that story was among the other individuals who were on that panel, which included his father Douglas Jay, the former President of the Board of Trade, Neild, as well as Michael Stewart and Peter Shore, both of whom had headed the old Department of Economic Affairs. Immediately, Neild responded that, "It was me. . . . I'd decided I'd had enough. I told Peter to watch out for Jim, because [devaluation] was going to come inevitably [and] he wasn't getting the proper advice" (*Contemporary Record: The Journal of the Institute of Contemporary British History*, Vol. 1, No. 4, Winter 1988.)
[30] PRO, PREM 13/2931. Note for the record from Sir Laurence Helsby, 5 December 1967.

stake, through his father-in-law as well as his father, in the success of government policies". Neild could not remember whether he had discussed the fact that all but one copy of the report, which had come from his office and had been critical of the government's determination not to devalue, had been ordered destroyed, but conceded that he might have.[31]

In addition, the documents suggest that Jay had been able to confirm the story four or five months prior to devaluation, which would have been the last impediment to publication. An under-secretary at the Treasury, David Walker said that Callaghan's son-in-law told him in July that he knew that Neild was "very angry" that all but one copy of the report on devaluation "had been forcibly withdrawn and destroyed".[32] Also, Jay said he had known that the other economic advisers had been equally upset that their advice was not being heeded. Walker, who had voluntarily come forward with his account to his superiors after Jay's column appeared, believed that Jay's knowledge came from Neild and feared that something he, Walker, might have brought up or left unchallenged "might have given Jay something he did not already know".[33] Also, when interviewed, Jay hints at having had the information confirmed well before the November devaluation. He mentions that on "one or two" occasions "there were things I might have written that would almost have precipitated a crisis, possibly a devaluation ... ".[34]

On the one hand, it is understandable that Jay, or for that matter any responsible reporter, would have been reluctant to divulge that information prior to devaluation, to avoid triggering a run on sterling. But it is harder to understand why it had taken several days to report that story once devaluation had been announced. The fact that a Labour government had had to devalue after the Prime Minister and the Chancellor had repeatedly pledged not to do so, in some cases forcing other governments into having to take action, was a major news story, not only in Britain but elsewhere in the world. Most reporters would have been eager to quickly get the disclosures into print to avoid those revelations being obtained by the competition; as it was, the *Financial Times*, with its vast influence in the "city",[35] pursued the same line of thinking and actually had published a similar, although less detailed, account

---

[31] Ibid.

[32] PRO, PREM 13/2931, behind Folio 4. Note for the record from A.M. Bailey, 27 November 1967.

[33] Ibid.

[34] Interview with Peter Jay, 11 December 2003.

[35] The name of London's financial district.

the same morning about Wilson's refusal to allow the subject to be raised.[36]

Rees-Mogg told the government inquiry that often after such a big story someone on the inside would contact a newspaper "spontaneously to give information in the belief that the record should be put right".[37] Yet although devaluation was announced the previous Saturday evening and *The Times* was at the centre of an intense battle to increase its readership, Jay did not report the story he had until Thursday, 23 November, the day of his regular weekly column and a day after Callaghan gave the speech that was viewed as a bid for the party leadership. That would suggest that Jay, who had written bylined news stories on the subject of devaluation as well, had withheld that information so it could have maximum impact by being first presented to the public not in a news story but in his regular Thursday column. In that way he had greater liberty to utilise those startling disclosures as a defence of his father-in-law. The comparisons between Callaghan and Cardinal Wolsey, the sixteenth-century prelate who lost all in his bid to please Henry VIII, and suggestions that Callaghan "in his heart" might have had deep reservations about the government's line of thinking, suggest that Jay was acting more like a surrogate for Callaghan than a journalist, whether Callaghan had had advance knowledge of Jay's intentions or not.

After the government had been forced to devalue and despite Jay's column in *The Times*, it was clear that Callaghan's tenure as Chancellor was over. In fact, he had secretly submitted his resignation to Wilson on 18 November, the night of the devaluation, and it had been agreed that a public announcement of his intentions would be delayed "until matters have settled down a little".[38] What was not clear at that point was

---

[36] *Financial Times*, 23 November 1967, p. 15. The account in the *Financial Times* strangely enough also appeared in a column that had been written by Samuel Brittan, who like Jay was a former civil servant. Crossman expressed the view in his diaries – *The Diaries of a Cabinet Minister*, Vol. II (London, 1976), p. 588 – that the appearance in the *Financial Times* of the related disclosures that same morning had made Jay's column "all the more sinister".

[37] PRO, PREM 13/2931, behind Folio 7. Note for the record from Sir Laurence Helsby, 14 December 1967. However, Rees-Mogg's comment had been meant to support his contention that the material had come to Jay after devaluation.

[38] Oxford, Wilson c.773. Callaghan's handwritten resignation letter to the Prime Minister, dated 18 November 1967, concluded: "I do not think it right that I should continue in the office and so with the deepest regret I must ask you to accept my resignation. We agree that it would not be right for this to be announced until matters have settled down a little, and I am ready to carry on for a short time before the resignation is made public."

whether Callaghan would remain in the government or who would succeed him as Chancellor. But although he knew that he could not remain at the Treasury, he continually lobbied against the idea of Jenkins succeeding him as Chancellor.[39] In a meeting that puzzled Jenkins, Callaghan invited the Home Secretary to visit him on 23 November, the same day that Jay's column appeared in *The Times*. Callaghan took it upon himself at that encounter and in meetings with Tony Crosland, the recently appointed President of the Board of Trade, to do two things to confuse the coming Cabinet shuffle: first he told Jenkins, for some unexplained reason and without having been asked, that it was "unlikely" that Jenkins would be his successor,[40] and secondly, he assured Crosland, one of Jenkins's closest friends, that he had inside knowledge of Wilson's intentions and that it was nearly certain that Crosland would be the new Chancellor.[41] Jenkins later wrote that the fact that he rather than Crosland had been named to that post – when Wilson at the end of November asked Callaghan and Jenkins to swap jobs – was a "devastating blow" to Crosland.[42] Jenkins implied that the way it had been handled did great harm to their friendship, which went back to their days together at Oxford, as well as to their future working relationship as the two economic ministers in the government. Jenkins had attributed at least part of that problem to Callaghan driving a wedge between the two men with his "busy-body activities".[43]

The bitterness between Jenkins and Crosland, which arose at the end of November 1967 and had been fuelled by Callaghan, continued throughout that Labour government, coming to a head with one particular incident in September 1969. Although Crosland, as President of the Board of Trade, had consulted the Treasury on the latest trade figures, when they were released to the press he had included his own evaluation of the data, which the Treasury had not seen beforehand. Jenkins fired off a note to Crosland. He told him that he found it "almost unbelievable" and that "if you do this sort of thing you can hardly expect

---

[39] *The Economist*, 25 November 1967, pp. 828–829. Its editorial said that "Mr Callaghan will not wish to delay his departure unduly, and *The Economist*, which has been advocating just that for a long time, has made no secret of its choice for his successor: Mr Roy Jenkins."

[40] Roy Jenkins, *A Life at the Centre* (London, 1991), p. 214.

[41] Callaghan, *Time and Chance*, p. 221. Callaghan conceded that he had put Crosland forward as his successor and "thought the Prime Minister shared my opinion".

[42] Roy Jenkins, *A Life at the Center* (New York, 1991), p. 206.

[43] Ibid.

good relations".[44] Crosland responded by implying that he had managed to get along with everyone else in the Treasury and that he was "saddened to receive so hectoring and pompous a communication from an old friend". Nevertheless, he assured Jenkins that "I personally intend now to forget this rather undignified correspondence".[45] But the jealousies and suspicions from the succession fight that Callaghan stoked two years earlier had not healed on either side; within a few days of that exchange, in a private memo to Wilson, Crosland urged the Prime Minister to allow him to play a bigger role in economic policy so as to act as a "counterweight" to the ever-increasing power of No. 11 Downing Street.[46]

It seemed that as soon as Callaghan moved from the Treasury to the Home Office at the end of November 1967, he was, for one reason or another, in the midst of controversy. It was Callaghan, in office as Home Secretary only a couple of weeks, who re-ignited the debate over the contentious issue of arms shipments to South Africa by making a public statement that urged the government to change its policy and permit the sale of arms to South Africa.[47] That public comment forced the item back on the Cabinet agenda. It caused major divisions within the government, and came at a time when Wilson's leadership was still reeling from the effects of devaluation and the controversy that had been triggered by Peter Jay's disclosures in *The Times*. Strangely enough, Crosland, who was obviously deeply disappointed by the appointment that had never materialised, shifted his position during the early stages of the renewed debate from the one that he had held only a few months earlier. This time he aligned himself with Callaghan and backed the arms deal to the consternation of Wilson.[48] The whole episode so annoyed the Prime Minister, who in the end had been able to keep the ban in place, that he took it upon himself to leak the contents of the Cabinet

---

[44] BLPES, Crosland 5/5. Note to the President of the Board of Trade from the Chancellor, 16 September 1969.

[45] BLPES, Crosland 5/5. Memo to the Chancellor from the President of the Board of Trade, 18 September 1969.

[46] BLPES, Crosland 5/5. Memo to the Prime Minister from the President of the Board of Trade, 22 September 1969.

[47] Callaghan did a similar thing six months later when he stepped out of his area of ministerial responsibility and made a contentious speech to the Fire Brigades' Union in Blackpool telling them that the time was near to eliminate the prices and incomes policy, which he had defended as Chancellor.

[48] BLPES, Hetherington 13. Supplementary notes of a meeting between Hetherington and the Prime Minister, 13 December 1967.

meetings to the press, but he chose to leak the material to the *Guardian*, not *The Times*.[49]

Callaghan, moreover, was among those who stirred the waters to help undermine the Chief Whip, John Silkin, a month later, while Wilson was away on a trip to Moscow. Silkin had blundered by suspending a group of Labour MPs, who had refused to support the government's position on cuts in social services, and did it without discussing the move with the Prime Minister or the Leader of the House. Although Wilson's trust in his Chief Whip, the individual responsible for maintaining party discipline and unity, was shaken by the episode, he viewed the attacks on Silkin as "an attempt by cowards to get at me."[50] Silkin told Castle that Douglas Houghton, an old friend of Callaghan's and the chairman of the Parliamentary Labour Party, had been "playing a double game. He is hand in glove with Jim to get rid of me".[51] In the end, it would take a much bigger crisis to finally bring down Wilson's Chief Whip and when that arose several months later, it would be Callaghan, too, who would play a role.

Right from the time he moved to the Home Office, Callaghan's hostility towards the new occupant at No. 11 Downing Street was evident as well. In a meeting of select ministers, Callaghan exhibited a lack of cooperation with the new Chancellor's early efforts to address some of the nation's pressing economic problems.[52] Oddly enough, Jenkins, having embarked as Home Secretary on one of the most ambitious agendas of social reform in Britain's history, made Callaghan's transition to the Home Office a bit smoother than it might have been by having helped to decriminalise abortion and homosexuality. By doing so, Jenkins removed from the debate two of the most heated issues during the turbulent 1960s. On the other hand, Richard Crossman felt that "Jim had left Roy a frightful legacy" at the Treasury, one that had been even worse than the economic problems that the Labour government

[49] (Manchester) *Guardian* Archive, C5/326. "Afterthoughts" from a meeting between Hetherington and Crossman, 26 January 1968.

[50] Oxford, Wilson c.936. Handwritten letter, unsigned and undated. But it is clearly Wilson's handwriting and the subject matter and the time references indicate that it had been written in January 1968.

[51] Castle, *Diaries, 1964–70*, p. 360.

[52] Roy Jenkins, *A Life at the Center* (New York, 1991), p. 215. Jenkins noted that in a meeting on the need for tough economic measures less than a month after devaluation, Callaghan surprisingly "opposed us on three of the controversial issues and gave only grudging acquiescence on the fourth".

inherited from the Tories on taking power in 1964. Crossman believed that Callaghan's promises to the IMF in the aftermath of devaluation had forced Jenkins in his early days as Chancellor "to go in for overkill".[53]

However, as soon as Callaghan became Home Secretary he had to deal with two other major social problems that had remained on the agenda – immigration and race relations. In many ways the legislation that had been enacted to stem what many feared would be a flood of Kenyans of Asian descent migrating to Britain and the corresponding Race Relations Bill, a counterbalancing measure to protect the minorities already in the country, was even more troublesome than the changes to the laws on homosexuality or abortion. That is because not only did race and immigration matters fuel discord between the left and the right, they fuelled discord within previously harmonious groups: for example, middle-class supporters of Labour and the working class; and popular trade union leaders, like Frank Cousins and Jack Jones, and their rank and file.

No doubt Callaghan put a Labour government in an awkward position when he blocked the entry to the United Kingdom of British passport holders fleeing a hostile administration in Kenya, a former British colony. As Home Secretary, he had no choice but to be at the centre of that unpopular debate, and at least initially it greatly undermined any effort to extricate himself from a potential legacy of failed policies. In the space of a few short months at the Home Office, Callaghan's overall popularity tumbled while Jenkins's popularity as Chancellor soared. In December 1967, shortly after the two men swapped jobs, Callaghan was seen as the most likely replacement for Wilson should the Prime Minister resign.[54] By the following April, Callaghan had fallen well behind Jenkins in the hypothetical succession fight. Callaghan had won the support of just 9 per cent of those polled, down from 17 per cent in December, while nearly a quarter had favoured Jenkins, up from 10 per cent. Even George Brown, who by that time had resigned in anger from the Cabinet and returned to the backbenches, had been slightly above Callaghan in popularity. The extent of Callaghan's fall from grace was even more startling among Labour Party supporters. In that category, the new Chancellor managed to maintain his impressive

---

[53] (Manchester) *Guardian* Archive, C5/334. Note of a discussion between Hetherington and Crossman, 21 March 1968.
[54] NOP Bulletin, April 1968.

15-percentage-point advantage over Callaghan, even though Jenkins had fewer ties to the party than Callaghan.[55]

On the surface, the polls were early evidence that Jenkins's consolidation of his new position had been swift and impressive. In the early period after devaluation, Peter Jay's column detailing Wilson's insistence on maintaining the parity of the pound helped his father-in-law's tarnished image and might very well have helped to keep him in the Cabinet. But it had been much harder for Callaghan to overcome the contrast between the old and the new way of doing business at the Treasury. Jenkins, a younger man, was perceived as a new style of political leader, a take-charge Chancellor who had total command over the Treasury and who was a strong figure in dealing with the Budget. Callaghan, on the other hand, was increasingly viewed as an ex-Chancellor who had made glowing speeches but, while not totally to blame for devaluation, had failed miserably in his understanding of economic and monetary matters.[56] In addition, there was a growing feeling in those early months of 1968 that Callaghan was not doing any better at the Home Office than he had done at the Treasury. Paul Johnson wrote in the *New Statesman*, the weekly journal that was influential with the political elite, that it looked as if Callaghan was shaping up to be the "worst-ever" Home Secretary,[57] while the columnist Alan Watkins called Callaghan's tenure "something of a joke".[58] Within the Cabinet, the mood was not very different; Crossman felt that things were now so bad that "Harold would leave Jim at the Home Office to moulder away and wreck his own reputation."[59]

But there was an element of political sophistication in the new Home Secretary's positions that was not evident from his dismal showing in the polls. Only by looking at the figures side by side with polls taken

---

[55] Ibid. However, nearly half of the respondents had no opinion at all and in a separate NOP survey, 50 per cent of all those questioned wanted Wilson to continue as Prime Minister. Among Labour Party supporters, that figure jumped to 91 per cent.

[56] Woodrow Wyatt, *Turn Again, Westminster* (London, 1973), p. 19. The mood was reflected in the MP Wyatt's summation of Callaghan's tenure as Chancellor as being a time when the "eloquence with which he presented his case blinded the House of Commons, and hence the lobby and press correspondents and the country, into supposing that he knew what he was doing".

[57] *New Statesman*, 1 March 1968, p. 264.

[58] *New Statesman*, 22 March 1968, p. 366.

[59] (Manchester) *Guardian* Archive, C5/334. Note of a discussion between Hetherington and Crossman, 21 March 1968.

that same month of the public's attitudes on racial equality do the numbers begin to make sense and begin to explain Callaghan's incredible resiliency, a quality that would be evident throughout his political recovery.[60] In early 1968, Callaghan – while clearly unpopular in comparison with Jenkins, who had seemingly done a better job as Home Secretary and now was seen as doing a better job as Chancellor – had taken a characteristically cautious stand on both immigration and race relations. As would be the case on so many issues in the coming years, there were no sudden, enterprising moves; even Peter Jay, in one of the few direct criticisms of his father-in-law, attacks the Labour government's crackdown on Kenyan Asian immigrants as a "shocking thing" and a "disgrace to any civilised legislature".[61] Nonetheless, Callaghan's position had *anticipated* public opinion.

In March 1968, despite the critical attacks on the Home Secretary's stance on the editorial pages of the quality broadsheets such as *The Times* and the *Guardian*, and the fact that Callaghan's popularity plummeted in the polls amid Jenkins's rise, more than two-thirds of the British electorate agreed with his tough stance on limiting the admission of Kenyans of Asian descent.[62] The crisis was triggered by Kenya's post-colonial Africanisation policy and in the first couple of months of Callaghan's tenure at the Home Office thousands of people fearful of losing their livelihoods in Kenya used their British passports to enter and settle in England. The crackdown was a policy that his colleague Tony Benn, then Minister of Technology, feels did have a "racist" element to it even though Benn agrees that something had to be done to prevent an influx of people coming into the country.[63] Regardless, the two-thirds figure in the polls had not only been true for the overall population but had been true as well for separate surveys taken of supporters of both the Labour Party and the Conservatives. Even the Liberals saw an astounding 73 per cent of their supporters agreeing with the tougher sanctions, although, no doubt, many

---

[60] Randall Hansen, "The Kenyan Asians, British Politics, and the Commonwealth Immigrants Act, 1968", *The Historical Journal*, Vol. 42, No. 3 (1999), p. 822. "The legislation was very much a triumph of Callaghan's strand of Labour ideology – nationalist, anti-intellectual, indifferent to arguments about international law and obligation, and firmly in touch with the social conservatism of middle- and working-class England ...."
[61] Interview with Peter Jay, 11 December 2003.
[62] NOP Bulletin, March 1968.
[63] Interview with Tony Benn, 21 July 2003.

of those surveyed would have been reluctant to voice those opinions publicly.[64]

Callaghan took a cautious approach on the Race Relations Bill right from the start, as well. A month after arriving at the Home Office, in a meeting with the Lord Chancellor, Gerald Gardiner, Callaghan agreed that the contentious issue of how to go about enforcing the new legislation "would have to be decided in Cabinet on political grounds".[65] While Callaghan wanted "sanctions", he had been equally, or possibly more adamant about protecting "an innocent person against whom an allegation of discrimination had been made".[66] Callaghan's private secretary Brian Cubbon thinks that "perhaps some of [Callaghan's] appointments to the Race Relations Board might have been more realistic and less idealistic than Jenkins" but otherwise the approach of the two Home Secretaries was one and the same.[67] Jones of the Transport and General Workers' Union (TGWU), who had caught the wrath of many of his members by his calls for stronger legislation that would levy meaningful penalties in cases of housing or job discrimination, agrees: "I think they regarded it as impractical.... There wasn't a strong attitude toward doing away with racial discrimination" in that Labour government.[68]

The real turning point for Callaghan, however, in that difficult first year at the Home Office came with his handling of the mass protest in London against the Vietnam War at the end of October 1968. It was the first indication that Callaghan's political comeback would be possible. Although Grosvenor Square, as it came to be known, was a single event rather than a great social issue, it had been the first time that Callaghan as Home Secretary had shown himself to be totally in command of a difficult situation. When that day ended, he had won the respect of the public and more importantly his colleagues in the Cabinet.[69] Callaghan's great success had more to do with what did not happen than anything that did happen. For weeks the press, in particular *The Times* and the *Guardian*, published story after story warning that groups of anarchists were determined to cause serious trouble. There

---

[64] NOP Bulletin, March 1968.
[65] PRO, HO 376/74. Minutes of a meeting at the Home Office between the Secretary of State and the Lord Chancellor, 3 January 1968.
[66] Ibid.
[67] Interview with Sir Brian Cubbon, 19 June 2003.
[68] Interview with Jack Jones, 18 June 2003.
[69] Richard Crossman, *The Diaries of a Cabinet Minister*, Vol. III 1968–1970 (London, 1977), p. 241.

were calls from Members of Parliament for the Home Secretary to ban the march or to put troops on standby. It was a time of great uncertainty amid fears that the demonstration might turn violent as had happened at the student protests in Paris earlier that year. The protest began with a march through central London that ended with a rally at Hyde Park and involved a much smaller group proceeding to the US Embassy in Grosvenor Square.

The talk of plots and anarchists was so prevalent in the press – oddly enough more so in the quality newspapers than the popular press – that Tom McCaffrey, Callaghan's press secretary, notified Cubbon on 8 October, more than two weeks before the march, that the date for an unrelated one-to-one interview that had been planned between Callaghan and Norman Fowler, the home affairs correspondent of *The Times*, should be moved forward. Fowler sought the interview as part of a review he was doing of the work that had been done at the Home Office over the previous year. But McCaffrey suggested to Cubbon that "in the light of current events", Callaghan should schedule the interview a week earlier "in order to include in the review anything which the Secretary of State would like to say prior to the demonstration on October 27". McCaffrey assured Cubbon that "this will not be a hostile interview".[70] All of the sabre rattling in the press had had an effect on public opinion as well. The man in the street was so sure of the evil intent of the protesters that one poll indicated that 87 per cent of those surveyed thought that if violence did materialise it most likely will have been caused by the demonstrators rather than the police.[71]

In the end, the fact that none of the predicted troubles – bombings, seizures of key installations in the capital, attacks on vital communications – had come to pass and that the march proceeded in an orderly manner made Callaghan a hero.[72] *The Times*'s Fowler praised Callaghan, saying he "had refused to be stampeded into banning the demonstration on the basis of some of the forecasts of violence".[73] The photographs

---

[70] PRO, HO 376/158. Memo to Brian Cubbon from PR Office, 8 October 1968. Although McCaffrey's name is not on the memo, the tone of the document and the directives within it make it clear that it emanated from him.

[71] NOP Bulletin, September 1968.

[72] British Parliamentary Debates, Fifth Series, Vol. 722, Col. 1060–1061. In fact, Callaghan told Parliament that foreign governments saw the British government's response as "a very useful lesson in how this kind of exercise should be conducted".

[73] *The Times*, 28 October 1968, p. 1.

of the jovial Home Secretary huddled with equally jovial bobbies in Grosvenor Square after the march was over helped Callaghan's public image and hence his dreams of a political recovery. No doubt, Callaghan demonstrated considerable political skills and page-one headlines like the ones in the *Daily Telegraph*, "Triumph for Law and Order",[74] and in the *Daily Mail*, "Yes, Our Police Are Wonderful!",[75] reflected that. On the one hand, Callaghan, who in his earlier days had been the union negotiator for the police federation, managed to appease the left by allowing the march to proceed as scheduled; on the other hand, he had calmed the concerns of the right by showing himself to be a reasonable law-and-order man.

Nevertheless, was the march a serious threat to public safety? The left-wing newspaper *Tribune*, editorialising a few days later, said that when the demonstration was over the country heaved "a sigh of relief". But the editorial was also critical of all the "scare stories" and the "atmosphere of hysteria" that had been allowed to fester in the press prior to the demonstration, saying *The Times* was "by far the worst offender".[76] *The Times* later acknowledged, after having received a barrage of complaints from its readers, that its earlier stories did turn out to be "greatly exaggerated"[77] in light of the "militant few"[78] who had caused trouble. Nonetheless, it defended its coverage, in particular the story that fuelled so much of the speculation that had gone on for weeks. That story, which appeared on 5 September, warned of a "startling" plot by "a small army of militant extremists" who were intent on "storming" key installations and buildings in London at the time that police would have had their hands full dealing with the demonstrators at Grosvenor Square.[79] In addition, the unattributable suggestions in that story that Home Office officials were fearful that if the anarchists prevailed "it may take several days to flush them out and regain control"[80] were more characteristic of tabloid journalism rather than anything the public should have expected from *The Times*.

---

[74] *Daily Telegraph*, 28 October 1968, p. 1.
[75] *Daily Mail*, 28 October 1968, p. 1.
[76] *Tribune*, 1 November 1968, p. 1.
[77] *The Times*, 31 October 1968, p. 11.
[78] *The Times*, 28 October 1968, p. 1. The headline in *The Times* the morning after the march was "Police Win the Day Against Militant Few in March".
[79] *The Times*, 5 September 1968, p. 1.
[80] Ibid.

After the march, Callaghan said the news media had fuelled a threat that had just not been there, and that the reports in the newspapers and on television had "created much of the public fear and semi-hysteria".[81] While Callaghan's comment[82] was accurate to a point, a review of the press for the weeks leading up to the march supports *Tribune*'s contention that it had not been newspapers in general that had fostered the anxiety, but one newspaper in particular – *The Times*.[83] But who had been the source of that initial inflammatory story? The explanation *The Times* gave its readers had been contradictory. On the one hand, it said it had received the information from dissidents as well as unnamed "officials" who had reason to believe the threat was real. It described the officials only as being those who were "responsible for watching the situation", suggesting the story had come from either the police or the Home Office. On the other hand, *The Times* acknowledged that when "official spokesmen" had been presented with the "facts", they had not given much credence to the reports.[84]

Nor apparently did the *Evening Standard*, a popular newspaper traditionally far more prone to sensational reporting than a quality newspaper like *The Times*. While it did report the same information on its front page the afternoon of 5 September, it apparently had second thoughts a day later, and ran another page-one story debunking the talk of plots and anarchists.[85] But that did not stop *The Times*, which continued to fuel what it described as "the growing war of nerves"[86] with an exclusive page-one story about how Callaghan was going to ban the entry of some foreign students who were planning to attend the march.[87] The situation

---

[81] Callaghan, *Time and Chance*, p. 261.
[82] Oxford, Wilson c.1395. Callaghan was not above using rhetoric tied to the student protesters for his own political purposes as well. During the 1970 general election campaign he gave a speech in Liverpool on 5 June saying the Selsdon man, the quintessential Tory, "invented the bash 'em brigade. Bash the unions, bash the workers, bash the demonstrators, bash anyone who gets in his way...".
[83] The *Guardian*'s reporting and that of the popular newspaper the *London Evening News* were in a similar vein, although it had been *The Times* that had been the first of the quality newspapers to give extensive and continuing coverage to the "rumours" of the plots.
[84] *The Times*, 31 October 1968, p. 11.
[85] *Evening Standard*, 6 September 1968, p. 1.
[86] *The Times*, 16 October 1968, p. 1. The *Guardian* ran a similar story the following day inside the paper.
[87] Ibid. *The Times* had also scooped the competition with a page-one story the day before the march headlined, "Students Enter Britain Illegally for Rally" (*The Times*, 26 October 1968).

was so out of hand that Max Hastings of the *Evening Standard*, who had covered the violence between the police and demonstrators that summer at the Democratic National Convention in Chicago, charged a week before the London march that the warnings of impending trouble were being "artificially created".[88] The *Daily Express* sent a team of reporters to look at just who was behind the march and discovered that rather than the demonstrators being a grave danger to society, they were a motley crew who spent much of their time at "ludicrous" meetings arguing among themselves.[89]

Meanwhile, the editor of the *Daily Mail*, the Conservative popular newspaper, found that "much of the information" he had been receiving about the pending march was so questionable that he had refrained from publishing it at all for fear of inciting violence.[90] Although the march was targeted against the United States and not the British government, the whole issue of US involvement in Vietnam was a contentious one for the Labour government and caused deep divisions within the party. Callaghan mirrored the position of Wilson and the then Foreign Secretary Michael Stewart, a position that had avoided any criticism of the Americans while at the same time resisting US approaches to provide any financial or military support.[91] Regardless, McCaffrey, Callaghan's press secretary, says Grosvenor Square was "a wonderful thing", recalling how his boss was "strolling about amid all the rioters".[92]

The romantic way that McCaffrey depicts Callaghan's role in that event is the way the public perceived it as well, given the flattering coverage in the media and the laudatory reactions in Parliament, which had been the icing on the cake of Callaghan's triumph. In reality, when McCaffrey along with Callaghan and Brian Cubbon, his private secretary, strolled across Hungerford Bridge and towards Hyde Park, the streets were nearly empty. They were surveying the area before the march began. The police had warned Callaghan and he had heeded their advice to keep away from the demonstrations. It was only at the end of the day, when it had become clear that matters were well under control, that the Home Secretary appeared before the newspaper photographers

---

[88] *Evening Standard*, 18 October 1968, p. 31.
[89] *Daily Express*, 24 October 1968, pp. 6–7.
[90] Letter to the editor of *The Times* from Arthur Brittenden, editor, *Daily Mail*, 31 October 1968, p. 11.
[91] Gallup Public Opinion Polls, November 1967. An astonishing 82 per cent of those surveyed disapproved of the idea of sending British troops to Vietnam.
[92] Interview with Sir Tom McCaffrey, 3 July 2003.

and television cameras in Grosvenor Square to congratulate the police on keeping the event peaceful.[93]

Meanwhile, that same day several miles from the march, the political columnist Alan Watkins recalls that he and his wife were entertaining Callaghan's daughter Margaret and her husband, Peter Jay, at the Watkins's home in Surrey. Watkins remembers that while they were not "glued to the TV" they had "kept up with what was happening" and when it was clear that everything turned out well for the Home Secretary, Peter and Margaret Jay were "terribly relieved".[94] But Watkins must have been relieved as well; prior to having the Jays to lunch and a few months before the events at Grosvenor Square, he had gone out on a limb and rather boldly declared in the *New Statesman* that Callaghan "had now made a full recovery".[95] Watkins shifted in the space of a few short months from saying that Callaghan was "completely unfitted to fill the post of Home Secretary"[96] to praising Callaghan's "thoroughgoing political professionalism". That change of heart was built around the rather questionable premise that the Race Relations Bill, which Watkins had characterised "a responsible political exercise", had somehow been a turning point for Callaghan.[97] Also, Watkins in that same column on 26 July 1968, said Callaghan had been urging his associates to "rally round and be loyal to the leader" and on that point, the columnist felt "there is no reason to doubt the Home Secretary's sincerity".[98]

However, there would have been plenty in the Cabinet as well as the occupant at No. 10 Downing Street who would have strongly disagreed with Watkins on that point, having witnessed the Home Secretary's "sincerity" at the National Executive two days earlier, on 24 July 1968, when he had said one thing and done the other. Callaghan, who was still feeling a bit of an outcast in the Cabinet in this period just prior to Grosvenor Square, broke his pledge to support Anthony Greenwood, the consensus candidate, for general secretary of the Labour Party. Instead, Callaghan quietly manoeuvred behind the scenes with two former disgruntled Cabinet colleagues, Brown and the recently departed Ray Gunter, to get the National Executive to hand the post to Harry

---

[93] Kenneth Morgan, *Callaghan: A Life* (Oxford, 1997), p. 315.
[94] Interview with Alan Watkins, 6 November 2003.
[95] *New Statesman*, 26 July 1968, p. 99.
[96] *New Statesman*, 1 March 1968, p. 258.
[97] *New Statesman*, 26 July 1968, p. 99. The headline on the column was "The Rehabilitation of Jim".
[98] Ibid.

Nicholas, the former acting general secretary of the TGWU, who was politically attuned with Callaghan.[99]

Initially, Wilson refused to get involved in the endorsing of any candidate for that position when news of the opening came up in March 1968 and had only done so on the insistence of his political secretary and confidant, Marcia Williams. She quite accurately sensed that letting the post fall out of the Prime Minister's influence could spell trouble. When Williams first asked the Prime Minister, "What shall I do now on this?" his response was "Nothing". Williams fired back another memo to Wilson suggesting some candidates, including Victor Feather, the assistant general secretary of the Trades Union Congress, the lobbying group for the trade unions, and closed with, "Really you must do something." This time the response was simply, "Vic Refuses." But Marcia Williams had been persistent, coming around yet again with a suggestion that the Prime Minister meet Len Williams, the current general secretary of the Labour Party, "despite not wanting to be involved and all that", and this time Wilson agreed.[100]

A week before the general secretary's post was decided upon, Wilson, in a private conversation with Alastair Hetherington, the editor of the *Guardian*, said he "had not taken an active part in it nor had he intervened" in anyway on anyone's behalf. But at the same time, Wilson had said that although the subcommittee agreed on Greenwood, "one or two people" had been attempting to back out of that agreement and that "he wasn't going to allow that" to happen.[101] In the end, the breaking of that agreement did happen and while it certainly had been duplicitous on Callaghan's part, it had been a move that would reap great

---

[99] At the Labour Party conference in October 1967, Callaghan ran for and won the post of Labour Party treasurer, which gave him an automatic seat on the National Executive. While four other members of Cabinet – Brown, Castle, Benn and Anthony Greenwood – had been elected to the NEC that year and the Prime Minister was an ex-officio member, none of them had obtained their seats with quite the unspoken string attached that the Chancellor had. The treasurer's post was the only position decided upon by all the various sections of the party – trade unions, constituency organisations, women members, and socialist, co-operative and professional organisations – and Callaghan could not have won without the blessing of the trade unions, whose voting power far exceeded that of any other section.

[100] Oxford, Wilson c.1279, series of memos between the Prime Minister and Marcia Williams. The exchanges are undated, but apparently are from March 1968 given the subject matter and related correspondence in the file.

[101] BLPES, Hetherington 15/16. Notes of a meeting between Hetherington and the Prime Minister, 15 July 1968.

political benefits to him over the next year. In light of the back-room dealing, one member of the Cabinet urged Wilson to "keep a stiff upper lip" amid the "disloyalty and utter lack of cooperation on the part of some of our colleagues".[102] The *Tribune* noted that while Brown and Gunter, having recently left the Cabinet in anger, had an excuse for their behaviour, Callaghan had none. It reported that after his vote on the National Executive and after Callaghan's man had won, Callaghan "went to the Parliamentary Party meeting and delivered a tear-jerking appeal for unity, loyalty and loving kindness all round".[103] It had been the very appeal that Watkins, the columnist, had taken at face value.

Despite his success at Grosvenor Square, by the time Callaghan's first year as Home Secretary came to a close, there were still three major obstacles that remained in the way of his political rehabilitation – obstacles that to a lesser politician would have been insurmountable: first, the ascendancy of Roy Jenkins. It was not just that Jenkins had been proving himself to be a far more successful Chancellor, it was the fact that Callaghan was having to deal with constant comparisons in the press between the two men. Jenkins had been an outstanding Home Secretary while Callaghan for much of his first year in office was seen as no more than adequate. Whether people had agreed with Jenkins's vast array of social reforms or not, he had been seen as circumspect yet decisive; until the anti-Vietnam protests, Callaghan as Home Secretary was seen as neither.

Secondly, Callaghan had to deal with the obstacle created by the emergence of Castle in the newly created post of Secretary of State for Employment and Productivity. In April 1968, she had been handed a super-ministry and had been given the title of First Secretary, making her effectively the Deputy Prime Minister with a seat directly opposite Wilson at the Cabinet table. Callaghan resented Jenkins, who was the greater threat, given his elevation to the Treasury and his strength among the backbenchers. But Callaghan resented Castle even more because he felt that she was genuinely undeserving of the job.[104] Although her polling figures had been low, for the first time her name had appeared in national surveys among those who were being

---

[102] PRO, PREM 13/3416. Handwritten note to the Prime Minister from George Thomas, the Secretary of State for Wales, 24 July 1968.

[103] *Tribune*, 2 August 1968, p. 3.

[104] Anne Perkins, *Red Queen: The Authorised Biography of Barbara Castle* (London, 2003), p. 286.

considered as potential replacements for the Prime Minister.[105] At the Labour Party conference that autumn, Castle surprised the conference, and certainly must have surprised Callaghan, by getting re-elected to the National Executive with the biggest vote in the constituency section, even though she had been under attack a day earlier for the government's incomes policy. On the other hand, although Callaghan had won re-election as treasurer that year, he had had to do it without the support of Britain's biggest trade union, the TGWU.

The paths of Callaghan and Castle did not really cross until January 1969, simply because their legislative concerns and agendas were so different. But for most of 1968, Castle's star had been ascending rapidly[106] while Callaghan's had been descending and therefore she had become an ever-increasing threat to Callaghan's standing in the government and in the Labour Party. Crossman had even given a speech touting Castle as someone who would likely be Britain's first woman Prime Minister. Callaghan had seen how Castle had effectively consolidated and overridden Ray Gunter's once substantial role on labour relations, effectively bringing an end to Gunter's influence and his career as Minister of Labour. Crossman had told Hetherington that Gunter's resignation from the government, after only a short time in his new post at the Ministry of Power, came because he "had been uniquely suited to the Ministry of Labour" and had been "furious" over the way that it had been folded into the newly created Department of Employment and Productivity. "'That filthy woman' had got hold of it."[107]

Finally, despite Grosvenor Square, Callaghan still had no compelling issue of his own on which to rebuild his reputation. On the contentious battles over immigration and race relations, there had been no easy way out for the Labour government collectively, but it had been even more difficult for Callaghan individually. That is because in those early months of 1968 there had been little time for anything other than race and immigration matters and little opportunity for Callaghan to break out on his own. As we shall see with some inside help from the *Guardian*,

---

[105] NOP Bulletin, May 1968.

[106] Gallup Public Opinion Polls, February 1969. Castle came first in a survey of the most admired women, beating Queen Elizabeth II. Unfortunately, Enoch Powell, the architect of the racist "Rivers of Blood" speech, led the list of the most admired men, followed by Wilson.

[107] BLPES, Hetherington 15/18. Note of a meeting between Hetherington and Crossman, 2 July 1968.

he had been able to put a better face on the Race Relations Bill in much the same way that, with the help of his son-in-law's column in *The Times*, he had been able to put a better face on his role in devaluation. But in some circles, there had been a sense that if there was anything at all progressive in the new Race Relations Bill it was being credited to the groundwork laid by his predecessor; if there was anything less than laudatory, the blame was attributed to Callaghan.

Conclusion

So the road back had not been by any means assured. Nor should it be forgotten that in the early years of the Labour government, there had been three other senior ministers with strong ties to the trade unions who at one point or another had been at least as influential as Callaghan. By the time of Callaghan's success at Grosvenor Square, however, not one remained in the Cabinet. No doubt the most controversial had been Cousins, the general secretary of the TGWU, who had been the first to go – resigning as Minister of Technology two years earlier, in July 1966, after having had a falling-out with the government over its wage policies. Next, it had been George Brown, the deputy leader of the Labour Party and a former TGWU official, who after countless threats finally broke with Wilson and quit as Foreign Secretary in March 1968, never to return. Finally, there had been Ray Gunter, the former head of the railway clerks, who as Labour Minister since 1964 had been among the early influential members of the Cabinet along with Brown and Callaghan. After having to make way for Castle's expanded ministerial role, Gunter quit the government altogether in July 1968.

In not one of these cases had the minister been sacked, but in nearly all, they had left – with the exception possibly of Brown, whose troubles were also rooted in personal problems – because they had seen the writing on the wall. In other words, when Callaghan had moved from No. 11 Downing Street to the Home Office on 30 November 1967, there had been cases of other strong Labour ministers with trade union ties having been pushed aside, belying the argument that Callaghan had been somehow immune from such treatment because he was such a strong figure in the party and the trade union movement. Although Callaghan had gained another of the great offices of state, he had gained it in such unfavourable circumstances that it seemed improbable that he would be able to use it as the way back from the greatest defeat of his political career. The Home Office had been seen as a post that "can easily injure if not do irreparable damage" to a politician.[108] The fact that Callaghan had been able to survive for nearly a year, before Grosvenor Square had provided the first indication that his political recovery would be possible, had made the feat all the more remarkable.

Peter Jay contends that in the early days at the Home Office, Callaghan had been so disheartened that had it not been for his wife, Audrey, he might very well "have chucked it in".[109] But despite the criticism in the press, and his sharp drop in popularity, it is hard to believe that Callaghan had ever had any such intention. The evidence shows that almost immediately after he had tended his resignation as Chancellor, he already had an eye on rehabilitating his political career, helped by his son-in-law's determination to set the historical record straight[110] and give him at least some respectability on the issue of devaluation. Jenkins had been one of the most progressive Home Secretaries in years and Callaghan had had no choice but to follow through with much of what Jenkins had begun. But the deft way Callaghan had dealt with some of the toughest legislation that any Home Secretary had faced in years brings into question the popular perception that Callaghan had been a broken man in those early days and weeks at the Home Office.

For example, Callaghan had known just how far to go on immigration – a harsher, more restrictive approach than the one his predecessor would have followed – and on race, where many of the policies he had pursued had been remarkably similar to what Jenkins had intended to do. Callaghan, by being willing to take the heat from the left and face charges of "racism" early on for his rather brutal crackdown on the Kenya Asians, had shored up his base of support on the right. It had been done with full knowledge that his subsequent Race Relations Bill would at least make up for some of that injustice and move him back towards the centre. The population had been split down the middle over the race bill[111] and Callaghan had been very sensitive to public opinion. While using the legislation to project an image of tolerance to placate

---

[108] Comment from a lecture given by Callaghan in 1982 at the Royal Institute of Public Administration.

[109] Interview with Peter Jay, 11 December 2003.

[110] *The Times*, 24 November 1967, p. 1. *The Times* said Jay had felt "it was very important to get it on the record before 'the official' version of history became accepted...".

[111] NOP Bulletin, May 1968.

the left, in fact, he had been a party to blocking efforts to give the Race Relations Board or the courts any tools for enforcement.[112]

The column that Peter Jay wrote and *The Times* published five days after Callaghan announced that the pound was being devalued had been the very earliest attempt at a rehabilitation of Callaghan's political career. It is unclear how much of a lasting impact it did have, although it certainly had shifted at least some of the blame for devaluation off the Chancellor's shoulders. Where it might have been more revealing is that it had been the first of many occasions during Callaghan's long political rehabilitation when he had managed to skirt around the concept – directly or indirectly – of collective Cabinet responsibility. If Callaghan had been the one who made the comments and disclosures that his son-in-law had made in *The Times*, it would have been the end of Callaghan's political career. But by cleverly refraining from taking issue with Wilson and distancing himself from *The Times* story after it had been published, he had enhanced his own reputation at the expense of the Prime Minister's.

In Callaghan's memoirs published 20 years after devaluation, he had said that he could not "write too highly of Harold Wilson's personal consideration and kindness during this period".[113] Peter Jay says that comment had not been just a case of Callaghan looking back nostalgically at the events but had "reflected the truth and that [Callaghan] did feel grateful to Wilson in that regard".[114] If so, Callaghan, had an unusual way of showing it. He inappropriately inserted himself into the whole issue of succession at the Treasury, adding to Wilson's troubles. Moreover, he apparently did it because he felt that Jenkins, rather than Crosland, would be the stronger Chancellor and therefore Jenkins, from that position, would pose the greater threat to his own chances of a political recovery.

Although Crosland, as the author of *The Future of Socialism*, had been one of the great thinkers within the modern Labour Party, he had been especially indecisive as a minister and junior minister.[115] That would have likely made his time at the Treasury not unlike Callaghan's tenure,

---

[112] PRO, HO 376/76. Memo to the Secretary of State from David Ennals, 20 March 1968.

[113] Callaghan, *Time and Chance*, p. 222.

[114] Interview with Peter Jay, 11 December 2003.

[115] Giles Radice, *Friends and Rivals: Crosland, Jenkins and Healey* (London, 2002), p. 141. Radice characterised that trait differently, saying Crosland "liked to read himself into a subject, consult experts and civil servants, and then take an informed view".

which had been marked by uncertainty and an inability to make decisions. Despite Crosland's belief that his advising Callaghan to remain in the government had amounted to him having "talked myself out of the job",[116] the last thing that Wilson wanted or needed at that juncture was another indecisive Chancellor.[117] Politics aside, the Prime Minister had to make a bold move to regain credibility for the beleaguered currency and the government, not only in the eyes of the British public but internationally as well.

---

[116] Susan Crosland, *Tony Crosland* (London, 1982), p. 189.

[117] Interviews with Lord Rodgers, 23 March 2004, and Lord Croham, 3 May 2004. Both men had worked closely with Crosland at the Department of Economic Affairs and later at the Board of Trade and confirm his indecisiveness.

3
A Political Opening: The NEC and Nigeria

Transport House, for much of the twentieth century, was located in Smith Square, a short walk from the Houses of Parliament. It was the home of the Transport and General Workers' Union (TGWU), the most powerful trade union in England, and the Labour Party had its offices in rented space on the upper floors of the building. It was there, on 26 March 1969, that the party's governing body, the National Executive Committee (NEC), met as usual. But what happened at that meeting, in the fourth-floor committee room, surprised even the Home Secretary's staunchest critics. Callaghan used the opportunity of that gathering, on the eve of Harold Wilson's departure on an overseas trip, to cast a vote that delivered a bold challenge to his own government's plan to radically overhaul the trade unions. He did this even though the Cabinet had, after several extended sessions and much debate, approved the plan to legislate two months earlier.

The Labour government had left open some of the details of the reforms for further discussion, and it was known that Callaghan, when the plan was first presented to Cabinet on 3 January, disagreed with some points in the White Paper. But it had been assumed that he, being a senior minister, would support Barbara Castle, his colleague, at the NEC meeting, and maintain the position that had been collectively agreed upon by the Cabinet.[1] Yet, the fact that he did not do that was extraordinary for two reasons: first, Callaghan undermined not only the pending legislation, but the principle of collective Cabinet responsibility. Under

---

[1] George Brown, the deputy leader of the Labour Party and a former trade unionist himself, chastised Callaghan's position on constitutional grounds and voted with Castle.

that convention, once the Cabinet agreed on a policy – which in this case it had, since the intention to legislate was outlined in a White Paper approved in Cabinet on 14 January and later presented to Parliament with Callaghan's name among the sponsors[2] – Callaghan, as a minister of the Crown, was bound publicly to abide by the decision. Secondly, his vote to join the majority on the trade-union dominated NEC, and approve a resolution to block the proposal, came as the Prime Minister was preparing to depart on a peace mission to try to end the civil war in Nigeria.

The White Paper, which became known as *In Place of Strife*, was the Labour government's reaction to the findings of the Royal Commission on Trade Unions and Employers' Associations, chaired by Lord Donovan. The commission had been established three years earlier to address a sticky political problem, particularly for a Labour government, i.e. the public's concern over the unbridled power of the trade unions. When the time came to put a plan into action, Castle, in her expanded role as Wilson's new Secretary for Employment and Productivity, ventured beyond the rather conciliatory recommendations of Lord Donovan's committee. Instead, she unveiled a set of no-nonsense measures to prevent wildcat strikes, including the taking of a ballot before workers could walk off the job, a government-imposed four-week cooling-off period to minimise disruptions in certain industries and, if all else failed, the threat of jail sentences to get strikers back to work.

When Wilson arrived in Lagos the day after the NEC meeting, hundreds of thousands of Nigerians gathered along the motorcade route from the airport to the capital to greet him.[3] The outpouring reflected, at least in part, the hope that Britain might be able to do something to end the civil war. By then, the conflict had killed tens of thousands and caused widespread famine in Biafra, the newly named eastern region of the former British colony, which had seceded from the Nigerian federation two years earlier. But over the next few days Wilson's peace mission was overshadowed and hampered by what turned out to be Callaghan's shrewdest move in his bid to restore his political reputation. Callaghan, by exploiting the decision taken by the NEC while the Prime Minister was thousands of miles from London, cleverly repositioned himself in

---

[2] Peter Jenkins, *The Battle of Downing Street* (London, 1970), p. 79.
[3] Harold Wilson, *A Personal Record: The Labour Government 1964–1970* (Boston, 1971), p. 626. Wilson's memory of the greeting upon his arrival in Nigeria differed with that of the report of the BBC Home Service. Wilson recalled crowds 'cheering the whole way'; the BBC reported crowds gathered in silence.

the Cabinet. In doing so, however, he undermined any chance of Wilson succeeding in his effort to break the logjam and advance the cause of peace in one of most tragic episodes in Africa's history.

Nigeria's independence from Britain was less than a decade old, when its political system unravelled amid the troublesome exclusivity of its major political parties, which were organised along ethnic and regional lines. After an initial coup in January 1966, followed by a countercoup six months later, the Igbo people in the eastern region, which housed two-thirds of the nation's oil reserves, seceded in May 1967 and established the republic of Biafra. Shortly thereafter, the two sides went to war. As the fighting intensified, so did the attention of the international community. The Soviet Union supplied vital military aeroplanes to the Federal Republic and the Chinese provided Biafra with moral, if not military, support. The United States and the United Kingdom tried to stay on the sidelines.[4] But it was the growing impact of the Nigerian military government's economic blockade of Biafra and the resultant widespread suffering and starvation of the civilian population that focused public attention on the crisis and prompted Wilson to make his journey to try to "mediate" the crisis himself.

Some initial progress was being made. Page after page of diplomatic documents from the Prime Minister's six-day trip indicate that the weekend that Callaghan continued his challenge to the government, Wilson, amid the heat and humidity of Lagos, moved closer to the arrangement of a meeting with the rebel leader of Biafra, Colonel Odumegwu Ojukwu. In all those documents, many of which were drafted by career civil servants, there is barely a hint of Wilson's political troubles at home. But those papers become most revealing when they are compared with a separate group of documents from the Prime Minister's Office that comprise deciphered telegrams covering the same period.[5] In those exchanges, most of which were crafted by political operatives, there is page after page of cables that indicate the undercurrent of concern that

---

[4] Toyin Falola and Matthew M. Heaton, *A History of Nigeria* (Cambridge, 2008), pp. 172–178.
[5] Interviews with Lord Croham, 3 May 2004, and Sir Kenneth Stowe, 12 May 2004. Senior civil servants, including Douglas Allen, now Lord Croham, who was head of the Home Civil Service, and Kenneth Stowe, who was Cabinet secretary for Wilson, Callaghan and Thatcher, say that ciphered exchanges are reserved for high-level diplomatic documents and are almost never used for political exchanges. The use of such coding for the telegrams about the Callaghan affair supports the supposition that the problem was of the highest concern and was drawing attention away from the diplomatic crisis at hand.

Wilson and his chief political advisers at No. 10 Downing Street had with what Callaghan was up to while the Prime Minister was away.

Callaghan and others in the Cabinet were entitled to feel that they had been ignored by Castle and the Prime Minister in the formulation of a critical government initiative. After all, Castle, prior to presenting her plan to the full Cabinet shortly after the New Year, had worked behind the scenes for months on the legislation, and had deliberately avoided putting her proposals before the Cabinet committee that dealt with industrial relations, on which Callaghan sat.[6] Although the measure did allow plenty of time for "public" discussion, since the intention was not to legislate until the end of the year at the earliest, Callaghan and other ministers, who voiced initial concerns, believed they should have been brought into the debate far earlier. On that point, they were undoubtedly correct. The issue of industrial policy was the most important domestic problem that post-war Britain faced, dogging successive governments, both Labour and Conservative. Callaghan, though, was not motivated by principle alone.

While Wilson's Home Secretary dug his heels in back home that weekend and no doubt increased his stature with the trade unions on both left and right, the rebel leader of Biafra had apparently softened his hardline stance against the British Prime Minister. There are indications that Ojukwu was willing to leave the rebel-held territory during that first week of April and meet Wilson on neutral turf, without any preconditions.[7] Several problems arose over the next few days, however, and one of them was timing, and that is where putting the two sets of documents side by side becomes most revealing. Wilson, in the effort to lower expectations, wanted the meeting with Ojukwu to appear to be merely a routine part of his Africa tour,[8] albeit one that might provide

---

[6] Peter Jenkins, *The Battle of Downing Street*, p. 36.

[7] PRO, FCO 65/484. Telegram to British envoys detailing visit with President Julius Nyerere of Tanzania from Malcolm MacDonald, 6 April 1969. MacDonald said Nyerere had "indicated that his contacts with the Biafrans showed that Ojukwu had also sincerely desired a meeting". MacDonald's note implied that Nyerere felt great harm had been done "by the dropping of the alternative proposal that an emissary such as [MacDonald] would visit Biafra to arrange a meeting outside".

[8] PRO, PREM 13/2825. Telegram to Foreign Secretary Stewart from the Prime Minister, 30 March 1969. The Prime Minister rejected General Yakubu Gowon's original suggestion that the meeting take place after the OAU meeting in mid-April. He told Gowon "it would be far better to make the meeting only an incident in [the] present visit to Africa than give it separate and special status ... "

a breakthrough for peace talks ahead of the conference of the Organi-sation of African Unity, which was planned in Monrovia for mid-April. But the window of opportunity for Wilson was narrowed by two men: on the one side there was the military leader of Nigeria, General Yakubu Gowon, who as an ally of Britain had first to approve any invitation to his arch-rival Ojukwu and was understandably reluctant to do so. On the other side was Callaghan, whose manoeuvrings on trade union reform back home prompted Wilson's top political advisers and the govern-ment's Chief Whip[9] to urge the Prime Minister to cut short his African tour and return to London to deal with the unfolding political troubles.

At Wilson's first meeting with Gowon, shortly after his arrival in Lagos on Thursday, 27 March, the Prime Minister broached the sub-ject of Ojukwu, and added that he had not intended to mediate but only to help. Wilson told Gowon that senior British diplomats had been in touch with Ojukwu, who seemed to be serious about wanting to meet the British Prime Minister, and that he wanted Gowon's back-ing on the initiative before he proceeded with the invitation. Gowon had been reluctant to allow Wilson to visit Lagos, possibly because he wanted to avoid just such a meeting between Wilson and Ojukwu.[10] But Nigeria, amid the television news footage of starving children and the frustrations of relief agencies encumbered by the fighting, was losing the propaganda war waged by Biafra internationally. Gowon told Wilson that he would consider the proposal when it was put to him formally the following day.

In the meantime, Wilson as early as Friday, 28 March, received indi-cations of the trouble at home from Joe Haines, the former *Sun* reporter who had been brought in by the Prime Minister to overhaul press oper-ations at No. 10 Downing Street after the debacle over devaluation. Haines[11] told Wilson that the "line is being strongly peddled on [Callaghan's] behalf in London that he is waiting to see what industrial reform legislation is proposed, and that if it contains penal clauses

---

[9] PRO, PREM 13/2785, Folio 9. Telegram to the Prime Minister in Addis Ababa detailing a letter from the Chief Whip, urging that Wilson return early. The document is undated but was clearly sent on 31 March 1969.

[10] PRO, PREM 13/2817, Folio 11. Note of a telephone conversation between the Prime Minister and the Foreign Secretary, 7 March 1969.

[11] Although Haines's formal title was deputy press secretary, he was in reality Wilson's press secretary. At that point, his predecessor, Trevor Lloyd-Hughes, who was with the Prime Minister in Africa, still had the title but was being gently pushed aside to make way for Haines. Lloyd-Hughes became the government's chief information officer.

he will take the only honourable course, etc.... This attitude might be reflected in tomorrow's [newspapers]."[12] The mere suggestion that Callaghan might be contemplating resigning from the Cabinet and what that would mean for the Prime Minister in terms of a future challenge to his leadership of the Labour Party had to be profoundly distressing, even for someone like Wilson who could successfully compartmentalise his duties as Prime Minister.

The Economist, the influential business weekly, which at times had been critical of Callaghan's tenure at the Treasury, was quick to condemn the former Chancellor's disloyalty to the government, calling it a "serious matter".[13] The magazine was insightful in its understanding of his methods. In extracts of the account that were sent, via telegraph, to the Prime Minister from his staff that Friday, *The Economist* was quoted as saying that Callaghan's vote on the NEC against *In Place of Strife* "jeopardises the last big opportunity the Labour government has of pulling the economy around. He has been doing this for some little time behind the scenes: now he is being more open about it." The report concluded that the new Home Secretary "is back at the centre of the party stage from which devaluation had removed him", and that "if Mr. Wilson and Mrs. Castle falter now, they will be inviting Mr. Callaghan's friends to take over the party".[14]

That Saturday, while Wilson toured Port Harcourt in eastern Nigeria, the site of an oil refinery in which Shell and British Petroleum held a major stake, Gerald Kaufman, one of Wilson's closest political advisers, approached the Prime Minister in a "highly agitated" state. Kaufman told Wilson that a third party had informed him that the BBC was about to report that Callaghan had quit the government.[15] The level of concern that the Prime Minister's party felt is evident from the cable that was relayed to London: "Jim has done a Ray repeat Ray and George repeat George", references to Gunter and Brown who had recently quit the government. It continued, "Please give us facts, repeat facts... urgent answer required by telephone and flash telegram."[16] No doubt the sense of urgency was heightened by the tone of other press

---

[12] PRO, PREM 13/2785, Folio 2. Telegram sent to the Prime Minister in Lagos from Michael Halls, 28 March 1969.

[13] *The Economist*, 29 March 1969, pp. 17–18.

[14] PRO, PREM 13/2785. Telegram sent to the Prime Minister in Lagos from Michael Halls, 28 March 1969.

[15] Oxford, Wilson c.936, Folio 1. Note for the record on the Industrial Relations Bill, 3 April 1969.

[16] PRO, PREM 13/2785. Telegram sent to principal private secretary at No.10 Downing Street from Prime Minister's party in Lagos, 29 March 1969.

reports[17] like the one that bannered the front page of the final edition of the *Evening Standard* that Friday – "Jim Sets Off a Flaming Row"[18] – and the unpleasant thought of having Callaghan, Gunter and Brown huddled together on the back benches. After all, it had been that triumvirate that had placed Harry Nicholas in the job of Labour Party general secretary over Wilson's candidate the previous July.

The journalist Geoffrey Goodman contends that the axis forged when Nicholas narrowly won the party post was still in force during the debate over *In Place of Strife*,[19] something Wilson believed as well as evidenced by his personal notes from early 1969. In the end, Kaufman's source turned out to be unreliable; there was no such report. Nevertheless, before Wilson knew that, he expressed outrage at the thought of Callaghan tendering his resignation, even at one point questioning whether Callaghan could resign without "a recommendation from me to the Queen".[20] While the Prime Minister waited to hear back from the press office at No. 10 Downing Street he pondered how he would deal with the matter if it were true. He decided upon a "self-sealing" operation, a typical Wilson solution, with Denis Healey taking Callaghan's job and George Thomson, who was Minister Without Portfolio, replacing Healey at the Ministry of Defence.[21]

Meanwhile, that same day, a cable awaited Wilson back in Lagos from Haines, who told the Prime Minister that he had had conversations with three of his contacts: two of whom were journalists and all of whom had spoken to the Home Secretary, who was spending the weekend at his constituency in South Wales. Haines said that two of those individuals said Callaghan had told them he had no intention of quitting, and to the third Callaghan had repeated those words but with the disturbing caveat not "at the moment".[22] Haines, who having only recently left

---

[17] BBC Written Archives. Transcripts of news broadcasts from 26 March 1969. Although the BBC Home Service gave prominence to the NEC vote against the Industrial Relations Bill in its evening newscast, it was not until three days later – after the story exploded in the press – that the BBC mentioned Callaghan's role at the meeting. From that point on, the BBC Home Service gave the Callaghan angle extensive coverage.

[18] *Evening Standard*, 28 March 1969, p. 1.

[19] Interview with Geoffrey Goodman, 23 February 2004. Goodman acknowledges that in any such triumvirate, Callaghan typically would have been the behind-the-scenes player.

[20] Oxford, Wilson c.936, Folio 1. Note for the record on the Industrial Relations Bill, 3 April 1969.

[21] Ibid.

[22] PRO, PREM 13/2785, Folio 3. Telegram sent to the Prime Minister in Lagos from Michael Halls, 29 March 1969. Hall relayed a report from Haines.

the *Sun*, had impeccable sources in the party and during this period was one of the least reactionary of Wilson's political advisers. But he saw that caveat as yet another indication that Callaghan might make more trouble unless there were major changes in the industrial relations plan, including the removal of the section calling for fines for non-compliance, fines that if left unpaid could see union members being hauled off to jail.[23] The important point is that for the second time in as many days Wilson was left with the impression that Callaghan had hinted that he might quit and throw the government into disarray.

Yet the wheels of diplomacy continued to turn. On Sunday, 30 March, Wilson met yet again with Gowon in the vast rooms of State House, the former residence of the colonial governors-general. At the Prime Minister's insistence, Gowon, who was heavily dependent on British arms supplies to fight the war, finally agreed to Wilson's request and an invitation was dispatched from the British Foreign Office at 5.30 that afternoon to Ojukwu's emissary in London.[24] The fact that the Nigerian leader acquiesced on that request was a major diplomatic victory for Wilson; a week before the trip, the Prime Minister had been sceptical that Gowon would agree.[25] Nevertheless, valuable time had been lost and the political situation at home had deteriorated over the three days since Wilson first broached the subject with Gowon. The clock was ticking and a team of British diplomats were working feverishly at the Foreign Office in London, in Lagos and at British missions in capitals all across Africa to try and pull the logistics together to make the meeting happen.[26]

When news of Wilson's plans to visit Lagos were first announced in mid-March, Ireland's ambassador to Nigeria told Dublin that "colleagues" he had spoken to were of the opinion that the trip was

[23] Ibid.

[24] PRO, FCO 65/480, Folio 327. Telegram to Lagos embassy from the Foreign Office, 3 April 1969.

[25] BLPES, Hetherington 16/23. Notes from a meeting between Hetherington and the Prime Minister, 20 March 1969.

[26] John J. Stremlau, *The International Politics of the Nigerian Civil War 1967–1970* (Princeton, 1977), pp. 306–307. Stremlau argued that "by accepting Gowon's conditions pertaining to possible venues, Wilson destroyed the groundwork for his meeting with Ojukwu that had been quietly laid the previous week." But documents that have since become available suggest that the bigger obstacle was the lack of time rather than the location of the talks. (PRO, FCO 65/479. Telegram to Tebbit, Foreign Office, from Prime Minister's party in Addas Ababa, 31 March 1969.)

largely a "gesture" on Wilson's part "to distract attention from growing parliamentary opposition [to the supplying of arms to the Nigerian government] and to make it appear that Britain can intervene actively".[27] But British documents indicate that at that weekend preliminary plans were put forward to send senior British diplomats into Biafra to lay the groundwork for a meeting between Wilson and Ojukwu elsewhere in Africa.[28] Also, the leaders of several African nations were being contacted so as to allow Wilson to be able to offer Ojukwu the possibility of a meeting in any one of a number of venues in East or West Africa.[29] If a meeting was preferred in neutral waters off the African coast, the British Prime Minister was prepared to sit down with Ojukwu in the staterooms aboard HMS *Fearless*, which was docked in Lagos and was being used as a support ship for the Prime Minister's party in Nigeria.

The seriousness of Wilson's mission is given credence by the fact that he decided to remain in Africa and not attend the funeral of Dwight Eisenhower,[30] the US President, who as the Supreme Commander of Allied Forces in Europe played a decisive role in the defeat of Nazi Germany in the Second World War. Eisenhower had died that Friday and the funeral was to be held on Monday in Washington. But the BBC reported as early as Saturday that Wilson had decided not to attend because he feared that "if he did so he might lose for a long time the chance of bringing a new look to the Nigerian situation". Given the "special relationship" between the United States and Britain and the fact that Charles de Gaulle and other world leaders attended, Wilson's absence was notable. That Sunday, back in Britain, coverage of Wilson's Africa peace mission shared the front pages not only with the news of Eisenhower's death, but the continuing saga involving the Home

---

[27] National Archives of Ireland (NAI), DFA/EMB LAGOS P13/2/2/1. Letter to the Secretary, Department of External Affairs, from Ireland's ambassador to Nigeria, 14 March 1969.
[28] PRO, PREM 13/2825. Telegram to the Prime Minister's party in Lagos from Foreign Secretary Stewart, 28 March 1969.
[29] PRO, PREM 13/2825. Telegrams sent to British envoys in several African capitals that were relayed to heads of state or government, 30 March 1969. In the messages, Wilson sought possible venues for a meeting and said that before coming to Lagos he had had "some indirect approaches from Colonel Ojukwu suggesting that we should meet". Also, Wilson appealed for a quick response to his requests because he said he needed to be back in London on Thursday, although he actually returned a day earlier.
[30] BBC Written Archives. Transcripts from morning news broadcasts on Radio 4, 29 March 1969.

Secretary. Even Tony Crosland, the President of the Board of Trade and a Cabinet minister generally supportive of Callaghan, found himself caught in the crossfire that weekend. In a speech that Crosland gave in his constituency in Grimsby, Lincolnshire, he implied that anyone who did not want to live up to collective Cabinet responsibility ought to resign from the government. But those remarks, which did not mention Callaghan by name, were deleted from the text distributed to the press by Labour Party headquarters, prompting a heated exchange between Crosland and Percy Clark, the party's director of publicity, and arousing suspicions that Nicholas might somehow have been involved.[31]

Whether Nicholas had had a hand in that matter might never be known.[32] But comments Nicholas made that Monday in Scotland were of tremendous benefit to the Home Secretary in his hour of need. Just when Callaghan lost ground within the Parliamentary Labour Party for his actions at the NEC meeting the previous Wednesday, Nicholas came to Callaghan's rescue. In a press conference that Nicholas called in Glasgow, the Labour Party's general secretary, in his boldest statement yet, defended Callaghan's opposition to *In Place of Strife* in the National Executive. Nicholas told the assembled reporters that the fact that Callaghan was a minister of the Crown was "incidental" and that as treasurer of the Labour Party, he was "entitled to register whatever views he wishes to express in precisely the same way as I am, as general secretary".[33]

The comments are intriguing when compared with the tone of Nicholas's original remarks on the subject made in Aberdeen, Scotland, three days earlier, suggesting that something or someone strengthened his resolve. In those earlier comments to the Scottish Council of the party he praised the accomplishments of the government led by Wilson, pledged to raise money for the next general election and said the Home Secretary acted as he did because the White Paper on industrial relations at that point was simply a discussion paper. Nicholas added, in those

---

[31] *Evening Standard*, 1 April 1969, p. 1. The attempt to censor Crosland's remarks ignited a firestorm in the popular press. That story led the newspaper's afternoon's editions under the headline "How Crosland Foiled Censor". The smaller subheadline was "Attack on Callaghan Gets Through".

[32] *Daily Mail*, 2 April 1969, p. 1. The newspaper's political editor Walter Terry, who had close ties to Downing Street, reported that the "censorship move was decided at official level without consulting" Nicholas. But Terry also noted that Nicholas is "a supporter of Mr. Callaghan, who busily and successfully sponsored [his] appointment as general secretary last July ... "

[33] *Guardian*, 1 April 1969, p. 1.

comments made on Friday, that Callaghan "was well able to defend himself".[34] Nevertheless, the much harsher tone of the Monday press conference was perfectly timed for the return of Parliament after the weekend. It ensured that the Callaghan story would not die down and would rival the coverage coming out of Africa. *The Times* reported that Nicholas was "running the risk of precipitating an open constitutional clash"[35] between the Parliamentary Labour Party and the NEC. *The Times*, in a follow-up story a few days later, cited concerns of a "powerful alliance" between Callaghan and Nicholas that could be the "nucleus of a centre coalition far more threatening than the left-wing Bevanite coalition of the 1950s".[36]

The position Nicholas took, whether intentional or not, was a major break for Callaghan and shifted the focus away from the story that ran above the fold on the front page of Monday morning's *Guardian*.[37] The *Guardian*'s Patrick Keatley, a correspondent with good contacts on the continent, reported from Lagos that a meeting between Wilson and Ojukwu was imminent and said the Prime Minister had "grasped the prize that so nearly eluded him". In the end it did elude him, and the *Guardian*'s assessment of Wilson having emerged as the "catalyst and honest broker" in any effort to end the fighting turned out to be premature as well. Nonetheless, Keatley's story, which was dispatched to the paper on Sunday evening, called the expected meeting "a real triumph for British democracy". That evaluation suggests that a meeting might have been closer than the government later admitted.[38] It underscores a point that should not be overlooked, namely that had Wilson been successful in brokering a deal to end the suffering in Nigeria, his standing at home and abroad would have been elevated and he would

---

[34] *Guardian*, 29 March 1969, p. 1.
[35] *The Times*, 2 April 1969, p. 1. This was a reference to Aneurin Bevan, who resigned in protest from the Labour government in 1951, precipitating a major division in the party that lasted for several years. Bevan, who had set up the National Health Service, quit after the new Chancellor Hugh Gaitskell imposed charges on the NHS to pay for a rearmament programme in the wake of US intervention in Korea. Wilson, then President of the Board of Trade, joined Bevan in protest and quit the Cabinet as well. That move gave Wilson a bond with the party's left wing which endured throughout his premierships.
[36] *The Times*, 5 April 1969, p. 1.
[37] *Guardian*, 31 March 1969, p. 1.
[38] A.B. Akinyemi, "The British Press and the Nigerian Civil War", *African Affairs*, Vol. 71 (October 1972), p. 419. Akinyemi, who was highly critical of much of the *Guardian*'s coverage of the war, felt, nevertheless, that Keatley "maintained a high degree of professional integrity" in the work he did as a foreign correspondent for the paper.

have been a much more powerful adversary for Callaghan. It was also clear that Wilson, in the atmosphere of such a breakthrough, would have been in a much better position to shepherd his industrial relations legislation through Parliament.

The injection of Nicholas into the national debate at an opportune moment was further evidence that Callaghan's vote at the NEC, as the journalist Peter Jenkins put it, "had the effect of a smouldering match flicked casually into dry tinder. Within days, the flames were leaping up around the government."[39] So, as the press furore over Callaghan's misbehaviour grew, what Wilson himself describes as the press "in full cry"[40] that Saturday and Sunday, the Prime Minister's focus shifted as well. The extent of Wilson's concern with his Home Secretary's misbehaviour was not public knowledge at the time, nor did members of Parliament or the news media make any direct connection between what was happening in Africa and the Callaghan affair. But by Monday, 31 March, the morning that Keatley's story of an imminent breakthrough appeared in the *Guardian*, Wilson's commitment to the talks weakened. He quite suddenly became less concerned with meeting Ojukwu and more concerned with getting back home to deal with Callaghan. That was evident from several developments that occurred throughout that day in Lagos and later that evening in Addis Ababa, Ethiopia.

First, early that morning Wilson sent a ciphered telegram from Lagos to Fred Peart, the Lord President and the Leader of the House of Commons. The Prime Minister confided to Peart, who as leader oversaw the government's legislative agenda, that he was "watching [the] Callaghan situation carefully". Wilson asked Peart to keep a close eye on Douglas Houghton, the chairman of the Parliamentary Labour Party,[41] who was a close associate of Callaghan's from the two men's trade-union days and who was still angry with Wilson for having sacked him from his Cabinet post two years earlier.[42] In addition, the Prime Minister, in a clear indication that he feared the matter could escalate now that the weekend was over and members of the Parliamentary Labour Party were returning to London, told the leader of the House in no uncertain terms that it was

---

[39] Peter Jenkins, *The Battle of Downing Street*, p. 83.

[40] Oxford, Wilson c.936, Folio 1. Note for the record on the Industrial Relations Bill, 3 April 1969.

[41] PRO, PREM 13/2785, Folio 8. Telegram to the Lord President from the Prime Minister in Lagos via Michael Halls, 31 March 1969.

[42] Houghton had been in the Cabinet as the Chancellor of the Duchy of Lancaster from 1964 to 1966 and then was Minister Without Portfolio until he was removed by Wilson in 1967.

"essential that no repeat no party meeting on party situation takes place in my absence".[43]

Secondly, later that same morning as the Prime Minister's plane took off from Lagos for Addis Ababa on the second leg of his African tour, Wilson sent an unusual message from the plane to the captain of the HMS *Fearless*, where Wilson and his entourage had gathered until 1.30 a.m. the night before.[44] The message thanked the captain and crew of the assault ship, which was supposed to be standing by as a possible venue for a meeting with Ojukwu, for their hospitality in Lagos and wished them a "safe journey home" and a "swift" reunion with their families.[45] That happened despite the fact that a senior official at the Foreign Office had spoken with Ignatius Kogbara, Ojukwu's representative in London, that morning and assured him that "all the options offered including the West African ones remained open".[46] Also, a British diplomat met the following morning with the foreign minister of Benin, the West African nation bordering Nigeria, and secured approval "to pick up Ojukwu at [the port city of] Cotonou should he agree to a meeting on the HMS *Fearless*".[47] However, the ship's logs for that Monday and the following day confirm that it was sent out to sea on a westerly course early Monday afternoon, several hours before any response was received to Wilson's offer of a meeting with Ojukwu.[48] The next day's

---

[43] PRO, PREM 13/2785, Folio 8. Telegram to the Lord President from the Prime Minister in Lagos via Michael Halls, 31 March 1969.

[44] Wilson, *A Personal Record*, p. 635. Wilson writes that the plans to arrange the meetings were discussed aboard the HMS *Fearless* that night. He also mentions that earlier that Sunday Gowon raised no objections to a meeting at any of the possible venues, including the *Fearless* off the coast of neighbouring Benin.

[45] PRO, FCO 65/479, Folio 251. Message from the Prime Minister relayed from his aircraft to the captain of the HMS *Fearless*, 31 March 1969.

[46] PRO, FCO 65/479, Folio 241. Telegram to the Prime Minister's party in Addis Ababa from Foreign Secretary Stewart, 31 March 1969. The documents reveal as well that the Prime Minister's party notified the Foreign Office later that same day that they "had been given to understand authoritatively by Colonel Ojukwu's representative that although [he] would have preferred April 4, it would be possible for him to manage April 2". (PRO, FCO 65/479. Telegram to Tebbit from Prime Minister's party in Addis Ababa, 31 March 1969.)

[47] PRO, FCO 65/479. Telegram sent to Edward Youde, Prime Minister's party in Lagos and Addis Ababa, from McKeever, 1 April 1969.

[48] PRO, ADM 53/170. Logs from the HMS *Fearless* for March 1969. The captain of the *Fearless* left the ship and traveled by helicopter so that he could be among the entourage at the airport when the Prime Minister left for Addis Ababa.

log indicates the ship was en route to Plymouth where it arrived about ten days later.[49]

Thirdly, for some unexplained reason, the decision to send an emissary into Biafra to meet Ojukwu and make the arrangements for a meeting between Wilson and Ojukwu was suddenly called off.[50] That happened even though earlier that weekend the Foreign Office received assurances that the "Biafran authorities would be ready to authorise and facilitate such a visit".[51] The policy reversal, which Wilson only lightly addresses in his memoirs,[52] was later mentioned by both President Julius Nyerere of Tanzania, which recognised Biafra,[53] and by Group Captain Leonard Cheshire,[54] an unofficial British emissary, as being among the reasons that Ojukwu had not agreed to the meeting with the Prime Minister. Obviously, without knowing about the flood of cable traffic between the Prime Minister's party in Africa and No. 10 Downing Street, neither Nyerere nor Cheshire would have had any reason to suspect that Wilson's political concerns at home would have had any direct impact on the negotiations.

Finally, on the very day Ojukwu indicated that he had received the overture for a meeting from Wilson, the Prime Minister's influential political secretary Marcia Williams made an overture of her own. She made it clear to the Prime Minister in a ciphered telegram sent late Monday to Addis Ababa, and read by Wilson either late that evening or

---

[49] PRO, ADM 53/171. Logs from the HMS *Fearless* for April 1969.

[50] PRO, FCO 65/484, Folio 20. Memorandum to the Foreign Office and several African embassies, and embassies in Washington and New York from Malcolm MacDonald, 6 April 1969.

[51] PRO, PREM 13/2825. Telegram, marked "top secret", to Prime Minister's party in Lagos from Foreign Secretary Stewart, 28 March 1969.

[52] Wilson, *A Personal Record*, p. 637. In a statement issued to the press on 1 April 1969, after it was clear that the meeting would not take place, Wilson implied that his own willingness to meet Ojukwu negated the need for a visit by British emissaries.

[53] Ibid. MacDonald visited Nyerere as part of a tour of the region after Wilson returned to London.

[54] PRO, PREM 13/3372. Letter to Michael Palliser from Group Captain Cheshire, 10 April 1969. Cheshire felt that "possible sources of misunderstanding are Mr. Foley's recall on the eve of his intended visit to Biafra and the Foreign Secretary's statement in the House of Common's indicating that the Prime Minister would not rule out a visit to Biafra..."

when he was awoken at 3 a.m.,[55] that it was her "strong view" that he should return overnight on Tuesday "so that you may spend Wednesday at Westminster and be seen to be back in charge again taking situation in hand, not only with the Party but [with] colleagues". She warned Wilson that the political problem with Callaghan was "now breeding the fatalistic atmosphere [in the Parliamentary Labour Party] of which we read so much. Clearly not yet out of hand but dangerous and needs halting."[56]

That Monday, as Wilson continued to receive telegrams from his advisers about the political problems back home and continued to await a response from Ojukwu, Callaghan called on Peart, the Lord President and Leader of the House. Callaghan looked "uncharacteristically tense and uncertain", and in the course of their conversation said he "was emphatic that he was not interested in the leadership – all that he was concerned with was that the government should keep the support of the unions".[57] Callaghan said that others were deliberately trying to cause trouble, among them his nemesis Roy Jenkins, the Chancellor of the Exchequer, who wanted a "showdown" with him. Although, Callaghan had "no intention of resigning", he knew his vote on the NEC would come up in Cabinet upon Wilson's return. But he "thought it would be unfruitful" to go over what had happened at that meeting in detail in front of the other ministers. Callaghan said he was relying on Peart to relay this message "accurately" to the Prime Minister.[58]

Once again, there was an indication that Callaghan had no intention of quitting. Nevertheless, and this is an especially important point, for the third time a cable was delivered to the Prime Minister while he was on that peace mission that contained a hint of resignation; an implicit warning from Callaghan that he might well quit if Wilson carried this matter too far. Peart took the "chat" with Callaghan with a grain of

---

[55] Wilson, *A Personal Record*, p. 636. Wilson says he went to bed at midnight and was awoken by his private secretary Michael Palliser at 3 a.m. with word of an official statement from Ojukwu. The deciphered telegrams show that Michael Halls, who was the principal private secretary, had instructed from London that a telegram from Marcia Williams be given to Wilson as soon as he woke up as well.

[56] PRO, PREM 13/2785, Folio 10. Telegram to the Prime Minister in Addis Ababa from Marcia Williams. The telegram is undated, but it is clearly from 31 March 1969.

[57] PRO, PREM 13/2785, Folio 7. Memorandum from the Lord President to the Prime Minister, 31 March 1969. Document was relayed to Addis Ababa as a telegram on the same day.

[58] Ibid.

salt. But Williams, whose influence with Wilson was far greater than Peart's or anyone else's in the government, came to a rather different conclusion about that conversation. She told the Prime Minister that "the Lord President may take Jim with a 'pinch of salt' but he would be better employed using a slightly larger pinch. If what he says in his report is true, then this is a challenge to you."[59]

Healey, who was the Defence Secretary in that Cabinet, says Williams was shrewd on political matters during those years and was one of the rare individuals who could change Wilson's mind.[60] In this case, spurred by Callaghan's misbehaviour, she apparently did. Kaufman, who worked under Williams in the Political Office at No. 10 Downing Street and is now an MP, says he does not recall any of the particulars of that visit.[61] But a cable sent from Addis Ababa by Kaufman to Williams sometime on Tuesday makes it clear that the Callaghan affair was now at the top of Wilson's agenda. Kaufman wrote: "Himself enormously grateful for your telegram which put him in the real picture as others have not... [The Prime Minister] immediately looked into the possibility of travelling back overnight but Addis Airport close[s] at dusk. So we are leaving at dawn."[62]

The morning of that same day, Tuesday, 1 April, at a meeting with the Emperor Haile Selassie at Jubilee Palace in Addis Abba, Wilson recounted to the emperor how he had received a rejection of his initial offer, not through normal diplomatic channels but via Radio Biafra, the previous evening. Wilson relayed to the emperor, who as the president of the Organisation of African Unity was anxious for a breakthrough, how he had immediately "countered this move with a public statement repeating his earlier offer". However, the Prime Minister said a message received from Biafra in the middle of the night "made it virtually certain that no meeting would now take place", and that "this was a great pity".[63] Although a message was sent during the night from Biafra, Williams's first note, which raised the alarm about the Callaghan affair and urged the Prime Minister to return home, was received during the middle of that same night as well.

---

[59] PRO, PREM 13/2785, Folio 10. Telegram to the Prime Minister in Addis Ababa from Williams, undated but clearly from 31 March 1969.

[60] Interview with Lord Healey, 22 March 2004.

[61] Interview with Gerald Kaufman, 18 December 2003.

[62] PRO, PREM 13/2785/15. Telegram to Marcia Williams from Gerald Kaufman with the Prime Minister's party in Addis Ababa, 1 April 1969.

[63] PRO, PREM 13/2824. Record of a meeting between the British Prime Minister and the Emperor Haile Selassie at Jubilee Palace in Addis Ababa, 1 April 1969.

Given the great influence that Williams had with the Prime Minister it seems plausible that her note, with its grave concerns about Callaghan's threat to Wilson's leadership rather than any diplomatic exchanges from Biafra, would have been far more decisive in putting an end once and for all to any chance of the mission succeeding.[64] The normal diplomatic snags in trying to arrange such talks in a difficult political environment had been expected. It was known from the start that this endeavour was going to involve considerable give and take on both leaders' parts. In fact, an internal government document written just over a week before the trip conceded that even if Gowon should agree "it might take considerable time to persuade [Ojukwu] to emerge and it would almost certainly be necessary first to send an emissary to see him".[65]

Later that same Tuesday, Haines had a dour assessment for the Prime Minister of the developments in Fleet Street.[66] Wilson's press secretary was annoyed that the *Guardian*, by far the most influential newspaper in Labour Party circles, gave prominent page one coverage that morning to Nicholas's defence of Callaghan, a development the newspaper called a "startling" turn of events.[67] Even worse, the *Guardian*'s political correspondent, Peter Jenkins, levelled a harsh attack upon Wilson. Jenkins's column denounced Wilson's sloppy management style and said the Callaghan saga was a "new and ominous development for the Prime Minister".[68] But the column's most damaging salvo was the contention that the government had entered "its late-Macmillan phase", a reference to the backbiting and intrigue that marked Conservative Prime Minister Harold Macmillan's final days in office. Haines told Wilson

---

[64] BBC Written Archives. Transcripts of news broadcasts on Radio 4 made at 7 a.m., 8 a.m. and 9 a.m. on Wednesday, 2 April 1969. While the BBC reported that the Prime Minister was en route to London, it added that "hopes that Colonel Ojukwu would change his mind and accept Mr. Wilson's invitation to a meeting on neutral territory weren't entirely given up until midnight in Addis Ababa".

[65] PRO, CAB 164/409, Folio 6M. Memorandum to Michael Palliser from A.D. Brighty, 19 March 1969. The document details the logistics of arranging such a meeting.

[66] PRO, PREM 13/2785/12. Telegram to the Prime Minister in Addis Ababa from Michael Halls, relaying report from Haines. Telegram is undated but apparently was sent on 1 April 1969.

[67] *Guardian*, 1 April 1969, p. 1. The banner headline of Nicholas's defence of Callaghan that appeared the same day in the *Daily Express* – "Labour Chief Joins in Row" – was more typical of the popular papers than the quality papers.

[68] *Guardian*, 1 April 1969, p. 11.

that the *Guardian* "is clearly going through one of its periodic nervous breakdowns" and advised the Prime Minister not to attach too much importance to the story.[69] But Haines's note was not without some concern; he reminded Wilson that the *Guardian* "uniquely can create a mood" in the Parliamentary Labour Party.[70]

The extent of Wilson's concern with the unfolding drama back home, which was taking his attention off of the crisis in Nigeria, was reflected as well by an exchange between two senior civil servants which occurred just after the Prime Minister returned to London. Edward Youde in the Prime Minister's Office, who had made that trip with Wilson, told Donald Maitland in the Foreign Office that communications between London and the Prime Minister's party in Addis Ababa became "very seriously congested" during the two-day visit there and that there was a "major problem keeping members of the delegation informed". In addition, Youde said that the traffic in telegrams was "exceptionally high even for a visit of this kind".[71]

Nevertheless, the fact that a meeting never took place between the Prime Minister and the rebel leader of Biafra was blamed squarely on Ojukwu by the British government.[72] It is one of those "facts" that is repeated in document after document and in interview after interview, and its mere repetition gave it credence. It was the attitude that the press embraced as well; one that they repeated over and over again in the days and months ahead.[73] The three-column, three-line headline on the front

[69] PRO, PREM 13/2785/12. Telegram to the Prime Minister in Addis Ababa from Michael Halls, relaying report from Haines. Telegram is undated but apparently was sent on 1 April 1969.

[70] Ibid; Akinyemi, "The British Press and the Nigerian Civil War", in *African Affairs*, pp. 418–419. The author argued that the *Guardian's* view of the war was that "Ojukwu was the wronged party; as long as his demands fell short of secession they should be met." The newspaper also opposed British arm sales to Nigeria.

[71] PRO, FCO 65/480, Folio 327A. Note to Donald Maitland from Edward Youde, 3 April 1969.

[72] John W. Young, *The Labour Governments 1964–70, Vol. II, International Policy* (Manchester, 2003), p. 209. Young noted that both sides "seemed most concerned with avoiding the blame for failure".

[73] Akinyemi, "The British Press and the Nigerian Civil War", in *African Affairs*, p. 412. As Akinyemi pointed out, the impact of the British press in African politics was considerable. " ... anyone familiar with Africa, especially a journalist, is aware of how much attention African leaders used to pay to the British papers and the BBC as sources of information, often accepting everything they read and heard as gospel truth."

page of the *Guardian* on Tuesday morning was typical of the reporting: "Ojukwu Scorns Offer of Talks With Wilson".[74] But as the deciphered cables show, when viewed in context with the vast array of diplomatic documents, the reason a meeting never took place likely had as much to do with Wilson's eagerness to get back to London to deal with the misbehaviour of his Home Secretary as anything else.

In addition, a confidential letter from David Hunt, the British High Commissioner in Lagos, to D.C. Tebbit of the Foreign Office, written a few days after Wilson returned to London, calls into question the official line that Ojukwu really had no intention of meeting the Prime Minister:[75] "Ojukwu has obviously been disappointed," Hunt wrote. "I think he had two hopes. One was that the Prime Minister would actually agree to come to Umuahia, with all that that would have meant in added prestige. Failing that, and perhaps it was too much to hope for, he expected that if he came out to meet the Prime Minister a truce could be arranged, which has been his principal object for many months now. As it is he has got nothing, been put in the wrong and can only fall back on the sterile abuse which has gained him no advantage in the past."[76] Another letter nine days later between two senior civil servants boasted that "the responsibility for the failure to meet the Prime Minister has been quite successfully pinned on to Colonel Ojukwu".[77] Also, Tebbit, the senior British diplomat who was meeting Kogbara, Ojukwu's representative in London, said shortly after Wilson arrived in Lagos that he was under "the impression that Kogbara thought Ojukwu would not maintain his objection to leaving Biafra in order to meet the Prime Minister".[78]

In Wilson's private papers, there is an aide-memoire that confirms that on his arrival at Addis Ababa on Monday evening his attention was focused more on the troubles with Callaghan back home and less on any possible meeting with Ojukwu. Shortly after his plane landed he

---

[74] *Guardian*, 1 April 1969, p. 1.
[75] Stremlau, *The International Politics of the Nigerian Civil War*, pp. 306–307. In an interview with Ojukwu cited by Stremlau, the rebel leader "surmised that nothing could be gained from a meeting outside the enclave", and had "immediately rejected" Wilson's proposal. But the documents do not support that, suggesting that that statement might have been a face-saving device on Ojukwu's part.
[76] PRO, PREM 13/2820. Letter to D.C. Tebbit from David Hunt, British High Commissioner in Lagos, 5 April 1969.
[77] PRO, PREM 13/2820. Letter to Edward Youde from David Brighty, 14 April 1969.
[78] PRO, PREM 13/2825. Telegram, marked "top secret", to Prime Minister's party in Lagos from Foreign Secretary Stewart, 28 March 1969. Although that note mentioned that "this point was not directly discussed".

sent a message to No. 10 Downing Street letting them know that he intended to call a meeting of the parliamentary committee for Wednesday evening and "ask Callaghan for an explanation which the toughies on the committee would reject". He said that he planned to demand that the Cabinet the next day "endorse a statement by me on collective responsibility, and to reaffirm its decision on industrial relations policy".[79] The problem was that the situation had got out of hand and festered while Wilson was away and Callaghan had gained the upper hand. The Home Secretary was a deft political operator, but he was not the Prime Minister and had Wilson been in London that pivotal weekend it was doubtful that Callaghan could have ever gained the ground he did in the fight over *In Place of Strife*.

It should be pointed out that Wilson was also fighting with two other complications in dealing with Callaghan that possibly affected any meeting with Ojukwu and they both involved timing and the approaching Easter holiday. There would be no newspapers published on Good Friday and Parliament would soon be out of session for more than a week for the Easter break. So a quick return to Westminster was necessary if the Callaghan matter was to be dealt with firmly and quickly before Parliament went into recess. One has to wonder if the suggestion by Ojukwu for a meeting that Friday,[80] which would have entailed Wilson staying in Africa an additional day or two beyond his original schedule, would have been acceptable if the Callaghan saga had not reached such a crescendo. Indeed, a week prior to his departure, Wilson pondered just such an extension of the mission with likely visits to Liberia and Ghana planned for after his departure from Addis Ababa. On 20 March, the day after an internal government document indicates that the Prime Minister had called off the extension of his trip, the idea apparently was back on the table. Wilson told the editor of the *Guardian*, in a confidential discussion, that a plane was being chartered for journalists with those destinations in mind.[81]

---

[79] Oxford, Wilson c.936, Folio 1. Note for the record on the Industrial Relations Bill, 3 April 1969.

[80] PRO, FCO 65/479, Folio 257. Memo to the Foreign Office from Tebbit in Addis Ababa, 31 March 1969.

[81] BLPES, Hetherington 16/23. Notes from a meeting between Hetherington and the Prime Minister, 20 March 1969. But Wilson apparently told several leaders including William Tubman of Liberia, Jomo Kenyatta of Kenya and Milton Obote of Uganda, when inquiring about possible meeting places, that he had to be back in London by Thursday morning. (PRO, PREM 13/2825. Draft telegram to African leaders, 30 March 1969.)

As evidenced by the attention being paid by Wilson's Political Office to the reactions in the press, the Callaghan affair not only undermined the government's diplomatic efforts but brought to a boiling point the row over the reform of industrial relations, which after weeks of controversy had simmered down. The shifting of Fleet Street's attention away from Wilson's efforts to meet Ojukwu to Callaghan's misbehaviour managed to elevate Callaghan's role beyond that of just another minister, and created a public perception of Callaghan as someone to be reckoned with – a man of principle, a man who would risk all to stand up for the working man. The internal Cabinet conflict that Callaghan created came at the cost, however, of lowering the public's expectations for a successful conclusion to Wilson's trip. It dealt a blow to the prestige of the Prime Minister himself and broke the ever-important momentum in the build-up to a possible meeting with Ojukwu.

Just how serious the threat to Wilson's leadership was is debatable, but Callaghan, by openly defying the principle of collective Cabinet responsibility on this issue, saw a political opening: a way to gain the upper hand with Wilson, who had effectively demoted him; the current Chancellor Jenkins, who had usurped his place as the second most powerful man in the government; and Castle, who as First Secretary Callaghan felt had been promoted far beyond her potential. Callaghan took full advantage of the situation; the moves he made during those few days when Wilson was out of the country set the tone for the entire debate for the months to come. Tom McNally, who had just become international secretary of the Labour Party at that time, says that someone once referred to the future Prime Minister "as Lyndon Baines Callaghan and it wasn't totally unfair. Jim was a political wheeler-dealer."[82] Callaghan demonstrated his capabilities in that regard in an extraordinary way during the crisis over industrial relations and in so doing established the foundation on which his political rehabilitation would be built. The sad thing is that his political manoeuvrings undermined what has been called "the most high profile British peace initiative" of the Nigerian civil war.[83]

Group Captain Cheshire, who had gone into the rebel-held territory and met Ojukwu two days before Wilson's arrival in Lagos and played a quasi-official role in the effort to bring the two men together,[84] was

[82] Interview with Lord McNally, 17 July 2003.

[83] Young, *The Labour Governments, Vol. II*, p. 208.

[84] Stremlau, *The International Politics of the Nigerian Civil War*, pp. 306–307. Stremlau's account quoted Ojukwu as saying that Chesire was making detailed arrangements for a visit by Wilson to Biafra, but the tone of the documents from that period does not entirely support that contention.

unaware of the concerns being addressed to Wilson by his political advisers at No. 10 Downing Street. Nevertheless, several months after that trip he told the BBC's *World at One* radio programme that if the invitation made to the rebel leader that weekend "had been handled properly and not in the most unfortunate way it was handled, there could have been a meeting". Cheshire, a decorated Royal Air Force pilot who flew dozens of bombing missions over Nazi Germany and later devoted his life to the pursuit of peace, went on to say that "it was a moment of great hope that was lost. The path should have been prepared but it wasn't."[85]

Callaghan's move against the reform of industrial relations was a brash one and years later it still raises the ire of even those who grew to admire Callaghan as Prime Minister. Kaufman, looking back on the period of *In Place of Strife*, says some Labour ministers "never actually understood the concept of collective responsibility. Callaghan certainly understood the concept of collective responsibility but decided to flout it."[86] The argument that Callaghan should have known better is applicable to the Nigerian peace mission as well: first, Callaghan was present at most of the Cabinet meetings prior to Wilson's departure for Lagos where the situation in Biafra was discussed along with the hint of a breakthrough;[87] secondly, as Home Secretary, he had recently had experience of his own in dealing with a crisis in a former British colony, when Kenya had decide to expel Kenyans of Asian descent; and thirdly, Callaghan was not someone who was unaware of the broader African problem. From 1956 to 1961 he had been shadow Colonial Secretary and often boasted of his strong ties and friendship with the future leaders of the emerging African nations. In fact, he devoted an entire chapter of his autobiography to the subject.[88]

In 1979, when he was Prime Minister, Callaghan told an interviewer how Henry Kissinger "used to say to me: 'Well, you know much more about Africa than I do', which I'm bound to say, rather arrogantly, was true. [The former US Secretary of State] hadn't been there and didn't

[85] PRO, PREM 13/3372. Letter to Michael Palliser from Group Captain Cheshire, 10 April 1969.

[86] Interview with Gerald Kaufman, 18 December 2003.

[87] PRO, CAB 128/44, Part I. Minutes from the Cabinet meetings of 6 March, 12 March 1969.

[88] Callaghan, *Time and Chance*, pp. 118–146.

know it, and I knew it pretty well."[89] So Callaghan, who his "official" biographer cited as having had a life-long connection to Nigeria,[90] had to be aware that the mission that Wilson was on that weekend had broad implications not only for Nigeria but for the British government as well. The civil war that was raging there went to the heart of the post-colonial policy of Britain; in addition, there were fears in the late 1960s that what was happening in Nigeria would be the beginning of the "Balkanisation" of Africa and could breed instability elsewhere on the continent.[91]

That fateful weekend at the end of March 1969, however, there was apparently only one thing on the Home Secretary's mind and it was not the troubles of the emerging nations of Africa nor the delicacy of Wilson's negotiating position. It was how best to use the political mis-steps of Castle and Wilson and to a lesser degree Jenkins – all of whom had joined together to support the trade union reforms – to put himself back in the position as the heir apparent to the Prime Minister. Callaghan was less concerned with deposing Wilson than shifting the balance of power within the Cabinet back in his own direction, a process that began in the week Wilson was away. Despite the kudos the Home Secretary had received from the public, his fellow ministers and the news media for his handling of the anti-Vietnam war demonstrations in Grosvenor Square the previous October, that turning point had been a success of limited value to a man of Callaghan's ambition. While Grosvenor Square showed what Callaghan could do in a crisis, it failed to truly advance his career. That is because it did not clearly delineate Callaghan, who had failed as Chancellor after sterling was devalued in 1967, from his political rivals, all of whom were in their ascendancy. On the other hand, the controversy over *In Place of Strife* set him apart.

Did Callaghan intentionally throw down the challenge at that moment because he knew Wilson would be thousands of miles away and therefore vulnerable? It is hard to believe that Callaghan would not have known the impact of his vote on the NEC; there certainly had been other opportunities in the three months after the proposal was first unveiled when he might have publicly broken with the Cabinet. Even his most ardent critics, however, doubt that Callaghan would stoop to such a low level, although Castle felt her arch enemy "was capable of

---

[89] Kenneth Harris, *The Prime Minister Talks to the Observer* (London, 1979).

[90] Morgan, *Callaghan: A Life*, p. 64.

[91] Stockholm International Peace Institute, *The Arms Trade With the Third World* (London, 1975), pp. 115–118.

anything".[92] The evidence is unclear, but certain facts emerge. The journalist Peter Jenkins, recalling that critical meeting of the NEC, said "that in the opinion of someone sitting near to him [Callaghan] did no more than react spontaneously to the situation which developed within the Executive".[93] But that matter had been postponed from the previous meeting, so Callaghan and the others would have known that it was to be discussed at the March meeting.

Callaghan must also have known that Wilson sought to defer the debate yet again, an indication that the Prime Minister feared that a negative vote on the NEC might detract from his African mission. Two days before Wilson departed London, he appealed to Nicholas to try and entice the members of the National Executive to postpone the discussion by suggesting that they all meet out at the Prime Minister's country estate at Chequers along with the Cabinet to discuss the matter after his return.[94] However if Nicholas, who would have certainly relayed that information to Callaghan as soon as he received it, had undermined the Prime Minister, Wilson was not aware of it; he noted in that same memo, written a week after the meeting, that Nicholas did his best to get the matter sidelined but "the Executive seemed determined to press on with it".[95] In addition, the committee member who moved the initial resolution to challenge the White Paper at that meeting in the fourth-floor conference room at Transport House was the right-wing future leader of the mineworkers, Joe Gormley, another close ally of Callaghan.

At the time of the NEC meeting on 26 March, Jack Jones, the heir apparent to Frank Cousins at the TGWU, was arguably the most powerful trade-union leader in England. Jones initially felt that it would have been unlikely for Callaghan to have planned his attack on the legislation to coincide with Wilson's trip to Nigeria.[96] However, after he was shown evidence that the Prime Minister tried to have debate on the matter postponed,[97] and that Nicholas and Gormley were instrumental

---

[92] Castle, *Diaries, 1964–70*, p. 567.

[93] Peter Jenkins, *The Battle of Downing Street*, p. 80.

[94] Oxford, Wilson c.936, Folio 1. Note for the record on the Industrial Relations Bill, 3 April 1969.

[95] Ibid.

[96] Interview with Jack Jones, 5 May 2004.

[97] Oxford, Wilson c.936, Folio 1. Note for the record from the Prime Minister, 3 April 1969. The fact that Wilson had made that offer to try to delay a vote is corroborated by an entry in Castle's diaries from 24 March 1969. (Castle, *Diaries, 1964–70*, p. 625).

in bringing that agenda item to the floor, he had a different appraisal of the situation. Jones, who was adamantly opposed to *In Place of Strife* from the start, now concurs with the view that Callaghan had taken advantage of the fact that the Prime Minister was about to depart on an overseas mission.[98] Although acknowledging that the NEC was much broader than Callaghan, Gormley or Nicholas, Jones concedes that Wilson's request was denied because "people like Nicholas and Gormley would if anything want to do the opposite of what Wilson wanted", and Callaghan "would be party to anything that would undermine Wilson".[99]

Apparently Wilson embarked on the Africa trip because he had felt that if there were going to be any significant breakthrough in bringing the two sides together there would be a far better chance of it happening if it was brought about by him as Prime Minister rather than through an emissary. Michael Stewart, the Foreign Secretary, offered to go in his place. But Wilson conceded "this was an all or nothing job and partly a public-relations job", saying "he felt profoundly unhappy to sit doing nothing about Nigeria given the present troubles and growing uneasiness with the issue among the public".[100] But after he arrived in Nigeria, he must have been "profoundly unhappy" doing nothing, too, about the troubles that Callaghan had stirred up on the National Executive, in the Parliamentary Labour Party and in the news media over the few short days that he had been away. Any political crisis is distressing to a Prime Minister, but one that occurs when he is out of the country is even more disturbing, something Callaghan himself learned when as Prime Minister he was in the Caribbean at the time of a series of public sector strikes that became known as the "Winter of Discontent".

In situations like these, damage is done that can never be rectified.[101] Callaghan gained the upper hand in the Cabinet on *In Place of Strife* during that crucial week and Wilson, despite all his efforts, never regained it. "It was not wholly to his credit that *In Place of Strife* episode," says Brian Cubbon, who was Callaghan's private secretary at the time. "There was an element of I've got a good case for establishing myself and I'm

---

[98] Interview with Jack Jones, 5 May 2004.
[99] Ibid.
[100] PRO, PREM 13/2817/11. Note of a telephone conversation between the Prime Minister and the Foreign Secretary, 7 March 1969.
[101] Interview with Sir Kenneth Stowe, 12 May 2004.

going to push it for what I've got."[102] Wilson's private secretary, Michael Palliser, who was with the Prime Minister in Africa, agrees: "Callaghan was much more concerned with not going anywhere that he thought the party didn't want to go, and also, of course, with doing Wilson in the eye as well. I mean you know there were two considerations there. Again as I say that's not a value judgement. That's simply a statement of fact."[103]

One thing that Callaghan's handling of these events shows is that he was a skilled politician with an incredible ability to seize the moment and make the most of it. He would not make a move of such consequence without thinking it through and having at least a reasonable chance of success. But it is important to note that while he was incredibly perceptive, he was a politician who was not likely to get bogged down in deeper principles. The pragmatic approach that he took with Grosvenor Square, he took with *In Place of Strife* and he would certainly take that approach again in the crisis that emerged later in Northern Ireland. Another quality that Callaghan had, one that makes it difficult to retrace his tracks, was that he did many things out of the limelight and through surrogates.[104] Wilson's press secretary, Haines, says there were plenty of people working behind the scenes for Callaghan during the time of *In Place of Strife*, Houghton among them. But "Jim would have denied any contact.... Jim would never say we got to get rid of this man. You understand that. He isn't that type of politician. You might get other, less subtle, less experienced, less able politicians who would take the bull by the horns. Jim would never attack a bull from the front."[105]

Conclusion

Callaghan was a man of enormous ambition, and in that week that Wilson was away from London he began the process of laying the groundwork for his political rehabilitation. But it came in two stages. The first stage was the vote against the government on the National Executive and the general confusion that this action triggered. With

---

[102] Interview with Sir Brian Cubbon, 19 June 2003.

[103] Interview with Sir Michael Palliser, 31 July 2003.

[104] James Margach, *The Abuse of Power: The War Between Downing Street and the Media From Lloyd George to Callaghan* (London, 1978), p. 172. The reporter for *The Sunday Times* had referred to Callaghan as "a man who takes care never to get his hands dirty, let alone leave his fingerprints around".

[105] Interview with Joe Haines, 25 March 2004.

Wilson out of town, Callaghan was able to make his move on the NEC and follow it up over the next several days without having to deal with Wilson, a skilled and clever negotiator for the other side, who had the advantage of being the Prime Minister. Also, one thing that should not be forgotten is that Callaghan's vote on the NEC was not decisive. If he had missed that meeting or abstained, the resolution denouncing *In Place of Strife* would still have passed, 3 to 1.

The second stage was Callaghan's cleverly crafted attacks against *In Place of Strife* at several junctures over the next few months. Those attacks maintained Callaghan as a central figure in the opposition to that legislation and reshaped his role within the government, giving him a firm base upon which to rebuild his influence within the Cabinet and hence his reputation. No man is an island and in the next chapter we will take a more detailed look at how Callaghan solidified his gains by opposing *In Place of Strife* with the help of a few important figures both within and outside the government.

The initial strike against Wilson was an especially shrewd political move and carefully orchestrated; in the telegrams sent to the Prime Minister that weekend there was a pattern. In those notes there are indications, either from Callaghan himself or those who had had contact with him, that the Home Secretary had no intention of resigning. But in those exchanges, too, there was just enough doubt introduced to put Wilson on edge that Callaghan just might resign after all if the government did not modify its position. The fear that Callaghan would quit was with Wilson right from the start. When Wilson first heard the news of Callaghan's vote on the NEC, just as the Prime Minister was preparing to depart for Lagos, he considered demanding that his Home Secretary resign but on second thought "was not content to leave the country with a situation in which a senior minister would be able, for almost a week, to cause trouble from the backbenches and to elevate the policy issue involved into an issue of principle, a concept in any case alien to [Callaghan]".[106]

However, Callaghan managed to do just that, though he did it from the front benches. In that environment, certain events occurred which suggest that sometime either late on Sunday, 30 March, or Monday, 31 March, Wilson decided that the political threat from Callaghan had reached such a level that it had to be put down and the talks with

---

[106] Oxford, Wilson c.936, Folio 1. Note for the record on the Industrial Relations Bill, 3 April 1969.

Ojukwu gently sidelined. The evidence of that was the early departure of the HMS *Fearless*, the recall of emissaries who had been scheduled to go into Biafra ahead of any talks to meet with Ojukwu to set up the protocol for a meeting elsewhere in Africa, and indications that Wilson either planned to, or did in fact, return early. The fact that his flight departed Addis Ababa at daybreak on Wednesday, 2 April, might be evidence of his eagerness to return as well.[107] Nevertheless, there was so much attention being drawn to Callaghan for his defiance of collective Cabinet responsibility that his critics failed to see an equally troubling dimension to his opposition, namely that it was orchestrated to take advantage of Wilson's absence from London and without regard to the government's sensitive position in trying to bring about an end to the fighting in Nigeria.

Another puzzling point is that in 1970, when the *Guardian's* political correspondent Peter Jenkins published a definitive work on the whole saga of *In Place of Strife*, Callaghan, not one who was thought to be overly sensitive to press criticism, turned the matter over to his legal adviser. Amid fears of a lawsuit, the solicitors for the book's publisher agreed to the removal of several negative remarks about the motives of the Home Secretary from the text of *The Battle of Downing Street*; there was nothing in that book that suggested that Callaghan deliberately undermined Wilson's peace mission. On the contrary, the book was quite critical of Wilson and painted a fairly flattering picture of Callaghan as the "keeper of the cloth cap".[108] There is also the question of what role Tom McCaffrey, Callaghan's press secretary, played in this episode. McCaffrey contends that he had little to do with the whole debate over industrial relations.[109] However, interviews with several people close to Callaghan, including the permanent secretary at the Home Office who remembers McCaffrey having unfettered access to Callaghan,[110] would refute that. Also, Callaghan's biographer cites McCaffrey as among those who were the Home Secretary's most trusted advisers during the whole saga of *In Place of Strife*.[111]

Nevertheless, during that critical week Wilson made it clear that the individuals on whom he most relied to give him a proper assessment of

---

[107] PRO, PREM 13/2785/11. Telegram to Michael Halls from Edward Youde, Prime Minister's party, in Addis Ababa, 1 April 1969.

[108] Morgan, *Callaghan: A Life*, p. 341.

[109] Interview with Sir Tom McCaffrey, 3 July 2003.

[110] Interview with Lord Allen, 30 July 2003.

[111] Morgan, *Callaghan: A Life*, p. 339.

the situation back in London were: Fred Peart, the leader of the House; John Silkin, the government's Chief Whip; his press secretary, Haines; and the head of his Political Office, Marcia Williams. Of that group, Silkin and Williams advised the Prime Minister in separate telegrams on the Monday that the Callaghan affair was getting out of hand and that he needed to cut short his tour and return home; Haines and Peart took a less alarmist view, but both relayed hints of a Callaghan resignation. Though Wilson was getting counsel from many quarters it is clear that Williams was the person whose advice he relied upon the most. Williams, who worked briefly for Callaghan years earlier, understood Callaghan better than most people and had a grudging respect for his political timing, being a skilled operative in her own right. She summed Callaghan up years later as having the "agility to place himself with one bound at the head of the biggest column that is forming".[112]

In addition, Williams sensed that Callaghan was testing the waters and while he had to be put firmly in his place, she knew that any overreaction on the Prime Minister's part would ignite even more speculation in the press and undermine Wilson's leadership altogether. Bernard Donoughue, the senior aide to Callaghan when he was Prime Minister but who previously worked with Williams under Wilson's premiership, recalls that Callaghan "was fairly supportive of her. I didn't get on with her, but he didn't like me criticising her".[113] Haines, Wilson's press secretary, agrees that the relationship between Callaghan and Williams was good, although he feels that it was more a case of Callaghan having great respect for Williams and her shrewdness than her having any particular regard for Callaghan: "She never trusted him." Haines, who in later years was among Williams's toughest critics, concedes that her political skills, particularly during the period of *In Place of Strife*, were exceptional.[114]

There was another pattern here as well. Time and again there are indications that Callaghan expected of others what he failed to deliver himself. In 1977, nearly a decade after the end of the battle over *In Place of Strife*, Callaghan begged Peter Shore, the Secretary for the Environment, not to challenge the Labour government's commitment to membership in the European Economic Community. Callaghan, laying

---

[112] Marcia Falkender, *Downing Street in Perspective* (London, 1983), p. 218. Falkender is the name that Marcia Williams took when a rank of nobility was conferred on her in 1974 on Wilson's recommendation. Before leaving office, he elevated her to the Lords.

[113] Interview with Lord Donoughue, 9 July 2003.

[114] Interview with Joe Haines, 25 March 2004.

claim to "a horrible feeling that...full-scale war will break out", told Shore that a speech that he was about to make, one that no doubt would wind up on the front pages of newspapers across the country, "would be tantamount to saying (Britain) should leave the community if we do not achieve what you regard as the main task ahead, namely the revision" of the Treaty of Rome itself.[115]

The parallels to Callaghan's plea in September 1977 and the clash with the trade unions in the first six months of 1969 are uncanny. Shore was a member of the Labour Party's National Executive Committee, as Callaghan had been in 1969, and it was there that the matter was to be debated; the issue Shore proposed to contest was outside his ministerial responsibility, as had been the case with Callaghan, who as Home Secretary had been a thorn in the side of Wilson's efforts to reform the trade unions; and the problem of Europe in 1977 could as Callaghan told Shore "tear us apart" as had certainly been the case with *In Place of Strife*. There were two major differences, however: Shore acquiesced and never delivered that speech, and never became Prime Minister,[116] and Callaghan by 1977 was no longer the contentious bluff Home Secretary defiantly opposing the Prime Minister, but the Prime Minister himself.

---

[115] BLPES, Shore 722. Minute to the Secretary of State for the Environment from the Prime Minister, 28 September 1977.
[116] BLPES, Shore 444. Shore tried, without Callaghan's support, to gain the Labour Party leadership in 1983 but was among those who lost out to Neil Kinnock. (Handwritten letter to Shore from Callaghan, 22 September 1983.)

4
Setting the Stage: *In Place of Strife*

The manoeuvring that Callaghan had done on the industrial relations front while the Prime Minister had been away prompted Harold Wilson to do what many felt he should have done months earlier. Within hours of his return from Addis Ababa on Wednesday, 2 April 1969, the Prime Minister began secretly to put the wheels in motion for an abbreviated and, what his closest advisers had hoped would be, a more marketable version of *In Place of Strife;*[1] in other words, legislation that could make its way through Parliament far quicker than the original bill. On the advice of Barbara Castle and Roy Jenkins, he agreed to set aside the detailed White Paper that had triggered so much controversy in the National Executive and, instead, offer up an interim bill that could be included in the Chancellor's budget, the details of which were to be delivered to Cabinet in less than two weeks.

The short bill, for enactment before the summer recess, retained that part of the original proposal that gave the government the ability to step into a labour dispute and order a four-week cooling-off period. But it put off to future legislation the equally contentious requirement that called for trade unions to ballot their workers before ordering a strike. It kept in place the idea of levying "financial penalties" against workers who illegally stayed off the job, but "categorically ruled out" jailing anyone who refused to pay. In addition, the short bill put the whole matter of levying the penalties, which were no longer to be referred to as "fines",

---

[1] Labour History Archive (Manchester), Heffer ESH/3/4. The Labour MP Eric Heffer's handwritten comments on a copy of the original White Paper reflected the feelings of a significant segment of the Parliamentary Labour Party: "The soft sell for a hard deal. 80% acceptable – possibly more, but rest spoil the possible achievement..."

in the hands of an industrial board with representatives from both the government and the trade unions.[2] While this was to be presented as a further softening of the government's stance, the door remained open to the possibility that the civil courts might step in and order the seizure of a worker's personal belongings if he or she refused to pay.[3]

The fast-track approach that Wilson embraced within hours of his return from his African peace mission was not far removed from the earlier whimsical ideas of two of his closest political advisers, Gerald Kaufman and Joe Haines. Kaufman, having been with Wilson in Africa, experienced first-hand the Prime Minister's frustration at having been so distant from the developing political crisis; Haines, meanwhile, had used his contacts with the news media to try and calculate the political damage inflicted upon the government by Callaghan's intrigues. But six years earlier, they had been a pair of young comedy writers for *That Was The Week That Was*, the popular political satire programme on BBC TV. Then they had written a routine about the ushering into the Commons of the first vending machines for food and beverages and asked, Why stop there? Why not have vending machines at Westminster that can turn out "instant" government policies? In that skit, Kaufman and Haines had aptly noted that sometimes "MPs need a policy in a hurry"[4] and, oddly enough, in early April 1969 that was exactly the position that Wilson found himself in.

The sense of urgency explained why Castle and Jenkins had several meetings while the Prime Minister had been in Africa, including a private lunch at No. 11 Downing Street on Friday, 28 March, just two days after Callaghan's vote at the National Executive Committee (NEC) meeting.[5] By the following Monday, Castle and her advisers had begun to cobble together the short bill with the idea being that the remainder of the proposals in the White Paper would be addressed after the next general election.[6] The next day, Tuesday, the Chancellor, leaving little

---

[2] PRO, CAB 128/44 Part I. Minutes from Cabinet meeting of 14 April 1969.

[3] *Sun*, 17 April 1969, p. 1.

[4] BBC Written Archives, Script D421-172-0703. *That Was The Week That Was*, transcript from broadcast of 16 February 1963.

[5] PRO, LAB 77/15. Castle's ministerial appointments diary, 28 March 1969. The entry for that day indicates the urgency of the meeting. It appears the First Secretary had cancelled an earlier luncheon date with an unnamed individual at Escargot in London to meet with the Chancellor.

[6] PRO, LAB 77/15. Castle's ministerial appointments diary, 31 March 1969. Castle met on the interim bill with Roy Hattersley, her parliamentary private secretary, and several officials from her department.

to chance, lobbied for support for the early legislation from a wavering Peter Shore, who at that time had been overseeing the Department of Economic Affairs. Shore had been among those who had secretly met with Castle in the autumn of 1968, before the original proposal had been presented to Cabinet. Shore wrote in his diary of a "very unexpected invitation to lunch *à deux* with RJ [*sic*] at No. 11. Asked me not to say anything subsequently. Agreed. He is clearly waving an olive branch and I am slightly flattered. Difficult to form a real judgement over the claret and lamb chops but it sounded right to me ... "[7]

No time had been wasted; Castle and Jenkins in the wake of Callaghan's vote at the National Executive had been determined to have a definitive proposal to put before the Prime Minister as soon as he arrived back in London from Addis Ababa that Wednesday.[8] They had made it clear through Wilson's principal private secretary, Michael Halls, more than once that they needed to see the Prime Minister as soon as he returned and this message had been relayed to Wilson and Kaufman in Addis Ababa. But Wilson's first concern was limiting the immediate political damage to his own position.[9] As a result, it was Marcia Williams who Wilson wanted to talk to first, not Jenkins or Castle, when he arrived back in London, "to discuss who I should see and in what order".[10]

Meanwhile, Wilson, along with Kaufman and the rest of the entourage, had risen before daybreak that Wednesday, and had made their way out to the airport at Addis Ababa. They had climbed aboard a Royal Air Force jet, and after a refuelling stop arrived back in London in the late afternoon. The group returned just in time for the Prime Minister to address Parliament before the Easter recess, ostensibly to

---

[7] BLPES, Shore 71. Notation from the diary of Peter Shore, 1 April 1969.

[8] Wilson, *A Personal Record*, pp. 639–640. Wilson said he had received a telegram from Castle while he was en route to London on 2 April 1969 that indicated that she favoured a short bill, but that she thought there would not be enough time to prepare the legislation. Wilson said that after he arrived home and met with Castle and Jenkins, to his "surprise" Castle now thought that the timing would not be a problem.

[9] *Glasgow Herald*, 2 April 1969, p. 8. To show how much the situation deteriorated over the weekend, the hometown newspaper of Labour Party general secretary Nicholas headlined its lead editorial "After Wilson".

[10] PRO, PREM 13/2785, Folio 16. Telegram to Michael Halls from the Prime Minister in Addis Ababa. It is undated, as are some of the other telegrams in this series of documents. But related documents make it apparent that the telegram was from 2 April 1969.

report on his diplomatic mission to Nigeria. In reality, the trip straight from London airport to Westminster, with Haines having arrived at the airport, and Williams having joined Wilson and Kaufman further up the road for the ride back into London,[11] had less to do with Nigeria and more to do with Callaghan. The address to Parliament had been a smokescreen, an excuse so that the Prime Minister could assemble the parliamentary party without calling attention to what had been his real objective, namely to quickly reaffirm his leadership of the Labour Party. The Prime Minister and his top political advisers had agreed that there would be no press conference upon his arrival at the airport and hence no embarrassing questions.[12] Wilson was eager to get to the House of Commons with one overriding purpose in mind, namely to demonstrate that he was "in charge", without making it obvious that he had been deeply alarmed by what Callaghan had been up to.[13]

At the airport, Haines briefed the Prime Minister on the more immediate situation, which had deteriorated even further in the previous 24 hours. In particular, Haines told Wilson about the political fallout from the column that had appeared the day before in the *Guardian*.[14] Peter Jenkins had written that Callaghan "has now made effectively public a belief which he has long been mouthing in semiprivate. That is that Labour has no chance of victory under Mr. Wilson's leadership, and might have a sporting chance under his own."[15] It was clear that the insinuation of the *Guardian* column – excerpts of which had been featured on the front page and had given the column added significance[16] – had reverberated within the Parliamentary Labour Party, just as Haines predicted. Therefore the conversation between Wilson, Williams and Kaufman in the car as it raced along the route from Heathrow to

---

[11] Oxford, Wilson c.936, Folio 1. Note for the record from the Prime Minister, 3 April 1969.

[12] PRO, PREM 13/2785, Folio 16. Telegram to Michael Halls from the Prime Minister, apparently from 2 April 1969; Interview with Joe Haines, 25 March 2004.

[13] PRO, PREM 13/2785, Folio 10. Telegram to Prime Minister in Addis Ababa from Marcia Williams, undated, but clearly from 31 March 1969.

[14] Oxford, Wilson c.936, Folio 1. Note for the record from the Prime Minister, 3 April 1969.

[15] *Guardian*, 1 April 1969, p. 11.

[16] PRO, PREM 13/2785, Folio 12, undated, but apparently from 1 April 1969. The point had not been lost on Haines, who cited the "extract" that had appeared in bold type on page one as adding to the damaging impact of the newspaper's coverage.

Westminster in the late afternoon concentrated on controlling the damage being done by Callaghan, which had now become even more acute in the wake of Peter Jenkins's column.[17]

Wilson had had a gruelling week and looked tired as he arrived at the Houses of Parliament. Peter Jenkins later wrote that "devaluation had been a great trauma but this was perhaps the unhappiest and most unnerving period of his prime ministership to date. For once he seemed to his colleagues to be rattled."[18] Wilson met with Castle and Roy Jenkins "within a couple of hours" of his arrival at the airport to discuss the proposal for interim legislation, and again shortly after midnight and then again the following day.[19] Years later, Callaghan defended the actions that had precipitated the crisis by saying that Castle had unfairly singled him out and that it had not just been he who had opposed *In Place of Strife*. "It wasn't I who opposed her, I was certainly one of them. But it was also the parliamentary party, the trade unions themselves, the National Executive Committee. There was a whole area of the labour movement."[20] That might have been true, but Castle knew that Callaghan's intrigues and his significant influence within those very elements of the labour movement that he cited made his opposition to her White Paper unlike any other. Callaghan's opposition had been like no other for another reason as well. It had been a carefully calculated move on Callaghan's part to defeat the legislation but with a greater purpose in mind, namely to rebuild his own influence in the Cabinet.

Although Castle and Jenkins were the architects of the interim bill,[21] designed to head off the storm unleashed by Callaghan's vote on the National Executive, their recollections differ on Callaghan's reaction when the revised proposal was first presented to Cabinet two weeks later,

---

[17] Oxford, Wilson c.936, Folio 1. Note for the record from the Prime Minister, 3 April 1969.

[18] Peter Jenkins, *The Battle of Downing Street*, pp. 96–97.

[19] Oxford, Wilson c.936. Draft letter to Crossman from the Prime Minister, June 1969. (Notation on the original indicates that the letter was never sent.) Crossman was the only other individual at those private meetings. There were also more private meetings between Wilson, Castle, Jenkins and Crossman about the interim legislation just after the Easter recess.

[20] BBC2, *The Red Queen: A Film Portrait of Barbara Castle*, by Michael Cockerell, 29 January 1995.

[21] Interview with Lady Jenkins, 21 April 2004. Jennifer Jenkins recalls that even before *In Place of Strife* Castle and her husband "got on well" in that 1966–70 Cabinet. She says that they "rather agreed on economic policy, opposing Callaghan's management of the economy when he was Chancellor".

on 14 April, the eve of Budget Day. Jenkins contends that Callaghan was one of two ministers at that meeting, in the Prime Minister's room in the House of Commons, who opposed the interim bill.[22] Castle's recollection of the events of that afternoon is the exact opposite; it indicates that Callaghan offered no serious resistance to the change in strategy.[23] What might seem at first to be a minor discrepancy is actually of fundamental importance, especially given the critical roles played by Castle and Jenkins, both of whom were Callaghan's adversaries; untangling it is essential to understanding Callaghan's tactics. If Jenkins's recollection is accurate it gives credence to the argument that Callaghan had stood his ground on the issue and put principle before politics; on the other hand, if Castle's version is correct, it tells a different story.

Interestingly, even though Roy Jenkins was a prolific writer and an historian and was conscious of the importance of detail, an examination of the available evidence overwhelmingly supports Castle's version of what happened at that meeting. The discrepancy between the two accounts might be explained by the fact that Jenkins's version, which is included in his memoirs published in 1991, was written many years after the event. By that time Callaghan's overall opposition to *In Place of Strife* had become legendary, overshadowing the memory of specific details of specific meetings. On the other hand, Castle's account, which appears in her diaries, was taken from notes written in shorthand at the Cabinet meeting that afternoon.[24] Also, while the entry in Tony Benn's diary from that date is inconclusive on that particular point, Castle's description of events is supported by Richard Crossman.[25] Crossman told the *Guardian's* Alastair Hetherington in a private conversation less

---

[22] Roy Jenkins, *A Life at the Centre* (London, 1991), p. 288. "The Budget Cabinet on 14 April approved my announcement of early legislation with only the odd combination of Callaghan and Richard Marsh (who now seems a surprising defender of unfettered trade union rights) dissenting."

[23] Castle, *Diaries, 1964–70*, p. 635. "We had taken great care not to circulate any papers beforehand, knowing our Jim, but he must have suspected what was in the wind because he took the announcement of the short bill calmly enough. Indeed he was obviously looking for excuses not to make a resignation issue of it."

[24] Interviews with Lord Healey, 22 March 2004, and Tony Benn, 21 July 2003. Both Healey and Benn were in that Cabinet and had backed the legislation. While they question the accuracy of some of Crossman's diaries, which often had been recorded from memory on the weekend, they attest to the overall accuracy of Castle's diaries. Castle always kept shorthand notes of the meetings.

[25] Crossman, *Diaries*, Vol. III, p. 439. Crossman's entry for that afternoon said that Callaghan had "made a long speech about how we must now work together and how pleased he was at the decision ... "

than three weeks later that "there wasn't a member of the Cabinet who didn't share the Prime Minister's determination to put the short bill on the statute book" in that session of Parliament.[26] Although the actual minutes kept by the Cabinet Office are characteristically less specific and do not say who said what, there is no indication from those records that there was any fervent opposition to the bill. On the contrary, the minutes state that while some concerns were raised "the case for early legislation was very strong".[27]

In addition, a revealing and detailed memorandum on this point written at the time and found within Wilson's private papers indicates that the Prime Minister was amazed that "no one demurred" at that meeting. Wilson writes that the proposal for the short bill was agreed to "remarkably easily" and Callaghan "put one or two questions but raised no objection".[28] Wilson might have thought that his Home Secretary had turned a new leaf after he had given him a rather mild rebuke for his vote on the National Executive,[29] but Callaghan's acquiescence, supported by the evidence, had deeper roots. Callaghan was a shrewd enough politician to realise that there were great advantages for him in Wilson's sudden reversal of policy. By the Prime Minister urgently offering up the shorter version of the bill and tying it to the budget, four things happened that would strengthen Callaghan's ability to further exploit the issue and set the stage for his political rehabilitation.

First, Callaghan's political adversary Roy Jenkins now became entwined in the controversy with the trade unions in a more public way, seriously compromising his ability to be an alternative to Wilson in the broader political debate. From the start, Jenkins, who had always been the silent third partner with Wilson and Castle in the struggle to reform the trade unions, had favoured a quick solution having told Castle months earlier that unless they moved swiftly and put a bill before Parliament by July "the rats would get at the package".[30] By the time Jenkins's point of view had been finally embraced by Castle and

---

[26] BLPES, Hetherington 16/18. Conversation between Crossman and Hetherington at Prescote Manor, 4 May 1969.

[27] PRO, CAB 128/44 Part I. Minutes of Cabinet meeting of 14 April 1969.

[28] Oxford, Wilson c.936, Folio 2. Note for the record from the Prime Minister (following from note of 3 April 1969).

[29] Castle, *Diaries, 1964–70*, p. 631. While Wilson had left the impression with the news media that he had scolded Callaghan in Cabinet for his misbehaviour, in reality, as Castle noted in her diary, "the thunderbolt never came."

[30] Roy Jenkins, *A Life at the Centre* (London, 1991), pp. 287–288.

then Wilson, the dynamic in the country had changed. On 15 April, a day before Castle addressed Parliament with the details of the new measure,[31] the Chancellor announced in his budget speech both the intention to enact the short bill along with a plan to scuttle the unpopular prices and incomes policy. The elimination of that policy, which required that wage settlements be cleared by an independent board, was something which Callaghan, among others, had been urging for months. While the idea of offering such a compromise to make the Industrial Relations Bill more palatable might have worked in January, it was less likely to succeed in April, especially given Callaghan's vote on the National Executive and the ensuing controversy.

Secondly, the urgency for the short bill gave more credence to Callaghan's argument that changes had been pushed through without going through the normal deliberative processes and without the proposed legislation being properly thought out. Callaghan could argue, and in fact later did, that the initial agreement to debate all aspects of the proposal over several months had been abandoned, as had been the likelihood that the debate would continue at the Trades Union Congress in September and the party conference in October. In his autobiography, he refers to this as a "broken" promise and says that *In Place of Strife* "was suddenly to be turned into instant government",[32] a remark that was eerily reminiscent of the old comedy sketch written by Kaufman and Haines on *That Was The Week That Was*. One thing Callaghan leaves out of his recollection of those events, however, is the fact that he was among those who had unanimously backed that strategy. Not only did he agree to it, the overwhelming evidence suggests that he did not in any way qualify his support. What is evident as well is that this sudden speeding up of the timetable was something the Home Secretary proceeded to criticise in the months ahead even though Wilson, the day after his return from his Africa tour, had compelled Callaghan and the rest of the Cabinet to reaffirm their support for the principle of collective Cabinet responsibility.

Thirdly, the rush to legislate mobilised trade union opposition to the bill in a way that had not existed before, giving Callaghan the opportunity to consolidate his gains. *The Sunday Times* Insight team,

---

[31] BBC Written Archives. Transcript of the Radio 4 programme *Today in Parliament*, 15 April 1969. The BBC's parliamentary correspondent reported that Castle's speech about the interim bill "got a pretty cold reception from many Labour members".

[32] Callaghan, *Time and Chance*, p. 274.

which probed deeper into the big stories of the day, said the "short, sharp measure" was "enough to touch off the gravest conflict between the unions and the Labour Party since one created the other" at the turn of the century.[33] Instead of Callaghan warning his colleagues at the 14 April meeting of the impending dangers of such a move – given his closeness to Harry Nicholas, the former acting general secretary of the Transport and General Workers' Union (TGWU), and Joe Gormley of the National Union of Mineworkers, both of whom had played a key role at the 26 March meeting of the National Executive – he chose to deliver a statement of empty praise for the interim legislation. Behind the closed doors of that Cabinet meeting, Callaghan congratulated his unsuspecting fellow ministers for "a welcome readiness ... to negotiate with the TUC", something the Prime Minister noted that "Barbara in fact had always said".[34] This suggests the Home Secretary was setting a trap that his political adversaries would fall into one by one by agreeing to the proposal in the belief that Callaghan had somehow come around.[35]

The interim bill provided the perfect chance for Callaghan to grab onto the coat tails of the big union leaders, whom he knew would be incensed by such a move, and with their help indirectly regain his stature within the Cabinet. It is important to remember that Callaghan was now the only remaining senior minister with any trade union background in the Cabinet, since Ray Gunter, George Brown and Frank Cousins had all left the government. Later that same day, 14 April, the Prime Minister had got a hint of the extent of the opposition that was awaiting the proposal when he took Victor Feather, the acting general secretary of the Trades Union Congress (TUC), into his confidence to tell him of the government's plan to introduce the interim bill as part of the budget statement the next day. Wilson recalled that Feather, who was about to go on television to discuss the likely budget, agreed to pretend he knew nothing about the planned switch in strategy, but was "obviously disturbed" by the news.[36]

---

[33] *The Sunday Times*, 20 April 1969, p. 13.

[34] Oxford, Wilson c.936, Folio 2. Note for the record from the Prime Minister (following from note of 3 April 1969).

[35] *Daily Express*, 17 April 1969, p. 9. The newspaper's account on the day that the short bill had been introduced to Parliament was aptly headlined, "Mrs. Castle Walks Into a 'Roasting'".

[36] Oxford, Wilson c.936, Folio 2. Note for the record from the Prime Minister (following from note of 3 April 1969).

Finally, the fast-track approach with its determination to legislate in the current session played into Callaghan's hands by forcing the controversy over *In Place of Strife* into a much tighter timeframe. The interim bill sharpened the debate and made it far easier for Callaghan to propel a further dramatic showdown with Wilson without doing irreparable harm to the party's prospects in the next general election.[37] That showdown came a mere three weeks later, on Friday, 9 May 1969, at the day-long joint meeting of the National Executive and the Cabinet that was held behind closed doors at No. 10 Downing Street. Callaghan once again saved his onslaught for the moment of maximum political impact.[38] Despite the Cabinet having agreed a day earlier that it would not challenge the interim bill,[39] Callaghan, before his assembled ministerial colleagues and trade union leaders, once again delivered a blistering attack on the very legislation he had earlier supported.[40]

In an unvarnished appeal to the trade union leaders present, Callaghan told the gathering that the government had "a duty to prove that this policy is essential and they [had] not done so".[41] Peter Jenkins later wrote that the speech displayed such raw political ambition that even some of Callaghan's supporters had been disgusted by his behaviour.[42] Peter Jenkins argued in *The Battle of Downing Street* that the oration had been a "mistake" and a case of Callaghan going "too far". In addition, he blamed that speech for a split that occurred among Callaghan's own supporters in the Parliamentary Labour Party, some of whom thought that Callaghan's use of the occasion essentially to repeat a position that everyone was aware of, without resigning from the Cabinet over a matter of principle, had been utterly disloyal.[43] But that

---

[37] For Callaghan that would have been an important consideration; although he had not been loyal to Wilson, he was intensely loyal to the Labour Party.

[38] *The Times*, 17 April 1969, p. 1. After Wilson had returned from Africa, Callaghan had been sidelined on the issue. For example, the extensive coverage of the interim bill on page one of *The Times* had made no reference to Callaghan or any internal government opposition.

[39] Oxford, Wilson c.936, Folio 3. Note for the record from the Prime Minister (following from dictation of 10 May 1969).

[40] *The Sunday Times*, 4 May 1969, p. 12. Callaghan had caught the news media off guard as well. *The Sunday Times* in its lead editorial, five days before the joint NEC-Cabinet meeting, said that "already there are signs that the present attacks on [Wilson's leadership] are fading away..."

[41] *Sun*, 10 May 1969, p. 1.

[42] Peter Jenkins, *The Battle of Downing Street*, pp. 115–118.

[43] Ibid.

premise implies that Callaghan was actively able or seeking to replace the Prime Minister, a contention that the available evidence seems not to support. As the journalist Anthony Howard says, Callaghan did not have the reserves to remove Wilson from the leadership in the spring of 1969, "whereas Roy [Jenkins] jolly near did. Roy had about 100 MPs".[44] What is closer to the truth is that Callaghan was a risk-adverse politician who never took a position without having a pretty clear objective in mind.[45] Peter Jenkins is correct in saying that that speech was a repetition of Callaghan's earlier remarks. But because it was given at that particular time and before that particular audience, it served as an important element in setting the stage for his political rehabilitation. Having enticed his adversaries down a treacherous path, Callaghan used that speech to scuttle his Cabinet commitment to the interim bill, and to reaffirm his opposition to *In Place of Strife* so as to maintain his credibility with the trade unions.[46] In a clever sleight of hand, Callaghan, at that joint meeting of the NEC and Cabinet, brought himself back into the ranks of the fervent opponents to the measure by doing the exact same thing he had done before the National Executive in March, namely opposing the very legislation that he had earlier supported in Cabinet. This time, however, he attacked *In Place of Strife* with the Prime Minister present, rather than behind Wilson's back.

The Prime Minister was incensed by Callaghan's remarks, particularly the attitude he had taken in telling that gathering that ministers "seem to believe they have some divine authority to govern, irrespective of the effects on the movement".[47] Wilson noted that the Home Secretary acted "loftily",[48] as though he was detached from the Cabinet. In addition, what the *Sun* called the Home Secretary's "most serious challenge to his Cabinet colleagues"[49] had been broadcast on the evening news programmes of both the BBC and ITV, the BBC's commercial competitor,

---

[44] Interview with Anthony Howard, 12 March 2004.
[45] Interview with Lord Hattersley, 1 March 2004. Hattersley recalls Michael Foot telling him, after Hattersley's maiden speech in Parliament, that Callaghan was a politician who "does everything on purpose".
[46] While there had been several ministers – Richard Marsh, Crossman, Crosland, Peter Shore and Judith Hart – who had also broken ranks and voiced their displeasure with the bill at various times within the Cabinet, none of them had publicly undermined the White Paper.
[47] *Sun*, 10 May 1969, p. 1.
[48] Oxford, Wilson c.936, Folio 2. Note for the record from the Prime Minister (following from note of 3 April 1969).
[49] *Sun*, 10 May 1969, p. 1.

within minutes of the session ending. Callaghan did not leave No. 10 Downing Street that entire day, and later expressed his utter astonishment that the details of his speech had been leaked to the press before the meeting had concluded.[50] But the Prime Minister later discovered that it had been Douglas Houghton, the chairman of the Parliamentary Labour Party and Callaghan's old trade-union associate, who had been the informant. Wilson said that he had learned from "an unimpeachable source, himself relying directly on a journalist friend not unwilling to quote sources, that it was in fact Houghton",[51] who had leaked the details of Callaghan's remarks.

Houghton had left No. 10 just before lunch and shortly after Callaghan's speech.[52] Since that speech had been among the first delivered in the eight-hour long meeting,[53] it would have been ideally timed to make the afternoon's newspapers and that evening's TV news broadcasts.[54] Castle noticed that Houghton had not attended the luncheon and pointed that out the following day to Percy Clark, the Labour Party's press officer, after he had told her that he had been "shocked" that details of Callaghan's speech had appeared in newspapers being sold in the street as the participants had left Downing Street.[55] Nevertheless, the fact that Callaghan had immediately used a surrogate to leak the contents of that morning's speech, in other words to get his comments to the press before any of the other speeches might make their way into the newspapers, suggests he was less concerned with debating the merits of the proposed legislation than in maximising that platform for his own political advantage.[56]

After Callaghan's speech, which had drawn no applause, the Prime Minister said that "three junior members of the Cabinet had demanded that Jim be sacked, and even had threatened their own resignations if

---

[50] Oxford, Wilson c.936, Folio 3. Note for the record from the Prime Minister (following from dictation of 10 May 1969).

[51] Oxford, Wilson c.936, Folio 2. Note for the record from the Prime Minister (following from note of 3 April 1969).

[52] Ibid.

[53] *Guardian*, 10 May 1969, p. 1.

[54] Oxford, Wilson c.936, Folio 3. Note for the record from the Prime Minister (following from dictation of 10 May 1969).

[55] Castle, *Diaries, 1964–70*, p. 650.

[56] Minutes of NEC meeting at Transport House, 21 May 1969. Oddly enough, Callaghan and Nicholas were among those who "expressed their concern" at the NEC meeting over the leaking of the speech to the press apparently "during the lunch interval" at the joint NEC-Cabinet meeting.

he were not".[57] The story above the fold on page one of the next day's *Guardian*, however, struck a sympathetic tone[58] towards the Home Secretary's remarks and no doubt would have been of far more importance to Callaghan than the threats of junior ministers. Instead of drawing attention to the Home Secretary's betrayal once again of collective Cabinet responsibility, the *Guardian* focused on a different aspect of his behaviour – one that was summed up well by the three-column headline which read: "Callaghan Again the Union's Champion". The story by Ian Aitken supported the contention that after Callaghan's March NEC vote, his fellow ministers were under the impression that he "had been driven into acceptance of Cabinet policy on union reform". Aitken continued that Callaghan's speech before the joint session of the Cabinet and NEC, however, "makes it plain that he has in no way abandoned his hostility" to the bill.[59]

Wilson, of course, had no intention of sacking Callaghan, but this time the Prime Minister felt compelled to act. After he had pondered his response over the weekend, Wilson told Callaghan the following Tuesday, 13 May, that his colleagues wanted him removed from the Management Committee, or the so-called Inner Cabinet. The Inner Cabinet was the recently formed small group of top policy advisers that also included Castle, Jenkins, Crossman, Denis Healey, the Foreign Secretary Michael Stewart, and Fred Peart, the leader of the House.[60] Healey was the first to suggest to the Prime Minister on the Monday after the joint NEC-Cabinet meeting that Callaghan should be removed from the Inner Cabinet. When Wilson met later that evening with Jenkins, Castle and Crossman "they strongly took the same line".[61] The Inner Cabinet had only been formed at the end of April. Callaghan's inclusion in that circle – which Crossman said had been established to keep Wilson from talking "only to Kaufman and others of those negligible people

---

[57] Oxford, Wilson c.936, Folio 2. Note for the record from the Prime Minister (following from note of 3 April 1969).

[58] *Guardian*, 10 May 1969, p. 1.

[59] Ibid. The *Guardian* and *The Times* took a very different approach on 10 May 1969. While *The Times* briefly cited Callaghan's opposition to the penal clauses, it had focused its coverage on the broader meeting. On the other hand, the *Guardian*'s news story had been entirely about Callaghan's latest challenge to Wilson and Castle.

[60] Oxford, Wilson c.936, Folio 3. Note for the record from the Prime Minister (following from dictation of 10 May 1969).

[61] Ibid.

whom he had built around himself"[62] – might well have been because of his initial acquiescence on the interim bill, which Wilson had viewed favourably.

Regardless, the Prime Minister, who had chosen the less-intimate Cabinet room rather than his personal study for the face-off, told Callaghan just prior to the regularly scheduled meeting of the Management Committee that his colleagues had had enough of his behaviour. Wilson told Callaghan that the others had been especially irritated by the way he had referred to his fellow ministers at the joint NEC-Cabinet meeting as "they", acting as if he himself had not been part of the Cabinet. Callaghan responded, "Did I?" and added that if he had, it must have been a Freudian slip. Wilson countered that Freudian slips most often reflect an individual's true feelings. The Prime Minister implied that the other members of the Inner Cabinet did not trust Callaghan. Wilson said one of the ministers had told him that to have Callaghan at the Management Committee is "like a group of generals which included Pétain", a reference to the leader of Vichy France who was convicted of treason at the end of the war. The Prime Minister told Callaghan that if he remained among those in the inner circle "he would be too busy making sure that his baggage train was safe". Callaghan replied: "Not my baggage train... the party's baggage train."[63]

Wilson said that Callaghan offered his resignation not once, but twice that morning,[64] although there is no mention of that in the description of the meeting drawn from Callaghan's recollection of the encounter in his "official" biography.[65] That might be an indication that Callaghan knew he was conveying an empty threat – one that was not far removed from the hints of resignation that he had dropped in the immediate days after the March NEC vote. No doubt Callaghan was well aware that it would have been nearly impossible for the Prime Minister, given all that had happened in the previous six weeks, to remove him altogether from the Cabinet without creating a major split within the party. Philip Allen, the permanent secretary at the Home Office, had spoken to Callaghan that morning, just before he had left his office for No. 10. Allen, who was close to Callaghan, had gone back to his room and recalls it was not long before "my private secretary came in and said, 'The Home Secretary

---

[62] BLPES, Hetherington 16/18. Conversation between Crossman and Hetherington at Prescote Manor on 4 May 1969.
[63] Oxford, Wilson c.936, Folio 3. Note for the record from the Prime Minister (following from dictation of 10 May 1969).
[64] Ibid.
[65] Morgan, *Callaghan: A Life*, p. 336.

wants to see you.' I said, 'Rubbish, I've just seen him off.' 'He's back!' So I went in and he *was* back. And he had been thrown out of the Inner Cabinet and I sat there for about three-quarters of an hour while he ruminated. I don't flatter myself that I contributed anything at all. But it was interesting that he was prepared to philosophise and think in front of me. I was the first person really for him to talk to after this had happened."[66]

Over the next couple of days Wilson made an attempt to quell the storm in the newspapers, part of which Wilson implied had been created by Callaghan and "his friends".[67] The Prime Minister instructed Haines and Trevor Lloyd-Hughes, the government's chief information officer, to tell the press that Callaghan "was on parole and could work his ticket back. That he had lost a stripe, but could earn it back again by good behaviour and hard working."[68] Yet Wilson noted that some of the news stories reported that "I clearly wanted him out but didn't have the guts to sack him and that he was outwitting me by not resigning."[69] That was exactly the approach taken by the *Evening Standard* that Tuesday afternoon. The newspaper's late editions carried a two-line banner headline that dominated the front page and simply read "Callaghan Sensation". But a smaller headline over the banner and above a picture of a smiling Jim Callaghan was the one that played into the very image that had been reflected in the earlier *Guardian* story. It read: "The Unions' Friend Gets the Chop".[70]

No doubt, Wilson had to walk a fine line. On the one hand, Callaghan's behaviour at the joint NEC-Cabinet meeting required the Prime Minister to do something publicly to rein in Callaghan; on the other hand, Wilson had no intention of allowing the problem to turn into a full-blown crisis. While the *Daily Mail* called for Callaghan's resignation from the government,[71] the *Guardian's* editorial response was muted. It said that since Callaghan opposed his Cabinet colleagues at the joint NEC-Cabinet meeting "he can hardly expect to be in the government's front-line team not on this issue anyway".[72] While

---

[66] Interview with Lord Allen, 19 May 2003.
[67] Oxford, Wilson c.936, Folio 3. Note for the record from the Prime Minister (following from dictation of 10 May 1969).
[68] Ibid.
[69] Ibid.
[70] *Evening Standard*, 13 May 1969, p. 1.
[71] *Daily Mail*, 12 May 1969, p. 1. Its editorial concluded that if Callaghan "cannot support Mrs. Castle's bill then he must go. And if he will not go of his own accord then he must be forcibly pushed."
[72] *Guardian*, 14 May 1969, p. 8.

Callaghan's removal from the Inner Cabinet was big news in Fleet Street, the dismissal turned out to be more show than substance. Cabinet documents suggest that Callaghan was kept fully informed of what the Inner Cabinet was up to during the five months that he was barred from its meetings; during that time he received all the confidential papers. A memo by a senior civil servant to the Cabinet Office about the distribution of a "long-term strategy" that had been sent on 15 May, two days after Callaghan had been removed from the Inner Cabinet, said "The minute has of course been circulated to all the now members of the Management Committee, plus one!"[73]

Immediately before the combined NEC-Cabinet meeting that led to Callaghan's dismissal from the Inner Cabinet, Houghton – in a further example of the alliance that had been forged between the two men over this issue – laid the groundwork for the Home Secretary's belligerence. In a pronouncement that Wilson saw as a "pistol at the head of the government",[74] Houghton opened a meeting of the Parliamentary Labour Party on 7 May with a "sensational statement"[75] which said that there was no way the Parliamentary Labour Party would back the interim bill and that it should not be introduced. Houghton's policy shift got wide coverage in the news media, with *The Times's* political correspondent David Wood saying that Houghton had finally "stripped aside his public front of broker between Mr. Wilson and the backbenchers".[76]

Wilson was "extremely angry", primarily because the meeting had been an adjournment from a session two weeks earlier when the members, among them Houghton who had to take "off his spectacles to wipe his moist eyes",[77] had given Castle a standing ovation. In private notes, the Prime Minister appears to have been bewildered as to why Houghton, after having acted so conciliatorily, should have suddenly launched a broadside on the proposed legislation, an attack that came just before the joint NEC-Cabinet meeting. It is now clear that Houghton's strategy on the interim bill mirrored Callaghan's, that is initial acquiescence followed by a timely and sharp attack. But at the

---

[73] PRO, PREM 13/3077. Internal Cabinet Office memorandum to Burke Trend, 15 May 1969.

[74] Oxford, Wilson c.936, Folio 2. Note for the record from the Prime Minister (following from note of 3 April 1969).

[75] Ibid.

[76] *The Times*, 8 May 1969, p. 1.

[77] Oxford, Wilson c.936, Folio 2. Note for the record from the Prime Minister (following from note of 3 April 1969).

time, as far as Wilson could tell, nothing had happened to "justify" the change of tone. Although Wilson was able to get a "contrite" Houghton to clarify his position at a party meeting that evening and "one or two phrases were good, his choice of other phrases only served to give the screw another turn, and there were more press headlines".[78]

The industrial correspondent Geoffrey Goodman,[79] after having gained limited access to Houghton's personal papers, says there is evidence there that Houghton and Callaghan spent many an occasion in the spring of 1969 at Houghton's flat discussing ways to undermine the Prime Minister.[80] There is no mention in Callaghan's memoirs about multiple meetings on this issue with Houghton, who Callaghan had known since his days as an assistant secretary in the Inland Revenue staff federation, the union that represented clerks in the income tax collection offices. Houghton had headed the federation in the 1930s, and brought the young Callaghan along after he had left his post as a tax officer and moved into the ranks of the union's leadership. But Callaghan does allude to one meeting that spring between him and his old mentor over *In Place of Strife* and writes that they both agreed that if Castle's bill went ahead with the penal clauses remaining then Callaghan would have no alternative but to resign from the government.[81] But Jack Jones, the former general secretary of the TGWU who was active in the opposition to the White Paper particularly in its final stages, doubts that Callaghan would ever have resigned from Wilson's Cabinet. "I don't think Callaghan was the resigning type. I think he was realistic enough to realise that if you resign you indicate a sort of opposition that remains with you."[82]

Wilson apparently felt that way as well. In early 1969, at the height of the troubles over trade union reform, the Prime Minister wrote that

---

[78] Ibid.

[79] Geoffrey Goodman, *From Bevan to Blair* (London, 2003), p. 125. Houghton's papers are not publicly available.

[80] Oxford, Callaghan 341. Letter to Callaghan from Geoffrey Goodman, 30 November 1967. The extent of Callaghan's passion for the industrial relations debate must have surprised Goodman, who had written to Callaghan shortly after his move to the Home Office lamenting that contacts between the two men would be more limited from now on since "I doubt whether there will be many opportunities for you to get involved directly in industrial affairs from your new base".

[81] Callaghan, *Time and Chance*, p. 276.

[82] Interview with Jack Jones, 18 June 2003.

he doubted Callaghan "had the guts" to quit.[83] Although the unaffiliated white-collar Civil Service union that Callaghan and Houghton had belonged to was a minor player in the labour movement, the two men, nevertheless, had been union officials. They had to have enough understanding of the trade unions, and the impossible position that Wilson and Castle had put themselves in, to know that as the days passed any talk of resignation would have amounted to an empty threat. After all, once the short bill had been put in place, there was little likelihood that any penal clauses would get past Jones of the TGWU or Hugh Scanlon of the Amalgamated Union of Engineering Workers, the two central figures on the trade union side, or for that matter the considerable number of MPs who had been "sponsored" (i.e. given financial help) by the trade unions.

During the contentious month of April 1969, Callaghan found himself in the middle of another legislative controversy, namely a longstanding plan to reform the House of Lords. At the Cabinet meeting on 3 April, just after Wilson had returned from Nigeria, a ministerial committee, on which Callaghan had a leading role, was asked to assess the progress of the Parliament (No. 2) Bill that would eventually do away with hereditary peerages as well as limit the ability of the Lords to delay legislation and act as a check on the Commons.[84] The Labour Party, with its roots in the working class, had a natural inclination to want to curb the powers of the upper chamber. In the House of Lords, peers had no constituencies, tended to have ties to either the Conservative or Liberal parties and never faced a general election, having gained their seats either because of an hereditary right or because of a life appointment by a prime minister. The surprising thing was that the Parliament (No. 2) Bill had garnered some initial bipartisan support. But the day before Castle had unveiled the details of her interim Industrial Relations Bill on 16 April, that ministerial committee concluded that the government would likely have to scrap the plan to reform the Lords.[85]

Ministers had felt, however, that the root of the problem had not been the Lords Bill itself but "the general malaise"[86] in the Parliamentary

---

[83] Oxford, Wilson c.936, Folio 1. Note for the record from the Prime Minister, 3 April 1969.

[84] PRO, CAB 128/44 I. Conclusions of a Cabinet meeting in the Prime Minister's room at the House of Commons, 3 April 1969.

[85] PRO, CAB 128/44 I. Conclusions of a Cabinet meeting at No. 10 Downing Street, 16 April 1969.

[86] Ibid.

Labour Party, which with Callaghan's mentor Houghton at the helm had been making trouble at every turn for Wilson. In addition, the Lords Reform Bill had been reported out of the ministerial committee in such a way that the members had made it clear that if the Prime Minister had been ready to put his "whole prestige" behind it, in other words tie the bill to a vote of confidence in his leadership, they felt it could have passed. But no doubt that would have been a dangerous move amid the ongoing controversy over *In Place of Strife*. Even if the bill had passed, any erosion in support from Labour MPs, some of whom on the far left were urging not the chamber's reform but its elimination, would have threatened the Prime Minister's position. Wilson said that he had found out later that the suggestion for a vote of confidence had come from none other than Callaghan, "whose motives I suspected".[87]

The failure of the Lords Reform package cut short the career of John Silkin as Chief Whip. But Kaufman says that Wilson actually made it clear to him while they were on their African mission that Silkin's days were numbered and that Bob Mellish, a former dockworker from the far right of the party, would be his replacement.[88] Yet Wilson's private papers indicate that that decision was not finalised until several days after the withdrawal of the Lords Reform bill and that before appointing Mellish, Wilson had attempted unsuccessfully to get Healey, who had never been shy in his willingness to confront Callaghan, to take the job.[89] All of the trouble stirred up by Callaghan over *In Place of Strife* had convinced Wilson that a stronger personality was needed to guide the interim bill through Parliament. Kaufman to this day believes it was "a big mistake" to appoint Mellish because he thinks that Silkin being from the "soft left" of the Labour Party had actually been in a stronger position to get *In Place of Strife* through Parliament.[90]

---

[87] Oxford, Wilson c.936, Folio 2. Note for the record from the Prime Minister (following from note of 3 April 1969).

[88] Interview with Gerald Kaufman, 18 December 2003.

[89] Oxford, Wilson c.936, Folio 2. Note for the record from the Prime Minister (following from note of 3 April 1969). Wilson had been trying to get Healey more involved in party politics, as well as more involved with the National Executive.

[90] Interview with Gerald Kaufman, 18 December 2003. Kaufman says that since the "rebellions" in Parliament in the 1960s tended to originate from the party's left-wing, it made sense to have a Chief Whip who was from the left as well. Also Kaufman says that unlike Mellish, Silkin had had "a strong personal affinity" with Wilson.

When Wilson called in Houghton, a man he knew "to be at all times a loyal supporter of the Callaghan cause",[91] to discuss the decision to replace Silkin with Mellish, Houghton "warmly praised it". The Prime Minister asked him before the final decision was announced if he had another man who he would prefer in that job. Houghton replied "no", adding that "Bob was the best man. He would give him every possible backing."[92] Callaghan and Mellish had built up a close relationship over this issue, one that helped solidify Callaghan's own position – particularly when Mellish in the end told an angry Prime Minister that he could not deliver the votes to get Castle's reforms through Parliament. But indications of that intransigence had come in Mellish's first speech as Chief Whip before Houghton and the Parliamentary Labour Party. "Unfortunately," Wilson wrote, "though I had warned him against this – he three times – and in very strong language – said the government is beaten on the I.R. bill (or I think if we failed to get it upstairs) would have to seek a dissolution – there was no alternative."[93]

Although Wilson, Castle and the trade unions were engaged in talks on and off for weeks, the two sides failed to reach any compromise. Callaghan played only a minor role in the final episode of the saga on 18 June 1969, which involved a full day of meetings in the upstairs dining room at No. 10 Downing Street with Wilson and Castle on one side and the trade union leaders on the other. The Cabinet had been kept in abeyance downstairs and had been eagerly awaiting the outcome of this last round of negotiations, on which they, of course, had to pass final judgement. The loss of Roy Jenkins's support at the eleventh hour had given Wilson and Castle little ammunition going into the talks with the trade unions. Jenkins, while not changing his stance, had expressed a reluctance that he had not shown before. Wilson wrote that since the Chancellor "had asked me a day or two earlier to give my whole backing in what [was] likely to be a major Cabinet splitting exercise to cut government expenditure.... I was extremely cold and angry".[94] A day earlier, there had been a steady erosion of support for the interim measure in Cabinet and Callaghan in his bluff manner had again backed strongly anything the trade unions would be willing to give in the way

---

[91] Oxford, Wilson c.936, Folio 2. Note for the record from the Prime Minister (following from note of 3 April 1969).

[92] Ibid.

[93] Ibid.

[94] Oxford, Wilson c.936. Note for the record dictated by the Prime Minister, 22 June 1969.

of a "letter of intent".[95] Crossman said that Callaghan "behaved with an egregious smoothness and oiliness which was almost unbearable".[96]

In the end, Wilson and Castle were forced to accept a voluntary "solemn and binding" agreement from the trade unions to curb strikes. Wilson and Castle had returned to the Cabinet room downstairs with the news five hours after the ministers had been called together. The delay in reporting the result to Cabinet had been partly contrived by Wilson's anger with Callaghan and the rest of his colleagues and to keep them on the edge of their seats.[97] Wilson noted that "Jim Callaghan went into a state of ecstasy and promised his full support in what had been done. He would now throw himself into the campaign for a successful election which he was sure we would win, and under my leadership. Before the nausea became overwhelming I said that Barbara and I had work to do upstairs." As Wilson and Castle rose from their chairs, the ministers, in what can only be described as a collective sigh of relief, cast their ministerial dignity aside, "broke into cheers" and started banging on the table.[98]

Conclusion

There was no single event that did more to restore Callaghan's dominance within the Cabinet than *In Place of Strife*. He had used his opposition to the measure at critical junctures in the debate to strengthen his political position at the expense of Wilson, Castle and Jenkins, the main proponents of the legislation. In particular, the similarities between Callaghan's vote at the 26 March NEC meeting and his outspoken opposition to the interim bill before the 9 May joint NEC-Cabinet meeting suggest that Callaghan's opposition to trade union reform had been carefully calculated to catch his adversaries at vulnerable moments. For one thing, both events had been preceded by long periods of either acquiescence or only mild opposition on Callaghan's part to the government's plans. For another, both events had come after Callaghan had given his support to the measures in question – the original White Paper, in which he had been named among the sponsors, and the interim

---

[95] Ibid.
[96] Crossman, *Diaries*, Vol. III, p. 521.
[97] Interview with Joe Haines, 25 March 2004.
[98] Oxford, Wilson c.936. Note for the record dictated by the Prime Minister, 22 June 1969.

bill, which he had concurred with in the 14 April Cabinet meeting. Finally, both events had been followed by either hints or outright offers of resignation, even though Callaghan had known that it would have been nearly impossible for Wilson to agree to his resignation after he had thrown a protective shield around himself by ingratiating the trade unions by his opposition to the plan.

In the end, there were two winners in the defeat of the plan to reform industrial relations: the trade unions, which had blocked any chance of the legislation being approved, and Callaghan who, through a process of elimination, had established the foundation upon which he would build his political recovery. Although the public perception had been that the trade union leaders and Callaghan had been working towards the same goal, that had been only partially true. The opposition to the legislation that had been forged by influential trade unionists, such as Jones and Scanlon, was built on principle. During the first half of the century, trade unions had had an uneasy relationship with Parliament, which had enacted curbs on union financing and the right to strike, and they were reluctant to give up any hard-fought gains. In Callaghan's case, the defeat of *In Place of Strife* had been less a matter of principle than a way to shift the balance of power in the Cabinet back to where it had been before he had been forced to resign as Chancellor. Just how much plotting and planning had gone on behind the scenes might never be known, given Callaghan's propensity to use surrogates, such as Houghton and Nicholas, to advance his political ambitions. But at the end of the six months certain developments did emerge and invariably they had been favourable to Callaghan.

First, the political equation was entirely different than it had been a year earlier. The one thing that might have made Wilson a truly great Prime Minister and reshaped the Labour Party was no longer in his grasp.[99] Castle's ascendancy came to an abrupt halt and although she remained in the Cabinet she would never again be as influential a figure. Also, Jenkins had suffered immeasurably as well. By pushing for a fast-track version of the legislation in his spring budget speech, Jenkins had cornered himself politically. His mistake had been to believe that a strategy that might have worked a few months earlier could be resurrected after the setbacks inflicted upon the government by Callaghan's March

---

[99] *The Sunday Times*, 25 May 1969, p. 7. An Opinion Research Centre poll conducted for *The Sunday Times* found that although Wilson's image suffered from the controversy, there was also "disillusionment with Labour rule that goes beyond disillusionment with Mr. Wilson".

NEC vote. Jenkins had been a far more successful Chancellor than Callaghan, and had been arguably a far more effective Home Secretary, and many of his innovations at the Treasury had paid off as Britain's balance of payments improved. But the one thing that stood in the way of Jenkins's success at No. 11 Downing Street had been the government's inability to curb wages and increase productivity, the very thing that Castle's White Paper had aimed to bring about.

Secondly, Callaghan had benefited enormously from the fact that *In Place of Strife* inevitably brought opposing factions within the trade union leadership together, even though the battle over the plan had intensified a shift in public opinion away from the trade unions. In March 1969, on the eve of Callaghan's NEC vote, 62 per cent of the British electorate had felt that trade unions had "too much power",[100] a 12-percentage-point increase from August 1968. For years, Britain's trade unions had been led by right-wing figures – such as Arthur Deakin, Ernest Bevin's successor as head of the TGWU – who were less likely to challenge the political leadership within the Labour Party. But that had begun to change in the mid-1950s with the advent of Frank Cousins as general secretary of the TGWU. Cousins was a new breed of union leader. He fought passionately for social causes, like the Campaign for Nuclear Disarmament, that went far beyond the usual struggles for union benefits and pensions, and was often at odds with Callaghan and the right-wing trade unionists.[101] But *In Place of Strife* had slowed the growing divide between the left and right within the trade union movement. Callaghan, by advancing the arguments of the trade unions on this particular issue, was able to capitalise on this amalgamation and broaden his centre-right base, finding common cause with both right-wing and left-wing trade union leaders.

Thirdly, Callaghan had used this role of a quasi-spokesman for the opponents to the bill within the Cabinet to expand his scope beyond the Home Office in such a way as to help him begrudgingly to gain influence among the left wing of the Labour Party, which had strongly opposed the measure from the start and had been incensed by Castle's shift to the right on this issue. Although it would take his role in Northern Ireland to

---

[100] NOP Bulletin, March 1969. Meanwhile, 6 per cent of those surveyed had said the unions did not have enough influence and 22 per cent said they had just the "right amount".

[101] Oxford, Brown c.5023, Folio 49. Note for the record dictated by George Brown, 13 March 1968. Brown, whose trade union sympathies were close to Callaghan's, referred to Cousins as "the great left-winger".

complete the process, Callaghan's strategy had enabled him to begin to shed what had been his almost exclusive preoccupation with issues that had engendered criticism from the left – issues like race relations and immigration, which he had inherited from his arch-rival Jenkins and in which Callaghan had been perceived as being less progressive than his predecessor as Home Secretary. In addition, the polling data indicate that it had been the debate over industrial relations, rather than the Troubles that were just beginning to emerge in Northern Ireland, that had put Callaghan back into the spotlight nationally.[102]

Finally, Callaghan had emerged as a much more popular public figure by the time the saga had concluded. As we have seen, a poll taken in April 1968 had shown that if Wilson had left the premiership for any reason, Jenkins was heavily favoured to succeed him.[103] A little more than a year later, that same question put to a sample of the British electorate had indicated a remarkable turnaround for the Home Secretary. While Wilson and Castle might have found the Home Secretary's double-dealing intolerable, there had been an astounding change that had taken place in the public's perception of Callaghan. By the time the battle over *In Place of Strife* had concluded in mid-June 1969, Callaghan was at the top of the same national survey, this time polling 20 per cent, compared with Jenkins's 17 per cent and Castle's 4 per cent.[104] Even more amazingly, the belligerent Home Secretary had been garnering support from people who had totally disagreed with his views on trade-union reform, but had admired his sense of principle and unwavering opposition to the legislation.[105]

Despite the popular perception, Callaghan was "keeping his distance" from the TUC during much of the controversy,[106] and his support for the trade unions had not been as unwavering as it had appeared to be.[107] Jack Jones, of the TGWU, had been one of the most important players in the talks with the Prime Minister and Castle involving that measure. But Jones, who was affiliated with what was then the biggest

---

[102] NOP Bulletin, April 1969.

[103] NOP Bulletin, April 1968.

[104] NOP Bulletin, June 1969

[105] Ibid.

[106] Morgan, *Callaghan: A Life*, p. 341.

[107] *Daily Express*, 12 May 1969, p. 8. A column, headlined "Big Talk but Where's the Action", had suggested that it was time "for an end to Mr. James Callaghan's posturing in private as the trade unions' champion, yet shrinking from backing his protest with his resignation".

trade union in England, barely mentions Callaghan when referring to the intricacies of that struggle in the chapter of Jones's autobiography[108] devoted to *In Place of Strife*. Asked why, Jones says, "That's right.... We never found Jim all that enthusiastic about the trade unions, as I understood it, the shop floor because that wasn't his cup of tea."[109] Jones adds that Callaghan, "of course, opposed the *In Place of Strife* approach or at least he claimed he did, so in that sense we appreciated that. But it was an opposition that didn't I suppose mean a lot because the main force was Barbara Castle and Wilson himself."[110]

In other words, Callaghan's risk, if there was any, had been limited because he really took no direct part in any of the negotiations. He could be critical, but since it was not his department he had not been in any way obliged to help find a solution. Wilson's biographer Ben Pimlott is accurate in saying that "the victory belonged to Callaghan", but his notion that Callaghan had taken a "serious risk" by opposing Wilson and Castle is harder to accept.[111] Pimlott's supposition, which is shared by others, fails to address the opposite side of the coin. What if Callaghan had not opposed the reforms? Most likely after his move to the Home Office he would have been lost in the blur of Labour ministers, people like Greenwood and Stewart, who had been moved around like chess pieces by Wilson and had never been seriously viewed as prime-ministerial material.

Callaghan had not only staked out his ground on this issue, making himself clearly an alternative to Wilson, Jenkins and Castle, but he was well positioned in doing so. His allies within the political structure had been a formidable lot in formidable positions: Houghton at the Parliamentary Labour Party; Mellish at the Chief Whip's Office and therefore, uniquely among the three, within the Cabinet but not of the Cabinet; and Nicholas at Labour Party headquarters. While there is no evidence that Mellish had been a surrogate of Callaghan's, although he certainly had been sympathetic to the Home Secretary's views on a variety of issues, Houghton and Nicholas certainly had been. As the leader of the Parliamentary Labour Party, Houghton had been in a strong position to help Callaghan on *In Place of Strife* and did so on several occasions. The same can be said of Nicholas, the general secretary of the Labour Party, who had owed his job to Callaghan and only a month before all

[108] Jack Jones, *Union Man* (London, 1986), pp. 202–209.
[109] Interview with Jack Jones, 18 June 2003.
[110] Ibid.
[111] Ben Pimlott, *Harold Wilson* (London, 1992), p. 544.

of the turmoil had begun had sought and received Callaghan's help to get the Labour Party to supplement his pension.[112] Kaufman agrees that the fact that Houghton, Mellish and Nicholas had been in three particularly important posts at that particular time had been extremely useful to Callaghan.[113]

On the outside, of course, the biggest ally of them all was the trade union movement, which in the end had far more to do with the defeat of *In Place of Strife* than any politician or entity inside or outside the government. "The very fact that perhaps, unfortunately, he won the battle," says Leo Abse, a Member of Parliament who was also at the time a strong opponent of the White Paper, "is not an indication of a risk taker, it's an indication of a man who was a great manoeuvrer."[114] Tom McNally, who was a Labour Party official at the time, concedes that Callaghan "was not always a totally trustworthy ally politically because his political judgement would, perhaps, know it was time to settle before others did". Nevertheless, McNally admits "it might have been braver then [for Callaghan] to have thrown his weight on the side of reform rather than of appeasement because the problem did come back to bite him quite disastrously eight or nine years later."[115]

---

[112] Minutes of a meeting of the Finance and General Services Subcommittee of the National Executive Committee, 25 February 1969.
[113] Interview with Gerald Kaufman, 18 December 2003. But Kaufman believes that the three men were not "a kind of cabal. It just happened that each of them had those positions."
[114] Interview with Leo Abse, 20 May 2003.
[115] Interview with Lord McNally, 17 July 2003.

5
Fleet Street: A Special Relationship

The press barons, like Beaverbrook, Northcliffe and Rothermere, were no longer part of the landscape in Fleet Street by the late 1960s. But the great national newspapers that they and others had built in the first half of the century, many of which were located not in Fleet Street itself, but in the adjoining streets and adjacent squares, still dominated the news business. In those years, there were many influential newspapermen who covered the political and industrial scene – including Walter Terry of the *Daily Mail*, Geoffrey Goodman of the *Daily Mirror* and Anthony Howard of *The Sunday Times* – yet the reporters on the *Guardian*, which had its London offices on Gray's Inn Road, had the advantage of having worked on a newspaper whose attention was riveted to politics in a special way.

The *Guardian's* influence among the political elite on the centre left was deep and Barbara Castle, a former journalist, understood that as well as anyone. So much so that on 14 May 1969, the day after Callaghan had been sacked from the Inner Cabinet, she had arranged to meet Alastair Hetherington, the *Guardian's* editor, and some of the other senior staff for lunch in a private dining room at the Charing Cross Hotel in London.[1] Castle, who had met with the Parliamentary Labour Party that morning and had a further meeting on the Industrial Relations Bill scheduled for the House of Commons later that day, had sought that meeting because she had felt the *Guardian* had unfairly attacked her legislation. Callaghan, obviously, was not present at that meeting with the *Guardian* editors. But while he was on the right wing of the Labour Party and was never identified as being close to the press, his influence

---

[1] PRO, LAB 77/15. First Secretary's appointments diary for 1969.

was far greater at the *Guardian* than Castle, the Prime Minister or anyone else could have imagined. As a result, Castle, with all the trappings of First Secretary of State and accompanied by her press secretary, Bernard Ingham,[2] fought an uphill battle from the moment she stepped into the room.

Oddly, the target of Castle's venom that afternoon was not Hetherington, who had final say on editorial matters, but his news editor John Cole. Castle apparently knew, through her friend Mark Arnold-Forster, the chief editorial writer at the paper, who was also at that lunch,[3] that it was Cole who had penned the unsigned attacks on *In Place of Strife* that appeared regularly in the *Guardian*.[4] Cole had been the newspaper's labour correspondent from 1957 to 1963. As such, he had been the *Guardian*'s contribution to that small bevy of national reporters who covered the influential trade union movement and cavorted with the big union bosses and MPs with strong union connections, Callaghan among them. In those days, a labour correspondent was one of the two most important reporting jobs on many newspapers. Not only did they cover the trade unions and the employer organisations, but the meetings of the Labour Party's National Executive as well, along with any other party matters that occurred outside the House of Commons. The party's dealings within the House were covered by the individual who held the other top reporting post, that of political correspondent.[5]

But as had been Castle's mistake throughout the saga over *In Place of Strife*, her strategy in trying to win her opponents over at that lunch was flawed. Roy Hattersley, her former parliamentary private secretary, remembers Castle as being "an immensely persuasive person ... because she would attack you so much".[6] By this point, however, her proposals had been badly mauled by Callaghan and the trade unions and it was too late for that heavy-handed approach to work. Hetherington described the meeting as "fiery" right from the point before Castle "had a drink in her hand" to the finish. With Ingham, a former *Guardian*

---

[2] Ingham was a former *Guardian* reporter, who had actually been brought to London from Yorkshire by Cole to be the newspaper's No. 2 Labour correspondent. Ingham later went on to be Prime Minister Margaret Thatcher's press secretary.

[3] PRO, LAB 77/15. First Secretary's appointments diary for 1969. The other *Guardian* staff members at that luncheon were Hartford Thomas, the deputy editor, and John Torode, the Labour editor.

[4] Interview with John Cole, 25 February 2004.

[5] Ibid.

[6] Interview with Lord Hattersley, 1 March 2004.

reporter, at her side, she and Cole verbally attacked each other non-stop.[7] Cole believes that Castle "wanted to get the guy who was doing it" and to dress him down in front of his boss. "I think that was the object of the exercise and I wasn't taking that."[8]

Castle knew, too, that Cole as news editor was in a position to influence the coverage on that story and as such was a powerful ally for Callaghan's position. Not only was Cole writing the editorials, he was responsible for supervising the newspaper's reporting as well, right down to playing a role in deciding what stories were to be covered and how they would be displayed in the newspaper the following morning. What Castle did not know was that Cole was having "a lot of meetings with Callaghan in [Callaghan's] office or over lunch" during the early months of 1969.[9] Cole concedes that on the issue of *In Place of Strife* he was "wholly sympathetic with Jim Callaghan's point of view",[10] and, even if Cole had not been the news editor, editorial writers at the newspaper operated "as something of a law unto themselves".[11] Therefore, it is unlikely that Castle with her abrasive approach did anything to further her cause that afternoon, either with Cole or for that matter Hetherington, who actually saw some merit in her arguments, and more likely than not the encounter did Callaghan more good than Castle.[12]

In the early days of the fight over the reform of industrial relations, Castle and her supporters were buoyed by public opinion polls that showed the British people were tired of strikes and felt the government should take measures to prevent them. One national poll showed that two of the key elements in Castle's plan, the proposals for a secret ballot as well as the implementation of a cooling-off period prior to the taking of any industrial action, were favoured by as many as two-thirds of those surveyed.[13] In addition, approval for both ideas was equally

---

[7] Alastair Hetherington, *Guardian Years* (London, 1981), p. 213.
[8] Interview with John Cole, 25 February 2004.
[9] Ibid.
[10] Ibid.
[11] Guardian News & Media Archive. *Guardian* 150th anniversary booklet, May 1971, p. 9. The *Guardian*, unlike most newspapers, had a policy that kept their editorial writers well-grounded in the news. Not only would they write editorials but they would often give up their "anonymity by going off after news and coming back, as often as not, with scoops".
[12] It was a luncheon that Castle apparently wanted to forget. There is no record of it in her published diaries, her autobiography or the authorised biography of Castle by the *Guardian* reporter Anne Perkins.
[13] NOP Bulletin, January 1969.

strong among Conservative and Labour Party supporters. So in that sense Hetherington's early opposition to the proposals was daring. The same can not be said of Callaghan, however. Although Callaghan's name would often come up as one of a group of ministers who had concerns about the legislation, a review of the *Guardian* from late December 1968 until the end of March 1969 reveals a certain timidity on Callaghan's part. For three long months, Callaghan, the man who came to be so identified with the defeat of *In Place of Strife*, managed to stay on the fringes of the debate. He did not emerge from its shadows until the day he cast his vote on the Labour Party's executive just as Harold Wilson was preparing to depart for Nigeria.

Despite the *Guardian's* strong stand on *In Place of Strife*, Hetherington was not entirely convinced of the editorial position being espoused by Cole.[14] Hetherington was frustrated by his own experience with organised labour. He had had more than his share of problems with the Society of Graphical and Allied Trades, the largest of the newspaper's unions and "in many ways the most difficult",[15] and had been prevented from introducing new technology at the newspaper to keep costs down. Thus Hetherington had pondered taking a different editorial stance. In the end he bowed to the merits of Cole's arguments and allowed the *Guardian*, with its considerable influence, to come down squarely against the ideas outlined in Castle's White Paper. In doing so, the *Guardian* was the only national newspaper to oppose *In Place of Strife*.[16]

Once Callaghan did join the fray, however, the *Guardian* was supportive of his position, even giving him wide berth on the National Executive Committee (NEC) vote that was widely seen as a defiance of collective Cabinet responsibility. On 5 April 1969, just over a week after that meeting of the National Executive, the *Guardian's* lead editorial[17] amounted to a long diatribe on how the Prime Minister was right and that there "can be no compromise" on the issue of collective Cabinet responsibility. But the editorial managed somehow to take a complete U-turn and wound up attacking not Callaghan but Wilson for disregarding what the newspaper called "collective leadership". It concluded that

[14] Hetherington, *Guardian Years*, p. 213.
[15] Guardian News & Media Archive, Jean Stead papers, JLS 1/2. Confidential in-house memo to selective staff from Hetherington, 23 January 1967.
[16] The national socialist newspaper opposed the initiative, but it was not considered to be part of the mainstream media.
[17] *Guardian*, 5 April 1969, p. 8.

"if there were ample and open discussion in the first place then it would be realistic to expect collective responsibility to be accepted".[18] By comparison, the *Daily Express*, which had originally defended Callaghan's right to speak out against the initiative,[19] was more to the point. It concluded in an editorial, also published on 5 April, that now that Wilson had made it absolutely clear that the White Paper was "government policy" ministers "must either accept the policy or resign".[20]

In addition, Hetherington's notes show that he was sympathetic with the column written by Peter Jenkins which fiercely attacked Wilson's failed leadership on the day the Biafran peace mission collapsed. Hetherington, told Judith Hart, the Paymaster General, that it was "a very good column", though he thought the missives on Wilson's strategy of management by committee might have been too harsh.[21] Callaghan's name does not appear in Hetherington's notes of that meeting of 28 April 1969, but there is a peculiar reference to the column in Hetherington's memoirs written many years later. Hetherington, in recollecting the column's impact, refers to it as an attack on both Wilson and Callaghan.[22] But Hetherington, given his understanding of the influence of the press, had to know that the column, displayed as it was across the top of the opposite editorial page, was a significant boost to the defiant Home Secretary, particularly since it concluded on a prophetic note saying that the "feeling may go on growing in the ranks that the man whose style brought victory in 1964 and 1966 is the man with the style of governing most likely to ensure defeat in 1970".[23]

The whole furore was ratcheted up a notch less than two weeks later when the *Guardian* editorialised on whether Wilson's days were in fact

---

[18] Ibid; PRO, HO 292/26. Letter to A.D. Gordon Brown from Callaghan, 15 February 1972. The *Guardian* editorial was a bit like Callaghan's defence of collective Cabinet responsibility given a few years later to a committee reviewing the Official Secrets Act of 1911. He returned the transcript, suggesting a few changes "to bring the meaning out more clearly". He had told the panel that "of course I believe very much in the doctrine of collective responsibility, and I think it would be very foolish and government would be bad government if people were to depart from it". In the amended copy, however, he made a slight alteration, in what may have amounted to a tacit admission of his misbehaviour, saying "if people were regularly to depart from it".

[19] *Daily Express*, 1 April 1969, p. 10.

[20] *Daily Express*, 5 April 1969, p. 8.

[21] BLPES, Hetherington 16/19. Note of a meeting between Hetherington and the Paymaster General, 28 April 1969.

[22] Hetherington, *Guardian Years*, p. 214.

[23] *Guardian*, 1 April 1969, p. 11. (In 1966, Labour's majority increased to 98 seats).

numbered. If they were, the newspaper, in a lengthy editorial, concluded the obvious: that Roy Jenkins was the likely front-runner for Wilson's job. But it offered two other intriguing possibilities: the "maverick" Richard Crossman or Callaghan. The *Guardian* called Crossman a "highly effective Housing Minister", but in another case of strongly supporting the beleaguered Home Secretary, it reserved its real kudos for Callaghan. While acknowledging that he was a "failed Chancellor", it called Callaghan an individual of "complete integrity".[24] No doubt that's the kind of accolade the *Guardian*, or for that matter any newspaper, reserved for very few politicians. There are two things that make this most significant, however. First, the accolade appeared on 14 April, the same day that Callaghan misled his Cabinet colleagues by supporting the interim Industrial Relations Bill, only to attack that very same legislation at the joint NEC-Cabinet meeting three weeks later. Secondly, the "endorsement" came from the newspaper identified with the intellectual core of the left of centre within the party. In those years the *Guardian* was read by nearly half of all MPs, a third of senior civil servants[25] and its editorials were so widely followed that the newspaper considered them one of its "best selling points".[26]

But what was at the root of the *Guardian's* affection for Callaghan? It was generally thought that Callaghan's press secretary, Tom McCaffrey, who was a career civil servant, did not have the connections nor the political savvy of Roy Jenkins's press attaché, John Harris, who had worked as the Labour Party's spokesman as well as a newspaperman in London and Glasgow, or someone like Joe Haines, Wilson's press secretary. Nevertheless, Callaghan had a distinct advantage. Records of private conversations between Hetherington and Callaghan indicate the two men kept in contact over the years and were closer than journalists or the public realised. In some ways it was a perfect fit, in that both Callaghan and Hetherington were men of simple tastes and remarkably similar political views. In other ways, an odd match, given that Hetherington's newspaper was really a conduit for social change and the forum for the Labour Party's great thinkers. If you wanted to make an

---

[24] *Guardian*, 14 April 1969, p. 8.
[25] Guardian News & Media Archive. *Guardian* 150th anniversary booklet, May 1971, p. 6.
[26] Guardian News & Media Archive, Stead JLS 1/2/2. Internal memo for staff only on the newspaper's serious financial concerns, 6 December 1966.

intellectual argument, Denis Healey says, "They were the people, they were the best."[27]

Geoffrey Goodman, who worked for years at the rival *Daily Mirror* and for a time worked alongside Cole covering the trade unions, acknowledges that the *Guardian* all through the 1960s and early 1970s – printing glitches, financial troubles and all[28] – maintained a special and powerful niche despite its much smaller readership. Its circulation of around 300,000 was minuscule, compared with the *Daily Mirror*'s sales of more than five million. Nevertheless, Goodman says the *Guardian* was "regarded as the more serious heavyweight broad-sheet paper of political and intellectual debate". With the demise of the Liberal *News Chronicle* in 1960 and the relaunch of the *Daily Herald* as the *Sun* in 1964, Goodman says the *Guardian* "became the paper of the Labour Party, the left of centre, the liberal left of centre, from about the time Wilson became leader . . . . It was a very important influence".[29] Yet it was Callaghan, a politician who had built his career around embracing right-wing trade-union leaders, who was able to access the newspaper that was at the philosophical core of the centre-left of the Labour Party and do it without most people having had any idea that it was happening.

In those years and for some years to come, the public identified Wilson with the *Guardian*, not Callaghan. But there is an interesting, unexplored history between Hetherington and Callaghan that has been often overlooked and goes back several years before Callaghan found himself in the good graces of the *Guardian* on the debate over *In Place of Strife*. In the fight for the party leadership in January 1963 after the untimely death of Hugh Gaitskell, the *Guardian* endorsed not Wilson, not George Brown, but Callaghan. It was not some independent editorial board that had made that decision, it was Hetherington.[30] The editor of the *Guardian*, who had virtually a free hand in the operation of the newspaper under the rules of the ownership trust, told Callaghan in a frank telephone call a few days before the vote that he would

[27] Interview with Lord Healey, 22 March 2004.
[28] At one point in the mid-1960s the *Guardian*'s financial troubles forced it to consider merging with *The Times*, a plan that Hetherington vetoed.
[29] Interview with Geoffrey Goodman, 23 February 2004.
[30] Interview with John Cole, 25 February 2004. Before Hetherington made that decision, he consulted with Cole, who was then the Labour correspondent, and Francis Boyd, the political correspondent. Cole says that both he and Boyd favoured giving the endorsement to Wilson.

"prefer" him to either Wilson or Brown, the deputy leader whose drinking problem had become an embarrassment to the party.[31] Hetherington told Callaghan, who expressed some reluctance, that "he ought to run if there appeared to be any reasonable prospect of his coming above George Brown".[32] The next day, in a meeting with Wilson, the editor of the *Guardian* was less candid and less specific, saying Brown would never do and that he favoured either him or Callaghan.[33]

The root of the affection between Callaghan and Hetherington is unclear, and many of those who were close to either Callaghan or Hetherington during those years say they were unaware of any special relationship, although they agree that both men were rather private individuals. John Cole, who acknowledges his own closeness with Callaghan, concedes that such a relationship could have existed between Hetherington and Callaghan without his knowledge since he was not totally in Hetherington's confidence. If it did, Cole believes it might well have been strengthened by the fact that Hetherington was enamoured of Gaitskell, who had been the youthful Chancellor of the Exchequer in the final days of the 1950 Labour government and had succeeded Clement Attlee as party leader in 1955.[34] In 1961, Gaitskell, in a measure of his utter distrust of Wilson, moved Wilson to the post of shadow Foreign Secretary "where he could keep a close eye on him"[35] and handed Wilson's old post of shadow Chancellor to Callaghan.

Hetherington mentions in his memoirs that he had been seeing Callaghan "quite often" in the years prior to that endorsement in 1963 and had grown to like him.[36] Hetherington was a member of Royal Police Commission from 1960 to 1962 at the same time that Callaghan was in the rather unusual position of being both a Member of Parliament and the consultant to the police unions in England, Scotland and Wales. But Callaghan's memoirs, which are characteristically guarded, do not contain a single reference to the newspaperman. In Kenneth Morgan's

---

[31] BLPES, Hetherington 4/25. Note of a telephone conversation between Hetherington and Callaghan, 22 January 1963.

[32] Ibid. Hetherington added that if Wilson were the victor he "thought his worst defects would disappear, once his ambition was realised".

[33] Ibid.

[34] Interview with John Cole, 25 February 2004.

[35] BLPES, Hetherington 2/20. Memo from a meeting between Hetherington and Labour Party leader Hugh Gaitskell, 15 November 1960.

[36] Hetherington, *Guardian Years*, p. 81.

exhaustive nearly 800-page biography of Callaghan's life, there is only one mention of Hetherington. It refers to the 1963 endorsement, but concludes that Hetherington's support was the result of the impressive campaign that Callaghan put together, not mentioning that it was in fact Hetherington who had urged Callaghan to run.[37]

Also, Hetherington, who had many private meetings with political figures of all persuasions when he edited the newspaper from 1956 to 1975, was offered behind-the-scenes help from Callaghan in dealing with the newspaper unions as early as July 1960.[38] That would have been a critical time for the *Guardian*, which was then "vigorously"[39] pursuing the idea, one carried out a year later, of printing the newspaper in London as well as in Manchester, its traditional base of operations. Hetherington wrote years later that Laurence Scott, the chairman of the trust that oversaw the newspaper, wanted no part of any such deal with a politician.[40] At the time, though, Hetherington appeared both grateful and uneasy about the overture, concerned that if it became public knowledge it might damage the *Guardian*'s independence and credibility. In typical Callaghan fashion, the offer did have a limited-risk clause, however: it was only good before any trouble with the trade unions began, not after.[41]

It was in that meeting in July 1960 that Callaghan received some valuable advice. Callaghan had been telling Hetherington that as much as people liked and read the newspaper, there were times when they were uncomfortable about the *Guardian*'s loyalty to the cause. Callaghan said that "when the chips were down they didn't know which way it would go" and he advised Hetherington that if the *Guardian* wanted to increase its influence in the Labour Party, the newspaper "had to make [its] commitment plainer". Hetherington replied that the paper's tradition would not allow for that. Anyway, the *Guardian*'s editor continued, a "too obvious commitment would not be helpful". He had "some doubt indeed as to whether Callaghan, although he appeared to agree, really did entirely

---

[37] Morgan, *Callaghan: A Life*, p. 182.
[38] BLPES, Hetherington 2/21. Note of a meeting between Hetherington, Callaghan and Morgan Phillips, general secretary of the Labour Party, 26 July 1960.
[39] Ibid.
[40] Hetherington, *Guardian Years*, p. 147.
[41] BLPES, Hetherington 2/21. Note of a meeting between Hetherington, Callaghan and Morgan Phillips, general secretary of the Labour Party, 26 July 1960.

relish the essential independence of the *Guardian*".[42] But Hetherington need have had no fear, that was advice that the rising star within the Labour Party never forgot and it reflected his entire relationship with Hetherington and the paper for the next 15 years.

It is important to understand that the *Guardian* for much of the twentieth century was really unlike any other British newspaper. Most of the other influential newspapers were larger and had had a tradition of being owned and operated by press barons, like Lord Beaverbrook of the *Daily Express*, who was a great personal friend of Churchill and a successful Cabinet minister, or the *Daily Mail*'s Lord Rothermere, who had held minor posts in the government during the First World War. In the 1960s, Cecil King of the *Daily Mirror*, who sat on the board of the Bank of England and was the nephew of Rothermere and his press baron brother Lord Northcliffe, was the last of that line.[43] But Hetherington, although given complete control of the newspaper under the rules of the ownership agreement, was following in a different tradition at the *Guardian*, one that had been laid down by C.P. Scott, who had been the editor for more than half a century, from 1872 to 1929, and A.P. Wadsworth, an historian, who was Hetherington's immediate predecessor. Throughout the century, the *Guardian* had been at the forefront of the great social causes. It had been a strong advocate for Irish Home Rule and the right of women to vote; and later, it had been equally strong in its opposition to the proliferation of nuclear weapons, being instrumental in putting forth the idea of the nuclear non-proliferation treaty.[44]

Hetherington's propensity to meet privately with those who shaped policy at the highest levels of government in the 1960s and 1970s mirrored the practices of C.P. Scott. In Hetherington's case, he would type up his notes late at night and file them away for later distribution to a few senior writers and editors;[45] Scott, on the other hand, kept a more formal diary of his meetings with the political elite, most notably David Lloyd George. But Hetherington and Scott, more than a generation apart, might have had a similar motive for their meetings, which tended

[42] Ibid.
[43] King played the role of the press baron, but he had had to answer to a board, which in fact fired him over a campaign to try to oust Wilson as Prime Minister in 1968.
[44] Guardian News & Media Archive. *Guardian* 150th anniversary booklet, May 1971.
[45] *Guardian*, 4 October 1999.

to be with power brokers from the Liberal or Labour parties. The historian Trevor Wilson, who edited the diaries of Scott, observed that the object of his meetings was less about getting the news than about influencing government policy: "To adapt Bagehot [the scholar of the English constitution], he wanted to be consulted, to encourage and to warn. So he spent little time with those who, though they might have provided him with information, were unlikely to respond to his advice."[46]

That analysis might be applicable to Hetherington as well, and it might help to explain the bond between him and Callaghan. On the other hand, from Callaghan's perspective, the relationship that he had quietly cultivated at the *Guardian* meant that he was assured of getting a receptive audience, and getting his side of the story heard, from those at the highest levels at the newspaper. In other words, he was not as much the outsider that he pretended to be. Jenkins, as influential as he was as the nation's Chancellor of the Exchequer, did not have the inroads at the *Guardian* that Callaghan had, nor did Castle, but Wilson certainly did – he was, after all, the Prime Minister. Nevertheless, the support that Callaghan got from the *Guardian* during the battle over *In Place of Strife* and other major crises at this turning point in his career was the thread that kept his political rehabilitation together.

Callaghan's press secretary McCaffrey, repeatedly maintains that the *Guardian* "was not particularly in favour of Callaghan",[47] but the facts dispute that contention. On nearly ever major matter of policy that was crucial to Callaghan's political recovery, Callaghan and the *Guardian* found themselves on the same side of the issue: that was true on the Vietnam demonstrations in Grosvenor Square; on industrial relations, the most critical issue to face any government since the war; on Callaghan's defiance of collective Cabinet responsibility; as well as on the Troubles in Northern Ireland. Even on the great controversy over Britain's entry into the European Economic Community (EEC), an issue in which the newspaper and Callaghan did not always agree, the *Guardian's* posture benefited Callaghan. On the Race Relations Bill, Callaghan actively sought the editorial backing of the *Guardian* in a private meeting with Hetherington in April 1968 and in the end he got it.

---

[46] Trevor Wilson (ed.), *The Political Diaries of C.P. Scott 1911–1928*, (Ithaca, 1970), p. 23.
[47] Interview with Sir Tom McCaffrey, 3 July 2003.

In this period, the only substantive issue over which the two men came to a sharp disagreement occurred just prior to the start of Callaghan's political rehabilitation. The *Guardian* staunchly opposed the new Home Secretary's position that had instituted the quotas that in effect blocked the entry of Kenyans of Asian descent into the United Kingdom. The agreement to allow a "meagre" 1500 immigrants into Britain was a shocking position from a Labour government that had portrayed itself as being especially sensitive on matters of human rights. Even the *Daily Telegraph*, on the far opposite end of the political spectrum, called Callaghan's initiative "an unholy mess" that "led to the separation of families".[48] When the *Guardian's* editorials critical of the government's stance fell on deaf ears, it raised the bar and on 4 March 1968 called for the Home Secretary to resign.[49] But it was muted in that the editorial referred to Callaghan as "an extremely hardworking and conscientious minister" and laid some of the blame at the doorstep of his predecessor Jenkins, who the *Guardian* said should have prepared the country better for the influx that was obviously coming amid the changes taking place in Kenya.[50] The editorial also placed culpability on the press, saying that cutbacks in the news coverage of East Africa had let an important developing story slip through the cracks.[51]

For all the calls of resignation, the headline on the editorial did not demand Callaghan's ousting. It simply read, "Who should resign?" In addressing that question the *Guardian* dealt with all sorts of possibilities, including protest resignations from members of the Civil Service or the Race Relations Board, before it got to the rather tepid call for the Home Secretary to quit.[52] The *Guardian* was obviously not determined to see Callaghan go. Only a few weeks after that editorial was published, Callaghan had two private discussions with two senior editors at the *Guardian* – John Cole on 3 April 1968, and a follow-up visit from Hetherington on 9 April. Those conversations reveal that Callaghan was upset by the *Guardian's* editorial, but they also show the depth of the relationship that Callaghan had with the newspaper. There were no

---

[48] *Daily Telegraph*, 2 March 1968, p. 10.

[49] *Guardian*, 4 March 1968, p. 8.

[50] Ibid; BLPES, Hetherington 20/15. Crossman told Hetherington that Jenkins had had plans to introduce a similar bill in March 1968 but "they were going to keep the quota flexible – probably 8000 or something like that, but with the freedom to vary it when they saw how things were working out."

[51] *Guardian*, 4 March 1968, p. 8.

[52] Ibid.

further calls from Hetherington that Callaghan should quit, nor was there any talk from Callaghan of cutting off relations with the newspaper. On the contrary, there was a reaffirmation on the part of the Home Secretary, Cole and, more importantly, Hetherington of the warm relations that Callaghan had with the *Guardian*. Callaghan, the shrewd political operator that he was, tried to play on the two men's sympathies by saying that his wife, Audrey[53] – who was generally loved and respected for her charitable works at the Great Ormond Street Hospital for Children – was so distraught by the editorial that she would not allow the *Guardian* into the house.[54] Callaghan had to read the paper in his room at the Home Office. Callaghan told Cole that "he was not an edgy person, but found himself opening the *Guardian* now in the morning to see if anything unpleasant was said about him.... It was always some kind of a snide comment." Cole told Callaghan "that there was nothing like a vendetta against him" and Callaghan "accepted that immediately". In what seems to be a heart-to-heart talk with Cole, a year before Callaghan would become immersed in the controversy over *In Place of Strife*, he told the veteran reporter that he was "no longer *burningly* ambitious", implying that Wilson had nothing to fear and could have him as a "friend", but he added that he "was not prepared to crawl". Nevertheless, in a reflection of the perceived danger to his own political fortunes, Callaghan told Cole in that same conversation that "the worst thing in his view which could happen was for Roy Jenkins, who was the only possible alternative leader at present, to take over".[55]

Callaghan made much the same pitch to Hetherington about a week later saying he could not understand "why the *Guardian* had turned against him", particularly since he and Hetherington "had been good friends for a long time". Callaghan said that the press, including the *Guardian*, had "whipped up" the whole issue over immigration. He was critical of photos that appeared in the *Guardian* showing "people arriving at Gatwick carrying bundles as if they were refugees". Hetherington told Callaghan that he would be "delighted" if the controversy over the Immigration Bill would die down and said that he "was very sorry,

---

[53] (Manchester) *Guardian* Archive C5/335. Notes from a discussion between Callaghan and John Cole, 3 April 1968.

[54] Margaret Jay, however, never remembers her mother expressing any such concern. (Interview with Lady Jay, 3 March 2004.)

[55] (Manchester) *Guardian* Archive C5/335. Notes from a discussion between Callaghan and John Cole, 3 April 1968.

personally, both at the time and now, that we had felt it necessary to write what we did".[56]

But before Hetherington walked out of the door the two men agreed to have lunch "one day soon" and Callaghan put in place an early first step in his political rehabilitation. He told Hetherington that whatever he felt about the Commonwealth Immigration Act, he badly needed his support on the Race Relations Bill that was coming before Parliament. He urged Hetherington to avoid "nit-picking" the bill, saying instead that the *Guardian* should "give it a cheer, and give it a welcome".[57] The move to legislate to curb racial discrimination was Callaghan's way out of the hole he had dug himself into with the controversy over the Kenyan Asians and he knew that he was facing stiff opposition from two different camps: first, those who felt he had gone too far by introducing a Race Relations Bill in the first place and, secondly, and more importantly, the critical centre left of the Labour Party who had urged tougher sanctions and felt that Callaghan had not gone far enough. That was the segment that Hetherington could keep in check.

The editor of the *Guardian* told Callaghan that it seemed a "good bill", but when it came to enforcement Hetherington thought it lacked teeth.[58] He believed that the Race Relations Bill's emphasis on using persuasion rather than fines or imprisonment to redress the obstacles facing a black man trying to move with his wife and family into a white neighbourhood just would not work. Hetherington told Callaghan that in his view if a homeowner or a property agent "was hauled before a conciliation committee, he could simply ignore it and nothing more would happen". But the Home Secretary said there were provisions for the matter to be appealed to a higher level and anyway he told the *Guardian*'s editor that the "scope of the bill was great" and said that in "99 per cent of the cases", in the example that Hetherington had cited, the complaints would not be justified anyway.[59]

---

[56] (Manchester) *Guardian* Archive C5/336/1. Notes from a meeting between Callaghan and Hetherington, 9 April 1968.

[57] Ibid.

[58] Ibid; PRO, HO 376/74. Note to Mr. Pile from David Ennals, 8 March 1968. Even within the Home Office, there was a recognition of the public-relations problem with the bill. A month before Callaghan met with Hetherington, Ennals confided to Pile, amid concerns over the lack of enforcement measures, that "we are going to face strong criticisms of the Race Relations Bill from the informed press..."

[59] (Manchester) *Guardian* Archive C5/336/1. Notes from a meeting between Callaghan and Hetherington, 9 April 1968.

As he was leaving, Hetherington pondered whether this was a good time to thank Callaghan for "our debt to him 15 months ago",[60] but decided to deal with the matter by writing him a letter given the lateness of the hour and the fact he had to get back to the newspaper's offices on Gray's Inn Road. It was a reference to the fact that a little over a year earlier the *Guardian* came perilously close to having to silence its presses forever, but in the end an arrangement was worked out, through job cuts and union give-backs, to keep the newspaper afloat and independent. In his memoirs, Hetherington acknowledged that "George Woodcock from the [Trades Union Congress] did a bit of private talking in the background, as did Jim Callaghan and Ray Gunter [Minister of Labour], and that helped us over the last hurdle".[61] But in that note, which Hetherington did get around to writing, he went further. He told Callaghan that "not many people know" of the crucial role that he had played on behalf of the *Guardian*, and Hetherington assured Callaghan that it was "something that I shall never forget".[62]

Callaghan's finesse with Hetherington and Cole demonstrated how much Callaghan valued those relationships and nurtured them during the years of his political rehabilitation. There were no indications of his famous temper tantrums[63] or of the cutting off of relations with the *Guardian* even on the one occasion when the newspaper gave him a well-deserved slap on the wrist over his handling of the Kenyan Asians debacle. Callaghan's careful cultivation of the *Guardian* and the preservation of those ties over the years was one of the reasons he made such an incredible political comeback. It was in stark contrast to the way Callaghan could treat others who disagreed with him, or the indiscretion shown by some other Cabinet ministers in their dealings with the press. For example, when the *Guardian* was at its lowest point in late 1966 and early 1967, word got back to Hetherington that Michael Stewart, who was at that time the head of the Department of Economic Affairs, did not much care if the *Guardian*, which Wilson and Callaghan and others were rallying to support, kept printing or closed

---

[60] Ibid.

[61] Hetherington, *Guardian Years*, p. 170.

[62] BLPES, Hetherington 14/6. Copy of letter to Callaghan from Hetherington, 10 April 1968.

[63] In this respect Callaghan and Hetherington were quite different. "Hetherington did not put people down. He never publicly issued a rebuke. He made suggestions rather than issued orders, and although the effect was the same, there was room for discussion..." (*Guardian*, 4 October 1999.)

its doors forever.[64] Stewart was quoted as making an off-hand remark as he was walking down the stairs after a meeting with several people in attendance, Hetherington among them, that "he didn't set much stock by the *Guardian* nowadays, because it had become so malicious and inaccurate".[65]

The financial well-being of the *Guardian* was a concern that Callaghan and Wilson shared. In January 1967, Douglas Jay, the President of the Board of Trade, told Wilson that the economic troubles that were plaguing the newspaper industry – amid a steep decline in advertising sales, which reflected the weak economy that Callaghan was then overseeing – were the fault of the newspapers themselves and that it was time for the industry "to put its own house in order". Wilson, in an indication of the high regard he had for the *Guardian*, replied "this is right", but said that from the talk he had had with Hetherington, the *Guardian*, which had plans to cut its operating costs by more than £500,000 annually,[66] could well be forced to cease publication if the trade unions refused to cooperate. "If that happens I would hope that the [government] would go straight in and help on that specific issue.... The *Guardian* must not be allowed to close."[67] The *Guardian* survived but Jay did not; Wilson sacked him later that year. Jay, though, had been out of favour with the Prime Minister for some time, particularly over his resistance to the idea of Britain joining the EEC.[68]

Nevertheless, after the conversation that Callaghan had had with Hetherington about the Race Relations Bill in the spring of 1968, the *Guardian* did write an editorial on 19 April saying that the legislation's "flaws lie in the weakness of its enforcement machinery", but it gave Callaghan his due by saying the bill's failings were "not in its scope", picking up on the Home Secretary's very assessment of the great "scope"

---

[64] BLPES, Hetherington 12/2. Footnote to Hetherington's notes from a luncheon at which remarks were made by the Secretary of State for Economic Affairs Stewart, 9 January 1967.

[65] Ibid. The *Guardian*, though, may have had the last word. In its 14 April 1969, editorial suggesting alternatives to Wilson, Callaghan among them, it said: "To take Mr. Michael Stewart, because he has fewer enemies, would be a mistake."

[66] Guardian News & Media Archive, Stead 1/2. Confidential memo to senior staff from Hetherington, 23 January 1967.

[67] PRO, PREM 13/3414. Internal government assessment on the state of the national newspaper industry. The report is unsigned and undated, but it is apparently from 1967.

[68] Douglas Jay, *Change and Fortune* (London, 1980), pp. 407–408.

of the legislation.[69] In the final analysis, amid the national furore over the Conservative MP Enoch Powell's "Rivers of Blood" speech, which warned of violence unless black immigration was controlled, the *Guardian* came down firmly in Callaghan's corner. On 23 April, the day that Callaghan's bill was coming before Parliament, the *Guardian*'s lead editorial carried a powerful headline: "To Free Ourselves of Prejudice". The newspaper urged passage of the Race Relations Bill as a "minimum first step" and completely dropped any and all references to its concerns over the fact that the bill provided little or no redress in dealing with matters of racial discrimination in the job or housing market.[70] The *Guardian*'s support on the Race Relations Bill was a critical boost for Callaghan, an essential counterbalance to his much-maligned Immigration Bill. Hetherington came through in the end.

Bernard Donoughue, who was a senior adviser years later to both Wilson and Callaghan at No. 10 Downing Street, says Callaghan would have been "aware – as a sort of right-wing Labour person – that he shouldn't be caught in too many right-wing positions. He would want to have some credibility on the more liberal *Guardian* side of the party [and] race would provide him with an issue like that."[71] But it was more than a single issue – it was on issue after issue after issue. Callaghan had sway over Hetherington in a way that few politicians did with the exception of Wilson. On 27 June 1966, for example, the Prime Minister suggested to Hetherington that if more progress was not made in talks over the future of Rhodesia, whose white minority government had six months earlier declared a "unilateral declaration of independence" from Britain, "we could float the idea of handing sovereignty to the United Nations". Hetherington said he was going to be out of town and suggested that the Prime Minister might want to talk with Mark Arnold-Forster, the chief editorial writer, while he was away. Wilson said "it would be very handy to talk to Mark and he would do that".[72] Indeed, two weeks later, on 11 July, the *Guardian* came out with an editorial in which it put forward several suggestions to alleviate the crisis amid Britain's insistence on majority rule, among them the proposition of turning over the predicament "unsolved" to the UN.[73] There are

---

[69] *Guardian*, 19 April 1968, p. 10.
[70] *Guardian*, 23 April 1968, p. 8.
[71] Interview with Lord Donoughue, 9 July 2003.
[72] BLPES, Hetherington 12/12. Note of a meeting between the Prime Minister and Hetherington, 27 June 1966.
[73] *Guardian*, 11 July 1966, p. 8.

indications that Wilson and Crossman on occasion leaked the contents of Cabinet meetings to Hetherington as well.[74] Callaghan's modus operandi was different from Wilson's; much subtler but just as effective. For example, in February 1967, when Callaghan was still Chancellor he had told Hetherington that growth in the economy could only be achieved by wage restraint and that it would have to be done through legislation, not voluntary arrangements with trade unions. At the same time, Callaghan disclosed to the *Guardian*'s editor "the thinking" behind a major economic package that had not yet been put before the Cabinet. According to Hetherington, Callaghan said that what he was about to say was "strictly not for writing about, except in the most indirect way". He then proceeded to outline plans for defence cuts, deeper reductions in the growth of domestic spending and the need for Britain to ask the International Monetary Fund to ease its terms on the repayment of loans.[75] An early sign of Callaghan's disregard for Castle emerged in that conversation. Callaghan told Hetherington that he had permitted the Welsh Office to exceed spending for roads in his constituency of South Wales, and had not discussed it with Castle, who was then Transport Minister. "Barbara would be furious when she found out, but she wouldn't find out until it was too late."[76]

In that same conversation with Cole, on 3 April 1968, less than six months after Callaghan had left the Treasury, Callaghan dropped a bombshell about the government's incomes policy. Callaghan, who had just spent three years as Chancellor and knew the impropriety of commenting even in confidence on very sensitive wage matters, told Cole that when he was at the Treasury the government was actually prepared to accept a 6 per cent increase with the trade unions rather than the 3.5 per cent rise it was now "pretending" was the outside figure it could tolerate. Cole surmised that Callaghan "genuinely regretted" disclosing that fact and took Callaghan at his word when the Home Secretary said he had "avoided saying this because it would only make things more difficult for Roy".[77] Callaghan might have added Castle as well, since two days later she was named Secretary of State for Employment and Productivity with responsibility for that same policy.

---

[74] (Manchester) *Guardian* Archive C5/326. Notes of a discussion between Crossman and Hetherington, 26 January 1968.
[75] BLPES, Hetherington 13/24. Notes of a meeting between the Chancellor of the Exchequer and Hetherington, 2 February 1967.
[76] Ibid.
[77] (Manchester) *Guardian* Archive C5/335. Notes from a discussion between Callaghan and John Cole, 3 April 1968.

Although the conversation with the *Guardian* would be kept strictly confidential, the sheer distance between the wage figures would no doubt undermine Jenkins's credibility among Cole, Hetherington and any other senior staff members at the *Guardian* who read Cole's notes. Thus the newspaper's editors were privy through the back door to confidential information that would certainly make them suspicious of any future pronouncements in the sensitive area of incomes policy vis-à-vis the trade unions coming from the office of Jenkins, the man who was Callaghan's chief rival and at that point the second most powerful man in the Cabinet. That suspicion made its way on to the *Guardian*'s editorial page – in what must have been an unpleasant jolt for the newly appointed Castle – a week after Cole had had that conversation with Callaghan. On 11 April, the *Guardian* informed its readers that despite what the government was saying, Castle really had "more room to manoeuvre". The editorial, without disclosing what Callaghan had said about the 6 per cent figure,[78] added "it would be naïve to think, after all of the 'guidance' of the past three months, that 3½ per cent means 3½ per cent".[79]

Yet Callaghan's press secretary, McCaffrey, says he could never remember Callaghan leaking information to a journalist. "No, I can't think of anyone who would be his favourite person that he would leak a story to. From the time I knew him, I can't imagine Jim leaking a story."[80] Callaghan's agent Jack Brooks, who was among Callaghan's close friends and was responsible for taking care of Callaghan's affairs in the ever-important constituency in Cardiff, says that of course Callaghan leaked, "Everybody would do it. I would do it if I wanted to get a policy through."[81] Cole understandably skirts around the question of whether Callaghan leaked, asking, "Well, it depends what you mean by leak. Help me with your inquiry?"[82]

Callaghan's press secretary is a mysterious player. Either McCaffrey – who says "all these smart guys on the *Guardian* would of course be pretty scornful of anything that somebody like Callaghan did"[83] – was not privy to the relationship that Callaghan had with Hetherington and Cole or he intentionally cultivated an image of his boss that threw

---

[78] Castle, *Diaries, 1964–70*, p. 427. The increase of 6 per cent was the same figure that the TUC had proposed.
[79] *Guardian*, 11 April 1968, p. 10.
[80] Interview with Sir Tom McCaffrey, 3 July 2003.
[81] Interview with Lord Brooks, 16 July 2003.
[82] Interview with John Cole, 25 February 2004.
[83] Interview with Sir Tom McCaffrey, 3 July 2003.

Callaghan's rivals and the press off the scent. McCaffrey might not have had a background in journalism, like Harris and Haines, but he knew how Fleet Street worked and the significant role played by the *Guardian* in the nation's affairs. McCaffrey concedes as much by agreeing that the *Guardian*'s "influence was great" in the late 1960s and early 1970s but adds "Callaghan was regarded within the party at that time as a pretty right-wing kind of person. So he wasn't the *Guardian*'s favourite person."[84]

McCaffrey, who had worked for a time under Harris when Harris was Jenkins's press secretary at the Home Office, tells a story that Callaghan tells as well.[85] It is about how he, McCaffrey, read the riot act to Callaghan in his early days as Home Secretary: "I was in his room in the House of Commons, and I shut the door and I said, Can we talk? And I told him he was screwing up on all sorts of things and annoying all sorts of people.... That's when he started thinking about things. Up until that time, all he thought about was himself." McCaffrey attributes that conversation with putting Callaghan on the road to his rehabilitation.[86] But it is hard to understand how anyone, especially a civil servant, would have succeeded addressing Callaghan in that fashion; that is unless his influence actually was far greater than most people had realised.

Callaghan concedes that throughout his critical years at the Home Office, McCaffrey was someone he "relied on more than most"[87] and that he brought him into the debate on major issues repeatedly. McCaffrey apparently was popular with reporters, and Callaghan explains this by saying that although McCaffrey had to sometimes hold back information, he "made it a point of principle never to mislead them or lay false trails".[88] That is a view with which Alan Watkins, who was a columnist for the *New Statesman* at the time, agrees. Watkins adds that McCaffrey was much less of a Labour Party man than Haines was and "much more of a personal emissary of Jim".[89]

McCaffrey's animosity towards the *Guardian* creates the impression that he knew nothing of Callaghan's closeness to Hetherington or Cole; yet at the least a man in his position would be aware of which

---

[84] Ibid.

[85] Callaghan, *Time and Chance*, p. 407.

[86] Interview with Sir Tom McCaffrey, 3 July 2003.

[87] James Callaghan, *A House Divided: The Dilemma of Northern Ireland* (London, 1973), p. 69.

[88] Callaghan, *Time and Chance*, p. 407.

[89] Interview with Alan Watkins, 6 November 2003.

Fleet Street: A Special Relationship   113

news organisations were supporting his minister's policies and which were opposed. It suggests that Callaghan, in possibly the only risk he ever took, was playing a dangerous game. If the trade unions and the working-class people he so identified with had known the extent of his cosiness with the organ of the party's intellectuals it could have well undermined the image that he and McCaffrey so carefully cultivated; that of the bluff, common-sense man who had a certain disdain for the Oxbridge crowd. It was just that disdain that created an advantageous contrast for Callaghan at the time of *In Place of Strife*, given that Wilson, Jenkins and Castle were all Oxford-educated and lacked strong union ties.[90] It is a disdain that McCaffrey, like his boss of so many years, seems determined to convey in comparing Jenkins, whom he worked under for a time at the Home Office, with Callaghan. McCaffrey, relishing the contrast, calls Jenkins "a foppish, various clubs in London kind of person, dined and friendly with Jacqueline Kennedy and all this kind of thing. Whereas Jim was a working-class lad."[91]

The closeness between Jenkins and Harris was legendary: the stories of how Jenkins brought Harris with him as he moved from one post to the other, how Harris became so identified with Jenkins that Harris even began to gesture and talk like his mentor. Yet, Callaghan did a similar thing with McCaffrey, but whereas Harris took on some of the trappings of Jenkins, McCaffrey maintained those "un-civil-service-like qualities"[92] that Callaghan so admired. From 1968 onwards, Callaghan elevated McCaffrey's role at the Home Office. Then Callaghan made him his press secretary when he moved to the Foreign Office in 1974. Thomas Brimelow, the permanent secretary at the Foreign Office, who admired the new Foreign Secretary's "candour in declaring what it was he wanted", conceded that Callaghan made the request for McCaffrey's transfer "right away, in the opening conversation".[93] Finally, when Callaghan was about to become Prime Minister two years later, he told his top political aide Tom McNally in no uncertain terms that McCaffrey

---

[90] *Sunday Express*, 2 December 1967. After Callaghan's resignation from the Treasury in November 1967, the columnist cross-bencher noted that "no other post-war Cabinet has been so stuffed with intellectuals" and that "among Labour's top people today, [Callaghan] is one of the last to have made it the hard way. Which gives him a very special place in the hearts of the party's rank and file. A place he could never have acquired by a first at Oxford."

[91] Interview with Sir Tom McCaffrey, 3 July 2003.

[92] Callaghan, *A House Divided*, p. 69.

[93] BLPES, Hetherington 21/22. Note of a conversation between Hetherington and Sir Thomas Brimelow at Nuffield College, Oxford, 22 March 1974.

would be moving over to head up the press operation at No. 10 Downing Street. McNally says that while other senior appointments, including that of Bernard Donoughue to head the Policy Unit, were open for discussion, that appointment was not.[94] It is difficult to believe that any politician would give that kind of attention to the appointment of a press secretary if that individual had been unaware of the politician's priorities; in Callaghan's case, the tremendous role the *Guardian* had played in the rebuilding of his political career.

McCaffrey attributes his own success and Callaghan's political rehabilitation to that frank talk he had with Callaghan in his early days in the Home Office. He says, "It's because I played the part in that and because I was with him as his adviser and his closest person in the Home Office at that time, that's why we became such good friends and why I became his spokesman all the way up." But at the same time McCaffrey says he knew of no journalists who were close to his mentor and contends that Callaghan was much less political when he moved to the Home Office. "To start with, I think when he was at the Treasury, he was very, very political and I think gradually over the years he became more [concerned with] doing what he considered was right for the country and about his place in history and all that. It's a bit hard to say exactly what motivated him; he obviously wanted always to do a good job and always to get things right. And felt himself big enough, and I think to be fair Jenkins did too, not to ignore public opinion but go against it if he thought he was in the right." But when asked to give an example of that, McCaffrey responds, "Not sure I can."[95]

Nevertheless, Callaghan's official biographer, Kenneth Morgan, who had many lengthy conversations with the former Prime Minister, alludes to the relationship with Cole, the journalist who was likely the closest to Callaghan. But Morgan leaves an inaccurate impression. In a passing reference to the *Guardian's* former news editor, Morgan says that Callaghan "used"[96] people like Cole to advance his political career. The relationship, however, was much more complex than that; it was one that involved considerable give and take and was beneficial not only to Callaghan, but, through Cole and Hetherington, to the *Guardian* as well.

Jean Stead, who worked as Cole's deputy on the news desk and who later became news editor herself, noted that in this period of

[94] Interview with Lord McNally, 17 July 2003.
[95] Interview with Sir Tom McCaffrey, 3 July 2003.
[96] Morgan, *Callaghan: A Life*, p. 292.

the *Guardian*'s history "the demand and encouragement for journalists to produce exclusives was unremitting".[97] Cole was supervising the reporting and he had an important source in Callaghan, one he is still protective of – and rightly so. The extraordinary value of Cole's having had a confidential source at the highest levels of government and the Labour Party leadership, especially in those days when Fleet Street was teeming with reporters eager to beat the competition, is illustrated by his agitation over the loss of another of his closest sources, namely Wilson. Back when Gaitskell was party leader, Cole first arranged for Hetherington privately to meet Wilson, a source Cole carefully cultivated in his years as the *Guardian*'s Labour correspondent. To this day, Cole is still annoyed by the fact that Hetherington came between him and Wilson, and admits he "slightly resented the editor taking [Wilson] over when he became party leader though he was still available to me".[98]

Nevertheless, Cole and Hetherington grew closer in the critical years that paralleled Callaghan's political revival. Cole was promoted from news editor to Hetherington's deputy in November 1969 in what was an acknowledgement of his ever-expanding role and influence at the *Guardian*. In the internal office memorandum announcing Cole's promotion to the No. 2 spot at the paper, the *Guardian* staff were informed by Hetherington that Cole's responsibilities "will overlap with mine and he will take charge in my absence".[99] This was confirmation of Hetherington's complete trust in his deputy, whose views deeply influenced Hetherington.[100] It is a point that Callaghan certainly was aware of when he was seeking Hetherington's help on the Race Relations Bill. At one point in their conversation, Callaghan appealed to Hetherington to "ask John Cole, he would certainly say the same".[101]

It is important to emphasise that Cole's rapid rise in the ranks of the newspaper's management quickly followed two big issues: the defeat of *In Place of Strife* in June 1969 and the initial success of British policy in Northern Ireland in late 1969 and early 1970. Those two big ongoing news stories, which Cole rode to success on, were two issues that

---

[97] Guardian News & Media Archive, Stead JLS 3/3. Original text of article for *British Journalism Review*, Vol. 9, No. 4, 1998.

[98] Interview with John Cole, 25 February 2004.

[99] Guardian News & Media Archive, Stead JLS 1/2/9. Memo to staff from Hetherington, 28 October 1969.

[100] Hetherington, *Guardian Years*, p. 294.

[101] (Manchester) *Guardian* Archive C5/336. Notes from a meeting between Hetherington and Callaghan, 9 April 1968.

he was ideally suited for and two issues that transformed Callaghan's political career. Years of knowledge in dealing with the trade union movement and the union bosses gave Cole an inside track on the controversy over industrial relations as it had aided Callaghan in his manoeuvrings on that issue as well. Also, Cole, having been brought up in Ulster and spent his early newspaper days in Belfast, had an understanding of Northern Ireland, which few British newspapermen had. The editorial that Cole wrote on the day that Callaghan ordered British troops into Northern Ireland in August 1969, which was neither totally supportive nor critical of the move, greatly impressed Hetherington and in the weeks and months ahead he repeatedly deferred to Cole as the story dominated the headlines.[102]

On Northern Ireland, Cole had made himself indispensable to Hetherington in the way that Callaghan had made himself indispensable to Wilson. Before moving to the *Guardian* in 1956, Cole had been a reporter for his hometown newspaper, the *Belfast Telegraph*. It was in Belfast in the early 1950s that Cole first met Callaghan, who was part of a parliamentary delegation visiting Northern Ireland.[103] Hetherington was aware that Cole was regularly "consulted" by the Home Office in the late 1960s and early 1970s on that issue and that he often met with people like Callaghan and his protégé Merlyn Rees.[104] Those conversations were not archived, suggesting that the extent of the contacts – whether they were telephone calls, unrecorded comments or casual encounters – were greater than the documents indicate.

It had been a long-standing policy at the *Guardian*, and one Hetherington maintained, that great weight be given to the judgements of the correspondents in the field when taking an editorial stand on major issues.[105] On both trade-union reform and Northern Ireland, Cole was the in-house expert. But Hetherington's near total reliance on Cole when it came to Ulster troubled Wilson's press secretary Haines,[106] a strong advocate for a united Ireland. At one point in early 1972, Haines privately advised the Irish government to invite Hetherington to Dublin "on his own". Haines felt such a visit might help wean Hetherington

---

[102] Hetherington, *Guardian Years*, p. 294.
[103] Interview with John Cole, 25 February 2004.
[104] Hetherington, *Guardian Years*, p. 294.
[105] Interview with John Cole, 25 February 2004.
[106] Interview with Joe Haines, 25 March 2004. Haines had actually worked briefly under Hetherington when Haines was a subeditor on the *Guardian* early in his career.

away from Cole's more traditionalist views on the Irish question.[107] Since Cole was writing one editorial after the other on Ireland, his ability to sway public opinion was substantial.[108] Not only that, his influence was broad on other matters as well. For example, in April 1971, Cole blocked a story that the newspaper was about to publish on government leaks. Stead, the *Guardian*'s news editor, noted that Cole "threw doubts on the story, raising a number of points, which led to its withdrawal from the paper for tonight and, I suspect, forever".[109]

Regardless, in those years, no legislative initiative had a more profound effect on British politics than those involving the troublesome issue of industrial relations and no single news event was more potentially damaging to Britain's image in the United States and in the international community than Northern Ireland, particularly before the re-emergence of the Irish Republican Army. Oddly enough, Callaghan emerged, at least initially, in a very advantageous political position because of those two big issues. For the most part, he was on the same side as Cole, whom the newspaper conceded was a man who "knows where he stands on most things and, arguing his case with force and conviction, he has largely shaped the *Guardian*'s editorial line on Northern Ireland, and on industrial relations..."[110]

Conclusion

The *Guardian* was an essential element of Callaghan's political comeback. The editorials that were sympathetic to Callaghan on issue after issue gave him a political respectability on the left and the centre-left and therefore much more room for manoeuvring. It was an important bond and a complex one that involved Cole as well as Hetherington. But it was Hetherington, because of his overwhelming influence at the *Guardian*, who ultimately solidified the relationship that would greatly

---

[107] NAI, DFA/2001/23/559. Memo detailing meeting between Haines and C. Howard of the Irish Embassy in London, 16 February 1972.

[108] Ibid. Among the other suggestions that Haines made were for the Irish government to steer clear of hiring an outside public-relations firm. He felt it should be kept in-house because "commitment and care is necessary and it is hard to get this" from an outside agency.

[109] Guardian News & Media Archive, Stead JLS 2/1. Entry in personal diary for 29 April 1971. However, in that particular case the story eventually did make its way into the newspaper and won a prestigious award for the *Guardian*.

[110] Guardian News & Media Archive. *Guardian* 150th anniversary booklet, May 1971, p. 8.

aid Callaghan's re-emergence as Wilson's eventual successor. The relationship was critical to Callaghan for several reasons.

First, it enabled Callaghan to infiltrate the philosophical core of the Labour Party. The *Guardian* was being read and commented upon not by the working class or the trade-union leaders,[111] with whom Callaghan so identified, but by the left and centre-left, the Oxbridge crowd, who saw Callaghan as anathema to nearly everything they stood for. Stead, Cole's deputy, remembered Hetherington as being "probably the first editor to take the youth culture seriously".[112] The surveys reflected that; nearly half of the *Guardian's* readership was under age 35 and it was the best-read daily in British universities – hardly the crowd that Callaghan was outwardly pursuing.[113] It was an odd match as well given Callaghan's traditionalist views. The *Guardian* in the 1960s and early 1970s was a bastion of liberal thought. It provided an influential forum for a country that in the post-war period was going through massive social changes, many of which Callaghan frankly found distasteful. Discussions of drug use, abortion, homosexuality and pornography found their way onto its pages, breaking many a taboo of a "family" newspaper. Even in its advertising policy, the *Guardian* refused to embark upon "the slippery slopes of censorship".[114]

Secondly, the *Guardian* was also extremely important to Callaghan because its influence in the country went far beyond its circulation. Other news organisations knew of the newspaper's close ties with the Labour government. As a result, any favourable coverage that Callaghan received in the *Guardian* would likely be multiplied many times over in the British press as well as in the coverage on radio and television. Oddly enough, it had added impact for Callaghan because the newspaper was not viewed as being sympathetic to him. This was certainly evident when Wilson was in Nigeria. The *Guardian's* front-page story of Harry Nicholas's defence of Callaghan and Peter Jenkins's column on

[111] Interview with Jack Jones, 18 June 2003. Jones says "the newspapers with the big circulations were more important to us that the *Guardian*." But he concedes he was viewing the press from a trade-union perspective and that "it may be [that] Wilson and Callaghan didn't regard the papers like the *News Chronicle* and so on in the same way that I did."
[112] Guardian News & Media Archive, Stead JLS 3/3. Original text of article for *British Journalism Review*, Vol. 9, No. 4, 1998.
[113] Guardian News & Media Archive. *Guardian* 150th anniversary booklet, May 1971, p. 3.
[114] Ibid, p. 6.

the crumbling of the Wilson government reverberated far beyond Gray's Inn Road and presented a serious obstacle to the government. Thirdly, the relationship was so precious to Callaghan because so few people were aware of it. Hetherington took great care that all of his private discussions with Wilson, Callaghan, Crossman and others remained private, a point that Callaghan himself alluded to in one of their earlier conversations, when he referred to Hetherington as the "soul of discretion".[115] Healey – who had private conversations as well with King, the publisher of the *Daily Mirror*, who for a time was promoting Healey as an alternative to Wilson – remembers Hetherington as being especially good at keeping confidences.[116] As early as 1965, there is a notation in Hetherington's papers that advised any of the senior staff at the *Guardian* who saw the notes of any of his private discussions to "please carefully remember that their mere existence is something I would rather not have discussed".[117]

Finally, it had special meaning for Callaghan because he knew how important the *Guardian* was to the Prime Minister and how closely he read it. There was no other British newspaper that had as deep an impact on Wilson's thinking, although other news organisations certainly tried.[118] Wilson was an avid newspaper reader, and an even more avid reader of the *Guardian*. That was something that Hetherington had confirmed on an overnight stay at Chequers in February 1967 when he conducted an unscientific survey of the Prime Minister's newspaper reading habits. After Wilson had dropped by Hetherington's room and had learned that the morning papers had not been delivered, he had the newspapers from his own room sent over to Hetherington. "The *Guardian* looked as if it had been very thoroughly read. *The Times* had been looked at and was open at the Sports page. The *Financial Times* also

---

[115] BLPES, Hetherington 4/8. Memo of a meeting between Hetherington and Callaghan, 19 June 1963.
[116] Interview with Lord Healey, 22 March 2004.
[117] BLPES, Hetherington 11. Note of a meeting between Hetherington and the Prime Minister, 13 December 1965.
[118] Oxford, Wilson c.1068. Letter to Marcia Williams from James Margach, 17 September 1967. Margach of *The Sunday Times* suggested to Williams that Wilson employ "saturation bombing" in his dealings with the press. He said Wilson could give him "some discreet hints" for a story for the Sunday paper, which would be followed up by the dailies the next day. Then the story could re-appear a day or two later when the Prime Minister made his own formal announcement to the press. Although Castle's diaries show Margach was the recipient of leaked material, it is not clear if Wilson entertained the offer.

showed slight signs of wear. The others showed no sign of having been more than quickly skimmed through (in spite of the *Mirror's* feature on Merseyside)."[119]

It is remarkable that beyond the initial endorsement in 1963, the *Guardian* and Callaghan followed essentially the same political line on issue after issue, particularly in the crucial years of Callaghan's political comeback, and what's even more astonishing is that the trend was not more apparent to political observers. With McCaffrey at his side, Callaghan successfully created an image and that image of the avuncular trade-union figure was so established in the British media that any deviation from it was seen as merely a blip on the screen. There is no doubt that in those days Callaghan was viewed as a man of the Labour Party right, while the *Guardian* was the bastion of the Labour Party left. They were at opposite ends of the political spectrum. Tony Benn, whose political career spanned much of the same period as Callaghan's and whose early moderate views moved increasingly left, says: "I mean Jim was a conservative figure, don't make any mistake about it. He was a genuine right-wing Labour leader.... He was on the right, he worked with right-wing trade unions leaders, he took the view that you had to keep the left under control..."[120] What better way to do that than from the point of having considerable inroads at the newspaper that was the philosophical core of the party's left and left of centre. And to think Callaghan did it without anyone really knowing it.

In some cases the *Guardian* backed Callaghan's position on the issues and in others Callaghan likely jumped on the bandwagon. But on one major issue after the other, Callaghan and the *Guardian* found themselves in agreement. When this was pointed out to Healey, a minister in both the Wilson and Callaghan governments, he was genuinely surprised.[121] Even reporters who covered those events and were interviewed for this book did not realise the extent of the support that Callaghan was getting from the *Guardian*, support that came at one critical juncture after another. Hetherington no doubt was influenced by Cole's relationship with Callaghan. But he might have been influenced as well by Crossman, who wrote a column for the *Guardian* before he joined the Wilson government and from whom Hetherington had rented a spare room when the *Guardian* was making its move to London.

---

[119] BLPES, Hetherington 13/22. An addendum to notes from a meeting with the Prime Minister at Chequers, 19 February 1967.
[120] Interview with Tony Benn, 21 July 2003.
[121] Interview with Lord Healey, 22 March 2004.

Crossman told Hetherington in January 1968, less than two months after Callaghan's departure from the Treasury, of Callaghan's unhappiness now that he was no longer in the inner circle. Crossman said Callaghan was "taking it easy at the Home Office ... he was sitting there out of his corsets and his great fat belly had flopped. He was talking far too much to too many people and, even if he didn't mean to, was stirring things up a bit."[122] But Crossman's view of Callaghan began to change, particularly after Callaghan's forceful show of leadership at the time of the Grosvenor Square demonstrations that October. Crossman, who was not shy about talking or "stirring things up" himself, had far more conversations with Hetherington than anyone other than Wilson in 1968 and 1969 – critical years for Callaghan's rehabilitation. The fact that Crossman, in those conversations, came to have a great admiration for Callaghan, particularly his ability to pull himself up from the bootstraps after his demoralising departure from the Treasury, might well have elevated Callaghan's stature with the editor of the *Guardian*.

Callaghan also benefited from the fact that the relationship between Wilson and Hetherington was not as close as people generally believed, as well as concerns that Hetherington had had about the *Guardian* being left "out on a limb"[123] if Wilson were suddenly removed. First, Hetherington might have had unfettered access to the Prime Minister, but Wilson's press secretary Joe Haines, while conceding that he has no knowledge of a relationship between Callaghan and Hetherington, disputes the notion that Wilson and the *Guardian* editor were close. Instead, Haines thinks it was a "marriage of convenience", and says that Wilson never regarded Hetherington as a friend. Haines says the only reason the Prime Minister saw so much of him was not because he was Alastair Hetherington, but because he was the editor of the *Guardian*.[124]

Secondly, although Hetherington had many more conversations with Wilson than Callaghan in the 1960s, at times there are indications of a strain between the Prime Minister and the editor of the *Guardian* on two points vital to any newspaperman, namely sources and credibility. That does not appear to be the case with Callaghan, although the number of recorded conversations is far fewer. For example, Wilson told Hetherington in September 1967 that Peter Jenkins's column was "the best study of government" around, but when Wilson asked

---

[122] (Manchester) *Guardian* Archive, C5/326. Notes from a meeting between Hetherington and Crossman, 26 January 1968.
[123] Ibid.
[124] Interview with Joe Haines, 25 March 2004.

Hetherington why Jenkins had not popped around to talk with him, Hetherington mentioned that he did not want Jenkins to suffer the fate of so many other reporters who had had "a sudden cutting off from government sources". The Prime Minister said "he kept a check on ministers who talked too much to *The Times* but he would like to see Peter 'if he will play' ".[125] At another point, Wilson complained to Hetherington about the paper's coverage of a trip the Prime Minister had made to a mining region of South Wales in February 1968, saying the correspondent, Keith Harper, "couldn't be expected to know it, [but] it was he [Wilson] who had saved the Cefn Coed Colliery many years ago". Hetherington parenthetically notes, however, that the reporter told him "it was doubtful if Wilson had ever heard of Cefn Coed until he arrived in South Wales that day".[126]

Finally, Hetherington was annoyed, too, that he often found himself having to sit for 15 or 20 minutes outside Wilson's office before he could go in.[127] It was a problem that Callaghan had alluded to as well years earlier, but Callaghan's problem was not so much that he had to wait, but that he could not get in at all in the early period when Wilson became party leader after Gaitskell's death. Hetherington, in his notes from June 1963, said that "with Hugh Gaitskell, Callaghan had been used to sticking his head round the door and asking if he could have five minutes. That was nearly always possible, and they could clear up any problem or difficulty quite quickly in a direct conversation. That wasn't possible with Wilson, because one simply couldn't get in to see him."[128] For Callaghan that problem cleared itself up when he was Chancellor of the Exchequer, living and working next to Wilson with the connecting door between No. 10 and No. 11 Downing Street. But it reintroduced itself

---

[125] BLPES, Hetherington 13. Notes of a meeting between Hetherington and the Prime Minister, 19 September 1967.

[126] (Manchester) *Guardian* Archive, C5/330/1. Notes from a discussion betweeen Hetherington and the Prime Minister, 19 February 1968. Also, during the December 1967 controversy over arms to South Africa, the Prime Minister in leaking information to Hetherington told the editor that it was the first time he had leaked "anything hostile [about] any of his colleagues". Hetherington parenthetically noted that "one might need to interpret the word 'hostile' rather liberally if one were to believe him." (BLPES, Hetherington 13. Additional notes from a meeting between Hetherington and the Prime Minister, 13 December 1967.)

[127] BLPES, Hetherington 18. Note from a meeting between Hetherington and Prime Minister Heath, 12 October 1970.

[128] BLPES, Hetherington 4/8. Note of a discussion between Hetherington and Callaghan, 19 June 1963.

when Callaghan moved to the Home Office, and, along with his resentment over his diminished role in Cabinet, contributed to the strain between the two men in the late 1960s.

Nevertheless, after the crisis over *In Place of Strife* ended in June 1969 and the Troubles began that summer in Ulster, Callaghan was uniquely suited to handle them. By that time he had consolidated his position with the trade unions, left and right, and quietly cultivated a relationship, which he used to good effect, with one of the most influential newspapers in the country. So at this point Callaghan's political recovery was entering a new phase. He had shown during the Vietnam protests in October 1968 that he could manage a sudden crisis as well as or better than anyone, and by taking advantage of the debacle over *In Place of Strife* he had in fact shifted the balance of power in the Cabinet and made himself a far more formidable player. Now the stage was set for Northern Ireland, the biggest challenge yet on Callaghan's long road back to political respectability.

6
Northern Ireland: Image or Substance?

When Callaghan became Home Secretary, Northern Ireland was the least of his concerns; it was not even an important part of his portfolio. That all changed by the summer of 1969, when the peaceful civil rights protests of a year earlier gave way to rioting in the streets of Londonderry and Belfast. As the violence between elements of the Catholic and Protestant populations worsened that August, the *Guardian* "vigorously" opposed the idea of sending British troops to restore order. It warned that any such deployment to the British province would be "foolish" and amount to "embarking on a commitment to which there is no visible end".[1] The newspaper viewed the Troubles from an historical perspective and understood the unusual nature of the partition of Ireland, which had never been satisfactorily resolved in the Anglo-Irish Treaty of 1921 that ended the war between the Irish and the British and led to the eventual establishment of the Irish Republic. On the other hand, Callaghan's outlook was less circumspect. He understandably was focused more on immediate concerns, both in dealing with the rioting and in keeping the issue firmly in his control. Even though he had had no interest "at all" in Northern Ireland prior to becoming Home Secretary,[2] he was the one key member of the Cabinet who was the least resistant to calling in the troops.

To understand how Northern Ireland became so intermeshed with Callaghan's political fortunes, it is important to look at how the British government arrived at the decision to deploy troops. The Cabinet,

---

[1] *Guardian*, 5 August 1969, p. 8.
[2] BLPES, Rees 10/33. Transcript from "Witness Seminar on British Policy in Northern Ireland, 1964–1970". There is no date on the 63-page document but it is apparently from the 1990s.

before departing on its summer break at the end of July, authorised Harold Wilson, Callaghan, Denis Healey and, "if available", Michael Stewart, the Foreign Secretary, "to take any decisions urgently required" if conditions deteriorated.[3] But two weeks later, when the Troubles worsened, that quartet of decision-makers was not in place. At the moment when Wilson, who interrupted his own holiday to meet with Callaghan, agreed to Callaghan's decision to send troops, the move was made without the active participation of the Foreign Secretary or the Defence Secretary. Stewart had remained on holiday; Healey was in hospital recovering from surgery. Therefore, Healey, the most outspoken critic of a troop deployment and someone not easily intimidated by Callaghan, was unable either to press his case with the Prime Minister or to argue the fine points with Callaghan, a tough opponent even in the best of circumstances. So, in the end, Callaghan's view prevailed and British troops were sent into Londonderry on 14 August and then Belfast a day later.

Callaghan later admitted that the fact that Healey was essentially unavailable, that Parliament was out of session, and that Wilson, Stewart and the rest of the Cabinet were on holiday was "the most enviable position"[4] he could possibly have been in. It was "enviable" from Callaghan's point of view because since his resignation from the Treasury two years earlier, he had been without a compelling issue from which to rebuild his political reputation, and he found that issue in Northern Ireland. The anti-war protests at Grosvenor Square required a deliberative approach as well and proved that his political rehabilitation would be possible, but that crisis was limited in scope compared with Ulster. And the fight over industrial relations, while greatly strengthening his position with the trade unions and shifting the balance of power in the Cabinet back in Callaghan's favour, was outside the ministerial responsibility of the Home Office. But Northern Ireland, once the troops were in place, had neither limitations of scope nor authority and the Troubles put Callaghan front and centre and gave him the position of influence that he so long craved.

Over a matter of hours on 13 August, the situation in Londonderry and then Belfast deteriorated as the fighting between the two sides escalated. There were reports of rioting and looting, of police stations being under attack and women and children being forced to cross the border

[3] PRO, CAB 128/44 Part II. Minutes of Cabinet meeting, 30 July 1969.
[4] Callaghan, *A House Divided*, p. 70.

near Londonderry to seek safe haven in the Irish Republic. The upsurge in violence prompted Dublin to call for a United Nations peacekeeping force to be sent to the British province, a move that stirred anger in Westminster. Callaghan said he came to a final decision about intervention the following morning while he was on board a military plane en route to meet Wilson at the Royal Air Force Base at St. Mawgam, near Wilson's holiday home in the Scilly Islands off the tip of Cornwall, England.[5] Callaghan told Wilson at that meeting, with Callaghan's press secretary Tom McCaffrey and four other civil servants present, that the British government "would have to accede"[6] if a request for troops were made by the authorities in Northern Ireland, which – given the worsening Troubles – looked likely. But in a letter sent to the author, Callaghan concedes the British government would have stepped in far sooner – suggesting an earlier troop deployment – had it not been for the fact that the government of Northern Ireland "in those days was very cool and unreceptive to any intervention from the British government".[7]

Callaghan's comments in the correspondence with the author and his exchanges with fellow ministers at the time indicate that he was more eager to intervene than Wilson, who, while agreeing to the deployment on Callaghan's recommendation, was inclined to see it as no more than a "short-term operation to restore law and order and not to maintain it".[8] It is true that Callaghan expressed much the same view at that meeting on the morning of 14 August, telling Wilson that "the objective should be limited to the restoration of law and order". But Callaghan also introduced the possibility of a longer-term role for the British government; one in which he, no doubt, would be the principal player.[9] The Home Secretary said if a quick solution could not be found, he envisioned "formal administrative arrangements" in Northern Ireland, including the possibility of a new police force for Londonderry, one that hopefully "would carry the confidence of both the Protestants

---

[5] Ibid., p. 41.

[6] PRO, CAB 164/577, Folio 8M. Note of a meeting between the Prime Minister and Callaghan held at R.A.F. St. Mawgan, 14 August 1969.

[7] Letter to the author from Lord Callaghan, 17 June 2003.

[8] PRO, CAB 164/577, Folio 8M. Note of meeting between the Prime Minister and Callaghan held at R.A.F. St. Mawgan, 14 August 1969.

[9] Ibid. Callaghan in a panel discussion later said that he "never" thought that British involvement in Northern Ireland would be a short-term action even in the early stages. (BLPES, Rees 10/33. Transcript from "Witness Seminar on British Policy in Northern Ireland, 1964–1970". There is no date on transcript but it is apparently from the 1990s.)

and the Catholics".[10] Oddly enough, six days earlier, Callaghan did not embrace a short-term solution at all, when some of the same matters were discussed with Northern Ireland Prime Minister Major James Chichester-Clark at the Home Office. At that meeting, which Wilson did not attend, Callaghan told Chichester-Clark that if the troops went in and "even if they restored the immediate situation, the underlying circumstances would lead to their continuing deployment".[11]

Although Healey was closely consulted in the days leading up to that decision, he suggested in an interview for this book that had he not been hospitalised, he would have resisted Callaghan's determination to send British troops to Northern Ireland,[12] but "I wasn't in a position to stop it".[13] Healey, who served as Defence Secretary from 1964 to 1970, viewed the Troubles in Northern Ireland in a broader context than Callaghan and had been "reluctant" to send troops without an exit strategy. As "a student of war", Healey believed that such commitments should never be undertaken "unless you know how and when you can get out. We never did with Northern Ireland."[14] In his autobiography, published in 1989, Healey recounted how he warned the Cabinet about the difficulty of removing the troops if they were deployed, but in that book he concluded that like his fellow ministers he could "see no alternative".[15] Now, two generations after the deployment, he insinuates that had he been able to, he would have put up a fight over the sending of troops. When asked if his hospitalisation prevented him from taking a stronger stance, he responds, "Yes, yes … yes."[16]

Roy Hattersley was in charge at the Ministry of Defence in Healey's absence and it was he who had signed the warrant that sent the first contingent of soldiers onto the streets of Londonderry. But Hattersley at that stage in his career was understandably no match for Callaghan, even if he had wanted to raise objections to any of Callaghan's decisions. Only a few months earlier, Hattersley, as Barbara Castle's parliamentary private secretary, had been on the opposite side from Callaghan in the

---

[10] PRO, CAB 164/577, Folio 8M. Note of a meeting between the Prime Minister and Callaghan held at R.A.F. St. Mawgan, 14 August 1969.
[11] PRO, CAB 164/577, Folio 5M. Note of a meeting between Callaghan and Northern Ireland Prime Minister Major James Chichester-Clark, 8 August 1969.
[12] Interview with Lord Healey, 22 March 2004.
[13] Ibid.
[14] Ibid.
[15] Denis Healey, *The Time of My Life* (London, 1989), p. 343.
[16] Interview with Lord Healey, 22 March 2004.

great fight over *In Place of Strife*. He had been in the No. 2 post at the
Ministry of Defence only a matter of weeks when the Irish Troubles
took a bad turn. Hattersley was working 12-hour shifts with Callaghan
in the early days of that crisis and his comments reflect Callaghan's
all-encompassing role; a role that greatly enhanced Callaghan's public
image. "Well, we didn't know how bad it was going to be. We began;
he began to establish – re-establish – [policies] to protect some civil
rights.... We proscribed or he proscribed the sectarian policies on housing and allocation. I mean, it was a beginning and I don't know whether
we could have gone further, but it did begin."[17]

Since Labour's ascendancy as a governing party did not take place
until after the partition of Ireland in 1921, a policy that Labour had
opposed at the time, the party was not as deeply mired in the Irish
problem as either the Conservatives or the Liberals. But Labour was
not entirely free from the entanglement either. In a gesture towards
the North, Clement Attlee, Churchill's successor as Prime Minister,
handed the Ulster Unionists, the governing party of Northern Ireland,
a major victory in 1949 by giving them what was essentially the right
to veto any future plans to reunify Ireland. By that move, Attlee and
the Labour Party solidified the prevailing policy of Churchill and the
Tories on the partition question, a disposition that was coloured, at
least in part, by anger over Dublin's neutrality in the Second World
War. For the next two decades, the consensus among the British parties that gave Stormont, the administrative seat of Northern Ireland, a
free hand on internal matters remained in place. The major parties continued jointly to contrive to block any debate in Parliament about the
injustices in employment, housing and electoral policy that would later
gain international notoriety.

However, as the 1960s neared the end, the political climate began
to shift with an ever-increasing number of Labour MPs demanding a
debate. The situation in Northern Ireland had changed. Callaghan's
private secretary Brian Cubbon says, "British troops had to go in, and
some changes had to be made and all sides had to be talked to – which
was a novel concept in Northern Ireland."[18] But was the decision to
deploy troops an overreaction that was influenced by Callaghan's political ambition? Might Stormont have had to come to terms with the need
for reforms sooner if it had had to work out its own security problems

---

[17] Interview with Lord Hattersley, 1 March 2004.
[18] Interview with Sir Brian Cubbon, 19 June 2003.

without the aid of British troops? After all, the Troubles in the province during the summer of 1969 were still limited in scope. Callaghan's successor as Home Secretary, Reginald Maudling, defended Callaghan's decision as "undoubtedly right" because despite the fact that the police were heavily armed, there were not enough of them.[19] Liam Cosgrave, who was leader of the opposition in the Irish government at the time and later Prime Minister, believes the troop deployment was "the lesser of two evils".[20]

But the day before the decision was taken, the *Irish Press*, like the *Guardian*, had opposed the move as premature. The Dublin newspaper, with long ties to the family of the Irish leader Eamon de Valéra and, as such, deeply entrenched in the debate, said that "at this stage [it] can only inflame the situation [and] could very rapidly re-introduce the gun to Irish politics".[21] The *Guardian*, too, had noted, ten days before the deployment, that "the rioting, serious as it is, flares down as quickly as it flares up".[22] Even after the troops were sent in, the *Guardian* was not fooled by the initial welcoming from the Catholics of Londonderry. Its lead editorial the morning after the troops arrived warned that "one false move on either side could release among Derry Catholics the ancient hatred against the English".[23] Yet one thing was different this time around: the civil rights movement in Northern Ireland was less confrontational; it had appealed for reforms *within* the political system rather than a redress of its grievances the way it had done in the past, i.e. by appealing for help from the Irish Republic and/or the international community.[24]

Even Callaghan, in his correspondence with the author, acknowledges the limited nature of the Troubles in August 1969, noting that it was only after some police detachments "in the Bogside [area of Londonderry] and one or two other areas were in danger of being overrun, that [the government of Northern Ireland] recognised that they

---

[19] Reginald Maudling, *Memoirs* (London, 1978), p. 178.
[20] Interview with Liam Cosgrave, 1 October 2004.
[21] *Irish Press*, 13 August 1969, p. 8.
[22] *Guardian*, 5 August 1969, p. 8.
[23] *Guardian*, 15 August 1969, p.8. That particular editorial made reference throughout to Derry, rather than Londonderry, a term that the city's Catholic majority view as an affront. But Londonderry was used in the *Guardian's* news stories and other editorials at that time.
[24] Brendan O'Leary and John McGarry, *The Politics of Antagonism: Understanding Northern Ireland* (London, 1993), p. 171.

needed British intervention, and indeed that of the Army".[25] Callaghan in his long career never embarked on a position without carefully weighing the political risks. It certainly had been the case in the fight over *In Place of Strife* and was true, as well, with Northern Ireland. It raises the question whether Callaghan's decision to deploy troops was based as much on his political aspirations as it was on a need to address the escalating violence. What is clear is that as soon as the first British soldier touched foot in Londonderry on 14 August 1969, Callaghan gained for himself broad powers that further elevated his influence in the Cabinet and gave him the opportunity to rebuild his reputation and make himself the logical choice for a future Foreign Secretary.

Callaghan had a genuine concern that the civil rights of the Catholic minority were being violated, and early on in the Troubles was concerned that the Belfast government might be turning a blind eye to the violence being perpetrated by the followers of The Revd Ian Paisley, the churchman who was a right-wing defender of the status quo.[26] Yet Callaghan also saw the crisis as a golden opportunity and admits it. Recalling the period after the troops were sent in, Callaghan wrote, "There I was in charge, pulling levers here, pushing levers there, saying get this, fetch so and so and the whole machine absolutely buzzed."[27] But what Callaghan was doing with Northern Ireland was the very thing that had so annoyed him with Castle's approach to *In Place of Strife*; he was taking matters entirely in his own hands.[28] While the two events are very different – the crisis in Northern Ireland certainly had an immediacy to it that trade union reform did not have and therefore often required a take-charge approach – Callaghan was determined right from the start to bypass the collective nature of Cabinet government and

---

[25] Letter to the author from Lord Callaghan, 17 June 2003.

[26] PRO, CJ3/74. Handwritten note to R.W.J. Hooper, which is apparently from Callaghan, dated 5 January 1969. "I don't wish to jump to conclusions on the basis of newspaper reports, but if [Northern Ireland Prime Minister] O'Neill is backing the police in maintaining law and order, the police must deal with the Paisleyites."

[27] Callaghan, *A House Divided*, p. 70.

[28] Ibid., p. 41. Concerning the deployment of troops, Callaghan said that "on the whole I find decisions are fastest when the fewest people are consulted. I was not altogether unhappy, therefore, that it would fall to Harold Wilson and me to reach the fateful decision."

make the issue his alone and in that way he used it to rebuild his political reputation.

Callaghan's enthusiasm for the intervention is reflected in *A House Divided*, the book he wrote when Labour was in opposition, having lost the 1970 general election. "There are very few occasions in politics," he wrote, "when you get the opportunity to handle something in your own way: action usually comes after a long process of consultation, whittling down, compromise, arguing here, consulting there."[29] In other words, the proper workings of the parliamentary system. Northern Ireland was such a quagmire that at times his fellow ministers – with the exception, of course, of Healey – were more than happy to leave the issue to Callaghan, particularly after he scored one success after another in the early days of the Troubles, a period when the troops were hailed as liberators. Indeed, Wilson seemed content to allow his Home Secretary to upstage him in the immediate aftermath of the troop deployment. Callaghan orchestrated what amounted to a quasi-royal tour of Belfast and Londonderry that elevated his role almost to that of a Prime Minister.

Earlier that summer of 1969, a "deputation" of MPs had come up with three scenarios regarding any official visits to Northern Ireland. It suggested that either Wilson should go there, or that the Home Secretary or a group of senior Home Office officials should be sent to observe the worsening situation.[30] Callaghan had told the Cabinet on 30 July, two weeks prior to the deployment of troops, that he did not favour any of those suggestions and in particular called the idea of the Prime Minister visiting Northern Ireland "ill considered".[31] At that point, Callaghan had said any such visits would get the British government too deeply involved in the Troubles, which had begun several months earlier after what had started as peaceful student protests degenerated into sporadic rioting between Catholics and Protestants amid the heavy-handed tactics of the police. But within a month of that statement to his Cabinet colleagues, the British Home Secretary would be mingling with crowds of Catholics in the battle-scarred Bogside neighbourhood of Londonderry, accompanied by a contingent of television and print journalists, and dining in Belfast with leaders from both sides. No doubt it was a public-relations coup that greatly boosted Callaghan's

---

[29] Ibid., p. 70.
[30] PRO, CAB 128/44, Part II. Minutes of Cabinet meeting, 30 July 1969.
[31] Ibid.

image.[32] As *The Times*'s Norman Fowler said, "it proved to be the kind of situation in which Mr. Callaghan thrives".[33]

Was Callaghan's resistance to the idea of a visit by the Prime Minister an effort to keep the Northern Ireland issue for himself? It was not only the deputation of MPs that proposed such a visit. A week before the 30 July Cabinet meeting, John Hume, an Irish Catholic representative at Stormont who became close to the Home Secretary as the Troubles intensified, also suggested that just such a trip should be made, either by Wilson or Callaghan. Hume met with Callaghan's Minister of State, Victor Stonham,[34] and according to an account of the discussion given by Hume to an Irish diplomat,[35] Stonham told Hume "that he accepted completely his interpretation of the situation and he would personally support his main recommendations". Hume said he told Stonham that Wilson or the Home Secretary should visit Derry *before* the scheduled march of the Apprentice Boys set for 12 August, a date that turned out to be an incendiary moment in the Troubles.[36] It was advice that Callaghan rejected, making his own trip two weeks after the troops were in place. It is interesting to note that while Wilson felt the march – the annual parade of Orangemen that commemorates the victory of the Protestants over the Catholics during the Siege of Derry in 1688 – should be banned given the tense atmosphere,[37] Callaghan, by not taking a strong stand,[38] ostensibly allowed it to go ahead.[39]

---

[32] Interview with Sir Brian Cubbon, 19 June 2003. Cubbon, Callaghan's private secretary who later was seriously injured in an IRA bombing that killed the British ambassador to Ireland, said Callaghan was "flattered" by the reaction of the crowds on that first visit to Londonderry and Belfast. "He felt progress was being made despite Healey's – well the whole Cabinet's – reluctance to put troops in."
[33] *The Times*, 30 August 1969, p. 6.
[34] NAI, DFA 2000/5/38. Internal memo from the Irish embassy in London, 24 July 1969.
[35] Ibid. Hume purposely sought out the diplomat at a tea at the House of Commons so as to discretely relay the information to the Irish government.
[36] NAI, DFA 2000/5/38. Internal memo from the Irish embassy in London, 24 July 1969.
[37] *The Times*, 5 August 1969, p. 9; *Guardian*, 5 August 1969, p. 8. Both *The Times* and *Guardian* addressed the banning of all marches in their lead editorials, although *The Times* called for an outright ban while the *Guardian* merely suggested it.
[38] *Irish Independent*, 13 August 1969, p. 8. While not specifically referring to Callaghan, the Dublin newspaper wrote in its lead editorial that "for want of a man brave enough to ban the marching in the North, there was more violence."
[39] Peter Rose, *How the Troubles Came to Northern Ireland* (London, 2000), p. 161.

Although the *Guardian* was initially opposed to the idea of the troop deployment, the newspaper's criticism of the Labour government shifted to support within a few days after the troops were sent in. It editorialised on 18 August 1969, that the British government and the Prime Minister in particular had "handled the situation with commendable caution so far" and felt that now that the troops were in place they could not be withdrawn "without adequate guarantees of reform from Stormont".[40] The guarded praise for the Prime Minister was short-lived, however, and once again it was Callaghan, not Wilson, who got a significant helping hand from the newspaper of the centre-left. This time it came not in an editorial but in a highly charged political cartoon by Les Gibbard that dominated the top half of the front page just as Callaghan was wrapping up his triumphant tour of Northern Ireland.

The contrast created in that cartoon between Callaghan and Wilson, the man Callaghan had been so bitterly at odds with earlier that year, could not have been more unflattering to Wilson. The cartoon depicted the Prime Minister as an anxiety prone little man wearing only shorts and sandals, an allusion to the fact that he was not letting the crisis interrupt his holiday, as he sat in an overstuffed chair and watched his jubilant Home Secretary on television surrounded by the adoring masses in Northern Ireland. The caption read: "You know I would have gone myself – but I can't stand cheering crowds."[41] It was a stinging rebuke to the Prime Minister. In the 1960s, political cartoons, which were once prevalent in the popular newspapers of the working class, became instead a much-anticipated feature of the quality newspapers, which appealed to the middle and upper classes.[42] Gibbard's satirical poke at Wilson, which followed in the tradition of David Low and Bill Papas who had also sketched for the *Guardian*, carried added weight because once again the criticism came not from the more conservative newspapers, but from the *Guardian*, the newspaper identified with Wilson's base of support within the Labour Party.

That political cartoon draws attention to another aspect of Northern Ireland that played into one of the great strengths of Callaghan, namely that the whole emerging saga was ideally suited to television and the fact that Callaghan made the most of the emerging medium did much

---

[40] *Guardian*, 18 August 1969, p. 8.

[41] *Guardian*, 29 August 1969, p. 1.

[42] Colin Seymour-Ure, entry on political cartoons in John Ramsden (ed), *The Oxford Companion to Twentieth-Century British Politics* (Oxford, 2002), p. 101.

to restore his standing.[43] Leo Abse, the Welsh MP and solicitor, says Callaghan "was capable of playing the part of the knight in shining armour. It was an image in his mind that led sometimes to him being quite bold in certain respects."[44] Callaghan was a man who knew the importance of "image"[45] and no doubt had great appreciation for television's impact in Northern Ireland. In the late 1960s the British news media was still dominated by the comings and goings in Fleet Street and television as a purveyor of breaking news was still a relatively new player. But just as searing televised images had turned the tide in the civil rights movement in the United States, similar images would bring the injustices in Northern Ireland into homes across the world. At the time, some ministers were not sure how to deal with the expanding influence of television. Although at one point in January 1969 the Cabinet feared that production crews in Northern Ireland might be persuading "demonstrators to stage prearranged clashes with the police",[46] Callaghan came around to the belief that "the presence of television cameras and reporters in Northern Ireland had made a substantial impact"[47] in opening the door to reforms.[48]

After Callaghan came back from that trip on 29 August, a visit the *Guardian* called "strenuous but very useful",[49] he gave Wilson a provisional report the following day. But Callaghan was said to be "rather allergic"[50] to the thought of sitting down with his fellow ministers and

[43] Anthony Smith, "Television Coverage of Northern Ireland" in *War and Words: the Northern Ireland Media Reader*, edited by Bill Rolston and David Miller (Belfast, 1996), p. 26. Smith noted that "television news-collecting created new facts of life for the politicians of Belfast. Until 1965 it had been possible to prevent reporters from London from ever setting foot in the province at all. After 1968, such a course became totally unthinkable."
[44] Interview with Leo Abse, 20 May 2003.
[45] *Irish Times*, 29 August 1969, p. 9. As the columnist Henry Kelly wrote, Callaghan's trip seemed "to have turned into more of a personal performance than a political act, with front-page pictures depicting the loving hands and arms cast around children as the Home Secretary moved through riot-torn areas and inspected cumulative devastation".
[46] PRO, CAB 128/44 Part I. Minutes of Cabinet meeting, 30 January 1969.
[47] Ibid.
[48] BLPES, Hetherington 5/16. Note of a meeting between Hetherington and Callaghan on 20 November 1963. Callaghan actually favoured televising Parliament years before it happened, making such a suggestion to the editor of the *Guardian*.
[49] *Guardian*, 30 August 1969, p. 8.
[50] PRO, CAB 164/577, Folio 17Q. Memo to Sir Burke Trend from R.W.J. Hooper, 29 August 1969.

briefing them at the next Cabinet meeting, which was scheduled not for the following morning but nearly a week later. It is ironic that Callaghan who was often critical of his successor, Reginald Maulding, for not keeping him fully informed in opposition,[51] had few qualms about keeping his fellow ministers at arm's length – if it suited his political ambitions. Richard Crossman, the Secretary of State for Social Services, summed it up well when he said that Callaghan was "restraining Harold and not letting him poke his nose in too far",[52] but Crossman might have added that this applied not only to Wilson but to himself and the rest of the Cabinet as well. By keeping Wilson and his colleagues at bay, an exercise in which the Home Secretary was not always successful, Callaghan was able to use the emerging Troubles in Northern Ireland as a way to rebuild his political reputation and he did it in several ways.

First, the Home Secretary who had blocked the entrance to Britain of countless Kenyan Asians and took a cautious approach on race relations, presented himself as the defender of the oppressed in Northern Ireland. Callaghan's concerns for housing and jobs for the Catholic minority wore well in the streets of London and Liverpool where people were genuinely surprised and shocked at the discrimination that was going on in this other part of the United Kingdom. Although Northern Ireland was part of the same country, for a host of reasons, including the fact that it is physically detached from England, Scotland and Wales, it was not viewed that way by most people in Britain. In the late 1960s, it was a lot easier for a British worker to sympathise with Callaghan's demands for equality for the Catholics of Belfast than for that same worker to accept his fellow trade unionist on the shop floor who happened to be Black or Indian. Callaghan knew that and knew too that his strategy was one that posed no risk to his right-wing base in Britain since not a single British worker was likely to lose his job to a Catholic across the Irish Sea. In other words, Callaghan could make the case for civil rights in Northern Ireland in a way that he would not have dared to back home.

Callaghan knew that the sympathetic ear for the Catholic minority played well to foreign audiences as well, particularly in the United States, where Callaghan had fostered the closest of relationships when he was Chancellor. The United States had a sizeable Irish Catholic population and its influence came to fruition in the 1960s with a string of important Irish-American politicians from the Kennedys to New York

---

[51] Callaghan, *A House Divided*, p. 144.
[52] Crossman, *Diaries*, Vol. III (New York), pp. 636–637.

Governor Hugh Carey. Callaghan was aware of the great value maintaining those ties would play in his political rehabilitation. The television and newspaper images of Callaghan being embraced by the Catholics in the Bogside of Londonderry did more to restore his reputation on social issues and hasten the possibility of his becoming a future Foreign Secretary than anything he had done in years. In one fell swoop he greatly minimised any lingering damage, at home or abroad, from his harsh immigration controls on Kenyan Asians. In addition, the Home Office and the Foreign Office had moved quickly to head off any possible image problem with the United States, its closest ally, by holding "regular sessions" with officials at the US Embassy in London.[53]

Secondly, with Wilson playing a secondary role, Callaghan through the crisis in Northern Ireland was able to show what he could do as a leader. After the troops were committed, Callaghan could and did manipulate the deeply flawed government in Belfast in a way that would have been impossible in the corridors of power back home. With the Northern Ireland government dependent on the continued presence of troops, Callaghan was able to make major demands of Belfast that led to early gains in the reform of policing as well as in the allocation of housing, which Callaghan wanted to take out of the hands of corrupt local agencies and place under the control of a "single authority".[54] Fifty years of oppressive rule from Stormont, with virtually no intervention on the part of Westminster, had produced a rather primitive political system that Callaghan was able to redirect to his own advantage, building on the sensible law-and-order image that he had forged in Grosvenor Square.[55] Callaghan's press secretary McCaffrey concedes that Callaghan ran the government in Northern Ireland after the troops were sent in. "He would phone every single morning and he would tell them how he felt it ought to be handled. He was actually controlling it."[56]

Thirdly, Northern Ireland restored Callaghan's access to the Prime Minister, something he had been craving ever since he left the Treasury. While Wilson remained deeply distrustful of his Home Secretary in the aftermath of *In Place of Strife*, the extent of the Troubles in the province meant that Wilson had to give Callaghan the same kind of unfettered

---

[53] PRO, CAB 164/577, Folio 19N. Correspondence between N.J. Barrington and R. Dawe, 3 September 1969.
[54] Callaghan, *A House Divided*, p. 77.
[55] Ibid., p. 57. Callaghan mentions in his book that he often drew a parallel between the events of Grosvenor Square and the Troubles in Northern Ireland.
[56] Interview with Sir Tom McCaffrey, 3 July 2003.

access he was giving Roy Jenkins, his Chancellor. Therefore, the door was reopened between Wilson and Callaghan, a development that paved the way for their cooperation over the referendum on Europe, the episode that would complete Callaghan's rehabilitation. The Prime Minister was above all a pragmatic politician and even though Callaghan dominated much of the agenda, Wilson knew that Callaghan's successes in Northern Ireland made him indispensable. In the rough notes of a speech for the 1970 campaign, it is evident that Wilson was eager to align himself with his Home Secretary. The Prime Minister, still an imposing figure in British politics and one with far broader popular appeal than Callaghan, said that it was he who had given Callaghan his "guiding instructions. We would be firm, we would be cool, we would be fair." Then Wilson proceeded to ask if a Tory Home Secretary could "have handled that dangerous situation with such manifest firmness and fairness"?[57]

Finally, Ireland provided Callaghan with the opportunity to regain a dominant policy role within the Cabinet, something that was reminiscent of his days controlling the budget as Chancellor of the Exchequer. In a sense he was freer in dealing with this issue than he had ever been before. As Chancellor he constantly had to contend with Wilson, a former Oxford don and economist, and George Brown, then head of the rival Department of Economic Affairs, as well as the rest of the Cabinet looking over his shoulder. But Northern Ireland in 1969 came at a time when he was politically on solid ground. He had just won major trade-union support across the board by facing down his adversaries, namely Wilson, Jenkins and Castle. Also, his great success in Grosvenor Square a year earlier was seen as proof of his uncanny ability to tackle difficult law-and-order problems. John Cole surmises that Callaghan was helped, too, by the fact that the government really did not know what to do: "They thought 'Oh God, What on Earth are we going to do about this?' They hadn't taken any interest in it for 50 years and suddenly it was blowing up."[58] Callaghan took advantage of that fact and at every opportunity he encroached on the ministerial responsibility of his colleagues to advance his own ambitions within the government.

Years later, Healey wrote that the "crisis in Ulster created a new unity in the Wilson government",[59] but the documents show that Callaghan's

---

[57] Oxford, Wilson, c.1395. Campaign notes with Wilson's hand written comments, undated.

[58] Interview with John Cole, 25 February 2004.

[59] Healey, *The Time of My Life*, p. 343.

138 *Callaghan's Journey to Downing Street*

solitary approach to dealing with Northern Ireland also troubled Healey, an individual who could be just as overbearing as Callaghan. The Labour MP Ian Mikardo, while acknowledging Healey's outstanding talents, said the Defence Secretary was "a political bully wielding the language of sarcasm and contempt like a caveman's cudgel".[60] At about the time that Callaghan was being seen on British television walking through the riot-torn neighbourhoods of Northern Ireland at the end of August 1969, Healey – who had recently returned to his post – was telling the Prime Minister that he had no intention of "having to implement decisions and policies on whose formulation he has not been fully consulted".[61] Robin Hooper, the deputy secretary in the Cabinet Office, who was trying to clear up the problem over who was responsible for what, conceded in a memo to the Cabinet Secretary Burke Trend that Healey's annoyance with Callaghan was "not without justification".[62]

It apparently was more than the "slight fuss" that Hooper referred to, in that Healey got the Prime Minister to agree that the "spheres" of the two departments were to be clearly delineated and "laid down in writing". Hooper urged his fellow senior civil servants to keep "the whole thing as low key and low level as possible" and even seemed to be suggesting that it might be better to leave the final agreement unsigned,[63] although in the end that was not the case.[64] Wilson's former press secretary, Trevor Lloyd-Hughes, then the chief government information officer, was raising concerns as well in September 1969 that press matters on Northern Ireland were being too tightly controlled by the Home Office, urging a bigger role for the Ministry of Defence and the Foreign Office.[65]

Callaghan also might have overstepped his bounds a few days after the troop deployment and dabbled in foreign affairs by making contact through an intermediary with Irish Prime Minister Jack Lynch, a role that was the responsibility of Stewart, the Foreign Secretary. The British government affirmed the position from the outset that the Six Counties of Northern Ireland were part of the United Kingdom and that

[60] Ian Mikardo, *Back-Bencher* (London, 1988), p. 202.
[61] PRO, CAB 164/577, Folio 17Q. Memo to Sir Burke Trend from R.W.J. Hooper, 29 August 1969.
[62] Ibid.
[63] Ibid.
[64] PRO, CAB 164/577, Folio 21. Memo from R.W.J. Hooper sets out the division of responsibilities as "directed" by the Prime Minister, 4 September 1969.
[65] PRO, CAB 164/577, Folio 30. Memo to Sir Burke Trend from R.W.J. Hooper, 16 September 1969.

the Troubles there were a domestic matter; when London made contact with the Irish Republic it should be through proper diplomatic channels. That was true despite the anomaly that British diplomats treated Ireland as if it had never left the empire; even after it had become a sovereign nation, it remained, well into the 1960s, in the portfolio of the old Commonwealth Office, rather than the Foreign Office. Therefore, when the Troubles erupted in 1969, Foreign Office officials tended to be less well informed on Irish matters than they might have been.[66] Nevertheless, on the evening of Saturday, 16 August 1969, the day after the troops had gone into Belfast, one of Callaghan's principal private secretaries, Graham Angel, took a phone call at the Home Office from a senior envoy at the Irish Embassy in London. The Irish diplomat, Kevin Rush, called to forward information about how the "Ardoyne district of Belfast, a Catholic area, had been surrounded by Paisleyites who were at that moment moving in, and that there were no troops in sight."[67]

Although the British civil servant angrily, and correctly, told Rush that "he had no right to deal directly with the Home Office, or to try to speak to the Home Secretary personally", Angel agreed after much pleading from Rush to pass along the information to Callaghan – but only if Rush would make his "official approach" through the Foreign Office.[68] The Irish diplomat received an unusual call three days later from Angel, who had a message from his boss. Making it clear that Callaghan's communiqué was being relayed in the strictest of confidence, a comment that certainly would not discourage future confidential exchanges, Angel now said "the Home Secretary wished to thank the Taoiseach [Ireland's Prime Minister][69] for having passed on that information so quickly, and wished also to express regret that the Taoiseach and he [the Home Secretary] should be renewing their personal contacts only in such difficult circumstances".[70]

The Foreign Secretary, Stewart, seemed less willing than Healey to challenge Callaghan's raw ambition and propensity to dominate the issue. But even he had his limits. In March 1970, the Home Office

[66] Paul Arthur and Keith Jeffery, *Northern Ireland Since 1968* (Oxford, 1988), pp. 81–82.
[67] NAI, DFA/2000/5/38. Internal memo from Kevin Rush of the Irish Embassy in London, 19 August 1969.
[68] Ibid.
[69] The Gaelic title for the head of government.
[70] NAI, DFA/2000/5/38. Note from Kevin Rush of the Irish Embassy in London, 18 August 1969.

circulated a paper on relations with the Irish Republic, obviously a most sensitive matter, and did not bother to consult the Foreign Office on the final document. Philip Allen, the permanent secretary at the Home Office who was close to Callaghan, oversaw the revision of the paper after the Home Secretary had "expressed reservations", then put with it a covering letter from Callaghan and distributed the materials to other ministers without the revision ever being approved by the Foreign Secretary. When the Foreign Office raised objections, Allen – who had great appreciation for the fact that being the permanent secretary to a powerful minister expanded his own role[71] – acknowledged that his behaviour "caused some distress and annoyance" but sought to dispel any notion that the Home Office was engaging in any attempt "deliberately to avoid proper consultation".[72]

This was not a single occurrence; Callaghan suggested to the Prime Minister in early November 1969 that he, rather than the Foreign Secretary, should send a congratulatory note to Lynch[73] after the Irish Prime Minister had taken a "very statesmanlike position" in support of British policy.[74] Somehow Callaghan managed to get Stewart to go along with his idea. But Wilson was firmly opposed, saying it violated "precedent and would carry the risk that Mr. Lynch would feel that he now had direct access to the Home Secretary on Northern Ireland matters". The Prime Minister concluded, "this could cause difficulties in the future".[75] By comparison, later in 1970, when the Tory government faced a similar situation after the Irish Prime Minister had been particularly helpful on another occasion, the then Foreign Secretary, Alec Douglas-Home, wrote a letter of thanks directly to Lynch.[76]

[71] Interview with Lord Allen, 19 May 2003.

[72] PRO, CAB 164/578, Folio 8. Note to Sir Edward Peck from Sir Philip Allen, 18 March 1970.

[73] PRO, PREM 13/2732. Telegram to British Foreign Office from A. Gilchrist, Britain's ambassador to Ireland, 19 November 1969. Less than two weeks after Callaghan had tried to send that congratulatory note, Prime Minister Lynch told the British envoy that "the Stormont men were letting Callaghan down, and badly" by undermining the reforms with "exaggerated fears" of a Protestant backlash.

[74] PRO, CAB 164/577, Folio 37. Letter to the Prime Minister from Callaghan, 5 November 1969.

[75] PRO, CAB 164/577, Folio 38. Memo to Faulkner of the Home Office from P.L. Gregson of the Prime Minister's Office, 6 November 1969.

[76] PRO, CAB 170/98. Telegram to the British Embassy in Dublin from the Foreign Office, 14 July 1970. Embassy is asked to relay a personal message of thanks to Lynch from Sir Alec Douglas-Home.

Although Wilson would step in on occasion when Callaghan overextended his reach,[77] Callaghan was able to use the Northern Ireland issue to such great political advantage because the Prime Minister's response to Northern Ireland was different than his method of dealing with other crises. For example, only six months earlier Wilson had turned down Foreign Secretary Stewart's offer to go to Lagos on his behalf to try and bring the two sides together in the civil war in Nigeria. Wilson argued that the crisis there was of such importance that only a Prime Minister could deal with it.[78] Around the same time, Wilson told Alastair Hetherington, the editor of the *Guardian*, that he just had to go to Nigeria, where unlike Northern Ireland not a single British soldier was deployed, because "he must see the situation for himself" and "couldn't rely on the advice of others".[79] Within weeks of Wilson's return from Africa, Crossman noted in his diary that the Prime Minister had had a "passion" to visit Northern Ireland "as soon as possible", that Wilson had "a passion for being on the spot, being in the news".[80]

Did Wilson give Callaghan a wide berth because of Callaghan's early success in dealing with the crisis in Northern Ireland? Or did Wilson's approach – and Callaghan's expanded role that led to his rehabilitation – have its root in the recent debate over *In Place of Strife*? In the immediate period after the troops had been deployed, Wilson did not return to No. 10 Downing Street over the following four days. His uncharacteristic response in the immediate aftermath of the deployment might be explained by an unwillingness to give any added attention to the crisis in the news media. On the other hand, it might have had something to do with some frank advice that Crossman had given Wilson after the failure of the government's plans to reform industrial relations six weeks earlier. After telling Wilson the "scars [from *In Place of Strife*] will take some time to heal", Crossman had urged the Prime Minister

---

[77] Oxford, Callaghan 175. Letter to Callaghan from the Prime Minister, 27 January 1968. Attempts to side-step his Cabinet colleagues happened before. Wilson admonished Callaghan, shortly after he became Home Secretary, for trying to meet privately with him on another department's business. Wilson told Callaghan "there is no 'formality' in our being joined for our discussion...by the colleague whose responsibility this is – just as I should naturally want you to be present if any of our colleagues who had no responsibility for Home Office questions said they wanted to discuss such business with me."
[78] PRO, PREM 13/2817, Folio 11. Note of a telephone call between the Prime Minister and Foreign Secretary Stewart, 7 March 1969.
[79] BLPES, Hetherington papers 16/23. Note of a meeting between Hetherington and the Prime Minister, 20 March 1969.
[80] Crossman, *Diaries*, Vol. III, p. 458.

"to consider the desirability of becoming less personally identified with particular aspects of Cabinet policy" and "more detached".[81] Crossman, who had played an important role in Wilson's leadership victory in 1963 and was always among Wilson's closest advisers, added that "I suspect that after this searing experience things will never be the same in this Cabinet."[82]

The dominant role that Callaghan took in August 1969 was an outgrowth of his earlier successes at Grosvenor Square. Cabinet papers from as early as late 1968, only weeks after his great triumph at Grosvenor Square, indicate that Callaghan saw the political advantage of keeping the Northern Ireland debate under his control months before it exploded into a crisis for the Wilson government. In December 1968, Callaghan resisted suggestions from Healey that a "machinery of government" be put in place for "urgent consultations" to deal with any possible requests for troops.[83] Reinvigorated by the October 1968 police action that put down the anti-war demonstrations, he told Wilson and Healey that he was opposed to the idea of a "formal committee" to deal with the matter, citing the possibility that the British government might be faced with a crisis "at an hour's notice on a Saturday evening".[84] Although Callaghan thought it unlikely that it would be necessary to call in troops without going through the normal channels, he was prepared to do it and said, "if it did occur the government here as a whole would have to defend it".[85] In a sense that was what he did and that was what the Cabinet belatedly did. Castle, the First Secretary of State who until the debacle over *In Place of Strife* was viewed as a Deputy Prime Minister, noted in her diary entry for 14 August that she was "astonished to learn from the news [reports] that British troops" had been sent into Londonderry.[86]

Even after the division of responsibilities between the Home Office and the Ministry of Defence were worked out in September 1969, Healey was still wary of Callaghan's motives and was determined not to let the

---

[81] Oxford, Wilson c.936. Minute to the Prime Minister from Crossman, June 1969.
[82] Ibid. Although Crossman's remark was intended to make the point that they could be either better or worse.
[83] PRO, CAB 164/576. Memo to the Prime Minister from Healey, 17 December 1968.
[84] PRO, CAB 164/576. Memo to the Prime Minister from Callaghan, 20 December 1968.
[85] Ibid.
[86] Castle, *Diaries, 1964–70*, p. 699.

Home Secretary run roughshod over the Ministry of Defence.[87] In early November 1969, Healey made it clear to Callaghan that he intended to assign his own political adviser to Northern Ireland, rather than having to depend solely on information provided through officials directly responsible to Callaghan.[88] The Home Secretary strongly and repeatedly resisted such a move.[89] In the end, however, Callaghan met his match in Healey; the Home Secretary gave in and a "point of contact for the Defence Secretariat" was established.[90] But that came only after Callaghan's appeal for Wilson to intervene failed and the dispute seemed headed for an embarrassing and "awkward" showdown in a meeting of ministers.[91] After the troops were sent in, Healey, as Defence Secretary, was really the only individual who was in the position to provide a counterbalance to Callaghan. Once soldiers are deployed, ministers are understandably reluctant to do anything that could be interpreted as undermining the troops.[92] That, no doubt, strengthened Callaghan's hand. But his great climb back to political respectability on the back of Northern Ireland was tied as much to two distinct media campaigns as it was to the events themselves: first, an overt campaign that centred around Callaghan's triumphal arrival in the Catholic neighbourhoods of Londonderry and Belfast in the immediate aftermath of the deployment of British troops and his follow-up visit to Northern Ireland six weeks later; and secondly, a covert effort that was conducted by Callaghan through continual close contacts and policy discussions with the *Guardian*'s news editor Cole as well as the dissemination of material that was being done on Callaghan's behalf by those who were closest to him.

Geoffrey Goodman of the rival *Daily Mirror* believes that Callaghan and Cole "being an Ulsterman"[93] became close as the Troubles in Northern Ireland intensified. Goodman acknowledges that Cole "had already

---

[87] PRO, CAB 164/577, Folio 43. Letter to Callaghan from Healey, 21 November 1969.

[88] Ibid.

[89] PRO, CAB 164/577, Folio 38M. Letter to Healey from Callaghan, 6 November 1969.

[90] PRO, CAB 164/577, Folio 49. Note of a meeting on Northern Ireland matters, 5 December 1969.

[91] PRO, CAB 164/577, Folio 44. Memo to Sir Burke Trend from R.W.J. Hooper, 28 November 1969.

[92] Gallup Public Opinion Polls, September 1969. In the immediate aftermath of the deployment, the British public were supportive as well, with 67 per cent of those surveyed agreeing with the decision.

[93] Interview with Geoffrey Goodman, 23 February 2004.

established a relationship with Callaghan before that, but I think it was consolidated" at that point.[94] It was an important relationship for Callaghan not only because of Cole's knowledge of the issue, but because Cole was well regarded by both major parties.[95] The *Guardian's* coverage of the Troubles was the "most consistent and reliable" of any British newspaper.[96] Callaghan knew how much Hetherington relied on Cole's views to shape the *Guardian's* editorial policy on the issue. That was true in 1969 and 1970 and remained that way at least as late as November 1973, when the then Conservative Home Secretary Robert Carr privately sought Hetherington's opinion on the idea of the new power-sharing executive for Northern Ireland.[97] Hetherington was not convinced that the arrangement would work. "John, however, thought there was at least a rather better than even chance and his judgement had been sound in the past."[98] Nearly two years earlier, William Whitelaw, then Lord President of the Council and later Secretary of State for Northern Ireland after the imposition of direct rule in March 1972, "most warmly commended the good sense of John's own judgement on Northern Ireland".[99]

That begs the question whether the Labour government's policy on Northern Ireland in that early period of the Troubles was being increasingly influenced by the *Guardian*, particularly given Callaghan's frequent contacts with Cole and Callaghan's propensity to keep matters of policy from his ministerial colleagues. Such a role for the *Guardian* would not have been without precedent. In 1921, C.P. Scott, the *Guardian's* editor, had many discussions on Ireland where he acted

---

[94] Ibid.

[95] NAI, TAOIS 2002/8/511. Letter to Irish Prime Minister Lynch from unidentified individual, dated 26 November 1971. Not everyone was convinced of the great depth of Cole's understanding of the problem. A prominent individual, whose name was removed from the document, felt that Cole had "only tinkered with the problem so far ... " From the tone of Lynch's response to the letter, suggesting a possible meeting in Dublin, it was someone whose views were being taken seriously by the Irish Republic.

[96] John Darby, "The Logistics of Enquiry: A Guide for Researchers" in *Northern Ireland: The Background to the Conflict*, edited by John Darby (Belfast, 1983), p. 231.

[97] BLPES, Hetherington 21/37. Notes from a luncheon meeting with Robert Carr, 28 November 1973. Hetherington said that "we lunched alone, at his invitation. He had said that he was having one or two lunches with individual editors."

[98] Ibid.

[99] BLPES, Hetherington 19/26. Notes from a discussion over lunch between William Whitelaw, Hetherington, John Cole and *Guardian* correspondent Francis Boyd, 25 January 1972.

in an advisory role with the then Prime Minister David Lloyd George, one of the architects of the Anglo-Irish Treaty.[100] Scott became "the close companion of men who were deciding the destinies of the nation" and had "sought the company of anyone who might assist the causes dear to his heart".[101] The *Guardian* in those days had taken up the plight of "dispossessed Catholic workers in Belfast"[102] and had campaigned against "Ulster extremists" who were intentionally trying "to bring the whole project of reconciliation to an end".[103]

In addition to Cole, Allen, the permanent secretary at the Home Office who had an impressive administrative track record at both the Home Office and earlier at the Treasury, was an important ally for Callaghan as well. In one of the mysteries of the Northern Ireland saga, Allen, who became Lord Allen of Abbeydale, has repeatedly stressed that his role was minimal in the Home Office's handling of the critical events of that summer and autumn. Allen says that while his boss was entirely devoted to the problem, "I didn't myself get terribly involved in Northern Ireland.... I don't know enough about it really to give you more than an impression."[104] Yet that contention is at odds with the Home Secretary's engagement diary for the first six months of 1970,[105] which showed that Allen was repeatedly conferring with Callaghan and other officials on that matter. In addition, Allen, in an interview[106] with Anthony Seldon in 1980, estimated that nearly two-thirds of his time was taken up with the crisis.[107] Also, Allen was the chairman of a "committee of senior officials" whose responsibility it was to "deal with general policy matters"

[100] Trevor Wilson (ed.), *The Political Diaries of C.P. Scott*, pp. 24–32.
[101] Ibid., pp. 21–24.
[102] *Manchester Guardian*, 30 November 1921, p. 6.
[103] *Manchester Guardian*, 26 November 1921, p. 8.
[104] Interview with Lord Allen, 19 May 2003. In a follow-up interview with the author on 30 July 2003, Allen added: "When I say I was always present [in Callaghan's office] that wasn't true when you come to talk about Northern Ireland.... I let Jim do a lot of talking directly to the people concerned. That was rather exceptional. Jim got so involved and I had to keep on running the office as a whole. A lot of the Northern Ireland exchanges were direct with the officials who had been involved. I never went to Northern Ireland."
[105] The earlier appointments' diaries for Callaghan's time at the Home Office are not at the Public Records Office.
[106] Letter to the author from Lord Allen, 14 June 2003. Lord Allen granted the author access to the material at the British Library of Political & Economic Science, which is restricted under an agreement with the archives.
[107] BLPES, LSE Oral History Series. Anthony Seldon talks with Sir Philip Allen, 28 May 1980.

on Northern Ireland,[108] a committee that still played a dominant role long after Callaghan left office.

John Clare, the reporter who was assigned to Northern Ireland by *The Times* from the start of the Troubles in 1968 and remained there throughout Callaghan's period at the Home Office, had few dealings with Callaghan at that time, seeing him only occasionally. However, Clare was getting unsolicited calls from Allen, who often provided him with information during the unfolding drama in Northern Ireland, "At times of his own choosing and on grounds of his own choosing."[109] What was noteworthy about Allen's dealings with *The Times* reporter is that it was not a case of a reporter trying to corner a senior civil servant to get him to hopefully confirm or deny information, it was a case of Allen, to whom Callaghan gave a peerage when he was Prime Minister, actually seeking out Clare and repeatedly volunteering material off the record. The permanent secretary "was not the most approachable of men by nature" although when it came to the Troubles in Northern Ireland, Allen would discuss matters "quite openly"[110] with Clare: "He would talk about Northern Ireland in a way that he wouldn't talk about anything else."[111] Allen, who "greatly admired" Callaghan and felt privileged "to see at close quarters a super-politician at work"[112], was one of the few people who remained convinced that Callaghan might have solved the problem in Northern Ireland if Labour had not been defeated in 1970,[113] even though the documents Allen was privy to made no such compelling case.

But was it a matter of Whitehall seeking to control the dissemination of information, a perfectly legitimate role for a senior civil servant, or was Allen, in fact, the perfect surrogate for Callaghan? Just as few people would have suspected Callaghan's close ties to the left of centre *Guardian*, few would have suspected that the soft-spoken, tall patrician Allen would be doing Callaghan's bidding with the press. Ironically, Wilson, who was always keeping a close eye on Callaghan, had a high regard for Allen's impartiality and ability to stay clear of politics. Wilson

[108] PRO, CAB 164/577, Folio 21. The letter from R.W.J. Hooper, dated 4 September 1969, which set out the division of responsibilities between the Home Office and the Defence Ministry, also clearly spells out Allen's role.

[109] Interview with John Clare, 19 April 2004.

[110] Ibid.

[111] Ibid.

[112] Oxford, Callaghan 175, Letter to Callaghan from Philip Allen, 23 June 1970.

[113] Interview with Lord Allen, 19 May 2003.

had asked Callaghan, when Callaghan had become Prime Minister, to name Allen to head up a leaks query tied to Wilson's questionable honours' list (the list of individuals who a premier recommends to the Queen for elevation to the House of Lords and other distinctions). That was not the only time that Allen was drafted to probe into examinations about leaks of confidential material to the press. Wilson singled him out to oversee such investigations on at least two other occasions. But when the tables were turned, Allen strongly resisted independent inquiries. Robert Mark, the former commissioner of the Metropolitan Police, told Hetherington that Allen "hated any outside scrutiny of civil service matters".[114]

Conclusion

Northern Ireland proved extremely beneficial to Callaghan. It was an issue in which Callaghan had considerable autonomy, and this greatly contributed to his ability to generate the maximum political capital from the Troubles. Of the group of advisers around Wilson, Healey, who stayed out of the more contentious battles over *In Place of Strife*, was the only individual who repeatedly confronted Callaghan on Northern Ireland and he did it on at least three critical occasions: first, by demanding and getting a clear division of responsibilities between the Home Office and the Ministry of Defence; secondly, by forcing the appointment of a political adviser to the General Commanding Officer in Northern Ireland, who would be answerable to him; and, thirdly, by demanding that Arthur Young, Callaghan's appointment to supervise police operations in the province, comply with the original understanding and regularly meet and consult with British military commanders in Northern Ireland.[115] All of this – along with evidence that supports the Defence Secretary's uneasiness about the deployment at the time – gives credence to Healey's contention that had he not been hospitalised on 14 August 1969, he might well have been in a stronger position to swing Wilson to his point of view. That argument gains further credibility given Wilson's unwillingness to come to Callaghan's defence by taking sides in any of these disputes between Callaghan and Healey.

---

[114] BLPES, Hetherington 20/23. Notes from discussions with Sir Robert Mark at Nuffield College, Oxford, 2–3 March 1973.
[115] PRO, CAB 164/577, Folio 43. Letter to Callaghan from Healey, 21 November 1969.

Callaghan realised that after the troops were deployed, he was operating in a "kind of twilight area constitutionally".[116] The legal foundation for the use of British troops in a civil policing matter was based "not so much on law as on mutual goodwill and co-operation"[117] with the government of Northern Ireland. One senior civil servant conceded in September 1969 that it was "a precarious basis [on which to deploy troops] maybe; but probably the best that can be devised in the circumstances".[118] Yet the troops were the cornerstone of Callaghan's success in Northern Ireland, and once they went in he had no intention of allowing them to be removed. In March 1970, the Cabinet secretary Burke Trend told Wilson that Healey might push for a timetable for troop reductions, but annoyingly noted Callaghan's "ominous" view that "we must maintain a substantial military and police presence at all times".[119] Trend, in his comments to the Prime Minister, was sceptical of any future scaling back of the military presence in the province, noting that the dates being bandied about kept becoming more distant. Despite the fragility of the situation, Callaghan was still able to rebuild his reputation on an issue that most other British politicians found debilitating. There were several reasons for that.

First, it was Callaghan who brought in the troops; all the other politicians were left with the insurmountable challenge of having to try to extricate them. It was a bold gesture of liberation that was heightened by his equally dramatic tour of the Catholic neighbourhoods of Londonderry and Belfast. The truth is that without the troops and all the ensuing publicity and leverage they gave him, particularly in the early stages when they were viewed as liberators, Callaghan would never have been able to command that issue the way that he did at home and abroad and his political rehabilitation might never have happened.[120] Healey, while minimising his own role, was, in fact, the counterbalance to Callaghan on Northern Ireland, and the fact that Healey was

---

[116] (Manchester) *Guardian* Archive. Memo entitled "The Home Secretary's Guidance to Editors on the Situation in Northern Ireland," 15 August 1969.

[117] PRO, CAB 164/577, Folio 23. Memo to Burke Trend from R.W.J. Hooper, 5 September 1969.

[118] Ibid.

[119] PRO, CAB 164/578, Folio 6. Note to the Prime Minister from Burke Trend, 18 March 1970.

[120] *Irish Independent*, 28 August 1969, p. 1. The Dublin newspaper concluded, after Callaghan had met with Cabinet ministers in Belfast, that "Mr. Callaghan, by controlling the army, controlled the real power in the North."

essentially unavailable to make his case in those critical days in August 1969, greatly strengthened Callaghan's hand.

Secondly, Callaghan had the advantage of being there first. Since he was the first British politician in the post-war period to deal with the Irish issue head on, his fellow Cabinet ministers and the opposition deferred to his leadership.[121] The bipartisan approach to Northern Ireland, which had been in existence for years at Westminster and actually contributed to the problem, remained in place in 1969, and with British soldiers at risk was actually strengthened. Also, Callaghan's counterpart among the Tories, Quintin Hogg, supported Callaghan's strategy and, given the unusual status of Northern Ireland, was slow to criticise him. At times Hogg's support was even unequivocal. After Hogg concluded a three-day visit to Northern Ireland in October 1969, he told a news conference, "I'm backing Callaghan for all I'm worth," and added that "the Unionists are mistaken if they think they would get a better deal from me".[122] Hogg never had the opportunity to put those words into action; when the Conservatives regained power less than a year later, he was passed over for the job and Maudling became Home Secretary. But the fact remains that Callaghan was not as supportive of the new Home Secretary as the Tory shadow minister had been to him.[123]

Thirdly, Callaghan, unlike his successors, was able to deal with Northern Ireland without having to deal with the Irish Republican Army (IRA), which did not become a serious player until after Labour left office in June 1970. The IRA, which had originally been an army of liberation in the Anglo-Irish war of 1919–21, had become less significant after it was outlawed by the Irish leader Eamon de Valéra in 1936 and after its failed border raids of the 1950s and early 1960s. Yet a heightened role for the more radical element within the IRA was inevitable given the slow pace of the reforms and the ever-increasing role of the British army. That eventuality was not lost on Britain's ambassador to the Irish Republic. While he believed in early 1969 that the IRA had no "peg or

---

[121] PRO, CAB 128/44 Part II. In Cabinet discussion on 30 July 1969, two weeks before the troops were deployed, it was noted that the "opposition had not sought to exploit the government's difficulties."

[122] *Irish Press*, 8 October 1969, p. 1.

[123] BLPES, Hetherington 19/2. Notes from a meeting between Wilson and Hetherington, 19 July 1972. Although Callaghan was quite critical of Maudling's lack of forcefulness on Northern Ireland, Wilson felt that Maudling's manner as Home Secretary was "deceptive". Wilson felt that "Reggie had a very quick mind and he adopted his sleepy way in order to camouflage the fact that he had seen round or through something a lot quicker than some of his colleagues..."

excuse on which to hang direct intervention by force", he thought that might change if British troops intervened. The envoy told Dublin six months before the deployment that any such commitment of troops "could give rise to a very dangerous situation from the point of view of peace in the area and he would be very worried if this should happen".[124] Nevertheless, the IRA's absence for most of the time that Callaghan was Home Secretary made the issue far more manageable for Callaghan, who himself challenged the Northern Ireland government's early tendency to blame the increasing violence on the IRA, saying it was not a factor.[125]

Finally, of all the leading British politicians of his day, Callaghan was perceived to be among the most anti-intellectual, and it was a perception he exploited. The man-of-the-people image made him perfectly suited to the job of dealing with the unsophisticated politics of Northern Ireland, in much the same way it had benefited him among the rank and file on *In Place of Strife*. Being surrounded by the adoring Catholics of the Bogside was a role with which his predecessor Jenkins would have been uncomfortable, but Callaghan revelled in it. Callaghan's anti-intellectualism had two dimensions that worked especially well in Northern Ireland: first, the avuncular public image which made him popular with the people and, secondly, the ability to take on anyone who stood in his way, which gave him an edge among rougher more reactionary politicians, many with whom his more cultured successors were unable to deal. Clare, who covered the Northern Ireland crisis for *The Times*, says that underneath the kindly and almost subservient public image that the Home Secretary liked to present, Callaghan was "tough, arrogant, overbearing, bullying. Most like Ian Paisley, not in politics but in manner . . . and therefore dealt with Ian Paisley better than anyone else up to that point."[126]

In one of the ironies of history, Wilson's loss at the general election in June 1970 was Callaghan's gain.[127] On that point, Callaghan was lucky because as subsequent events showed it would be only a matter

---

[124] NAI, DFA 2003/13/26. Note of meeting between H. McCann from Ireland's Department of Foreign Affairs and British Ambassador A. Gilchrist, 31 January 1969.

[125] PRO, CAB 128/46, extracts. Minutes of a meeting of the Cabinet, 19 August 1969.

[126] Interview with John Clare, 19 April 2004.

[127] J. Denis Derbyshire and Ian Derbyshire, *Politics in Britain: From Callaghan to Thatcher* (Cambridge, 1988), p. 30. The 1970 defeat was unexpected. "Labour's claims to have established themselves as the new 'natural party of government' lay in shreds and the nation turned to a new market-based experiment at economic regeneration . . ."

of time before the troops would wear out their welcome. An internal assessment made by the Irish government nine months before the troops were deployed concluded that British policy on Northern Ireland would be driven by party politics and "the longer term desideratum of cleaning up a 'back yard' which gives Britain a bad image in the eyes of the world".[128] That assessment proved to be as timely on the day that the Labour government lost power in June 1970, as it had been when it was written in November 1968. Had Labour won re-election and had Callaghan remained Home Secretary all the benefits that Northern Ireland provided to his political rehabilitation, the image of him as a decisive leader and champion of civil rights, would have unravelled.[129] Callaghan was a wonderful showman and a great police constable on the beat, but he was not a man with a long-term understanding of the Troubles in Northern Ireland, something he admitted himself years later.[130] That said, Callaghan was, however, a man with a long-term view when it came to enhancing his own political position although it seems likely that his strategies were confined to the crisis at hand rather than part of a grand scheme.

At some point between the end of the saga over *In Place of Strife* and Callaghan's successes on Northern Ireland, Cole says Callaghan and Wilson "more or less kissed and made up".[131] The *Guardian's* Cole believes they still were suspicious of each other, but he says Callaghan told him that after one of their meetings, Wilson asked Callaghan to stay behind. The two men had tea and a long talk and Callaghan agreed to support Wilson at least through the general election. After that, Callaghan told Cole "all bets might be off".[132] This was the start of the process that led to Callaghan eventually becoming Foreign Secretary, when Labour returned to power in 1974. But before he could reach that point, Callaghan still had work to do and Ireland would continue to be an important part of it.

---

[128] NAI, TAOIS 2001/8/1. "Note on North-South Policy", 11 November 1968.
[129] BLPES, Rees 10/33. Transcript from "Witness Seminar on British Policy in Northern Ireland 1964–1970", undated but apparently from the 1990s. Callaghan later admitted that the "honeymoon was getting a little dated by the time the election came along. And I don't know how long we could have kept it up."
[130] BBC2, *Timewatch*, 27 January 1993. Callaghan told the BBC, 25 years after the civil rights demonstrations that signalled the start of the Troubles: "I never flattered myself that I understood the situation fully and I think very few people do."
[131] Interview with John Cole, 25 February 2004.
[132] Ibid.

While there is no doubt that the Troubles in Northern Ireland sharply escalated after the Conservatives came to power and introduced a one-sided policy of internment without trial in 1971 to round up suspected IRA members, the solutions that Callaghan offered in 1969 and 1970 amounted to a short-term holding action that was politically expedient, and might have made matters worse. Austin Currie, a Nationalist MP, was among those who believed Britain should have "taken that extra step" in August 1969 and suspended Stormont as well. If it had, he later argued, "a lot of the trouble and a lot of the deaths that occurred after that would have been avoided".[133] But any sweeping changes in policy, namely direct rule or closer ties between Ulster and the Irish Republic, would have involved too much risk and that would have been anathema to Callaghan's political instincts. As early as 20 September 1969, five weeks after the troops were sent in and in the midst of general praise for Callaghan's decisiveness, a senior official in Dublin told Irish Prime Minister Lynch that the view that "all sides" are taking is that Callaghan's proposals for social reforms and overhauling the police services are "at best likely to emerge as an uneasy short-term compromise".[134] Jack Jones of the Transport and General Workers' Union believes Callaghan "might have been a little bit more daring" at the outset by working to bridge the differences between the North and the South and withdrawing a lot of support for the government in Belfast.[135]

Once the initial street battles died down in Londonderry and Belfast in the autumn of 1969, the issue slipped down the political agenda as far as the Labour government was concerned until violence flared up again in April 1970. It was during those months that critical time was lost. A review of Cabinet minutes from 13 January 1970 to the general election on 18 June, a total of two dozen meetings, shows there was not a single Cabinet meeting where Northern Ireland was a separate agenda item[136] with the exception of the disclosure that two Irish

---

[133] BBC2, *Timewatch*, 27 January 1993.
[134] NAI, DFA/2000/5/12. Memo to the Irish Prime Minister from Kevin Rush, envoy in London, 20 September 1969. Also, as early as mid-September, Callaghan told Mountbatten that he was "not overoptimistic about developments", citing the inertia from the government in Belfast. (Oxford, Callaghan 223/1508. Letter to Earl Mountbatten of Burma from Callaghan, 10 September 1969.)
[135] Interview with Jack Jones, 18 June 2003.
[136] There were, however, numerous meetings at the committee level.

Cabinet ministers were being accused of illegal arms shipments.[137] In other words, there were no new initiatives at Cabinet level and no discussion among ministers at No. 10 Downing Street now that the initial uprising was under control. Arguably, the expanding role of governments in the post-war period made it necessary for more policies to win final approval at committee level. But it is still hard to fathom why a matter as pressing as Northern Ireland was kept from the Cabinet, especially given the attention that that same Cabinet paid to *In Place of Strife*. In early May 1970, the Irish Prime Minister, who had restrained his public comments on the Irish Troubles to the great pleasure of Callaghan and the British government in the hopes that reforms would work, was being told by his advisers that Callaghan's strategy of working through the Unionist government and "whittling away" at its powers so as to overhaul the system "appears to us to be close to the point of failure".[138]

The contention of Callaghan's biographer, that Callaghan showed himself to be a statesman over his role in Northern Ireland, needs closer examination. Morgan's view that Callaghan came "tantalisingly close" to resolving the situation and that "in the next quarter of a century, that window of opportunity was not to return"[139] gives the former Home Secretary too much credit and turns a blind eye to Callaghan's use of the issue to advance his political ambitions. It looks past the fact, too, that even though Bloody Sunday[140] shamefully happened under the Conservatives' watch, the greater hope for peace in Northern Ireland came not from anything Callaghan did but the accord in December 1973 between the Conservative British Prime Minister Edward Heath and Irish Prime Minister Cosgrave. The Sunningdale agreement, while it was never ratified, recognised an "Irish dimension" to the Troubles. It brought all sides – the governments of Britain, Northern Ireland and the Republic – to the table for the first time in half a century, and led to the replacement of direct rule from London with the

---

[137] PRO, CAB 128/45. The arms controversy led to the removal of Charles Haughey and Neil Blaney from the Cabinet by Irish Prime Minister Jack Lynch. An investigation led to Haughey's arrest and he was tried and acquitted. He later became Prime Minister.

[138] NAI, DFA 2000/5/38. Internal Irish government memo prepared as an overview of the Troubles, 4 May 1970.

[139] Morgan, *Callaghan: A Life*, p. 354.

[140] On 30 January 1972, British troops opened fire on a civil rights march in Londonderry, killing 13 unarmed civilians. That same day rioters burned down the British Embassy in Dublin.

power-sharing executive made up of Protestants and Catholics. The returning Labour government's capitulation to the Unionist-inspired workers' strike in Belfast in May 1974, when Callaghan protégé Merlyn Rees was Northern Ireland Secretary, further undermined the carefully crafted power-sharing agreement that, while flawed, had for a short time actually begun to work.[141]

Cosgrave, reflecting on Callaghan's role in Northern Ireland, recalls: "Labour governments were generally not particularly helpful.... I think they feared the Conservatives would wave the flag of the Empire, that sort of thing and in the long run [Labour] hadn't the strength to do it."[142] Nevertheless, it was not the intricacies of Northern Ireland policy, which had ensnared political leaders from Lloyd George to Churchill, that contributed to Callaghan's rehabilitation; rather it was the image of strength and decisiveness projected by the deployment of troops and his highly publicised early tours of Belfast and Londonderry. Callaghan's press secretary McCaffrey says that on those early visits "the only person who [consistently] went around with him and spoke with him and attended different meetings [with him] was me".[143] The all-encompassing role that his press adviser played is evidence that Callaghan viewed the visits as an important part of his strategy not only in dealing with Northern Ireland but in dealing with his personal political goals as well.

While the visits that followed the troop deployments significantly enhanced Callaghan's public image, quickly elevating his stature within the government, the question remains how much lasting impact did they have? As was the case over *In Place of Strife*, Callaghan's very public role created a public perception of a man of great principle taking great risks. Callaghan's later behaviour on the issue demonstrated neither great principle nor an appetite for risk. Bernard Donoughue, who headed the Policy Unit at No. 10 Downing Street under the premierships of both Wilson and Callaghan, recalls that when Callaghan was

---

[141] BLPES, Rees 3/1. Letter to Merlyn Rees from James Callaghan, 2 April 1985. Callaghan acknowledged that the timing of the 1974 British general election was a "tragedy" as far as Northern Ireland was concerned because "it helped to destroy any credibility for the Sunningdale agreement by revealing the wide differences between the political groups".

[142] Interview with Liam Cosgrave, 1 October 2004.

[143] Interview with Sir Tom McCaffrey, 3 July 2003.

Prime Minister, he wanted to keep the matter "as quiet as possible".[144] Nevertheless, while he was in opposition, after the 1970 defeat of the Labour government, Callaghan cleverly kept himself at the forefront of that issue and by so doing kept alive the idea that he had somehow achieved in Northern Ireland what no other British politician had been able to achieve.

---

[144] Interview with Lord Donoughue, 9 July 2003.

7

In Opposition: Book Writing and Europe

The defeat of the Labour government in the June 1970 general election had come as a surprise. The front cover of *The Economist* the week before the election showed a confident Harold Wilson walking along the road with Roy Jenkins, his equally confident Chancellor of the Exchequer. Below the photograph of the two men was a headline that read "In Harold Wilson's Britain". But within a matter of days, and despite rising poll numbers that indicated a rally for Labour towards the end, it would be Edward Heath and the Conservatives who would form a new government. While Jenkins's "neutral" budget was seen by some as the reason that Labour had lost the election, others blamed the defeat on *In Place of Strife*, which Wilson and Barbara Castle, in particular, had backed to the bitter end. The only senior Cabinet minister who emerged from the defeat with his reputation burnished was Callaghan.

Although the Troubles in Northern Ireland intensified in the period leading up to the general election, Callaghan got out from under the escalating crisis just in time. When he left the Home Office in 1970, he was still seen as part of the solution rather than part of the problem. As a result, Northern Ireland proved highly beneficial to his political reputation. And, in the first few years in opposition, Callaghan was determined to exploit that conflict for political purposes as he did with a parallel issue, which we will explore later in this chapter, i.e. the debate over Britain joining the European Economic Community (EEC). On Northern Ireland, he kept himself at the centre of the controversy in several ways: first by being shadow Home Secretary for much of that time; secondly, by remaining as the Labour Party's spokesman on Northern Ireland even after Wilson had later moved him to the post of shadow Secretary for Employment; thirdly, by seeing to it that his protégé

Merlyn Rees eventually succeeded him in shadowing the province, and finally by writing a book about the Troubles.

Callaghan spent much of the first few years in opposition working on that book. Six months before *A House Divided, the Dilemma of Northern Ireland*, was published by Collins in September 1973, Callaghan on the advice of the Cabinet Office turned to his long-time associate, Philip Allen, who had recently retired from the Home Office, and sought his guidance on the manuscript.[1] As a former minister, Callaghan was required to clear the book with the Cabinet Office in much the same way that other memoir writers had, including most recently at that time Wilson and George Brown. But Callaghan's memoirs were unlike other such endeavours which had first begun with Churchill's breaking of the conventions on ministerial disclosures to write his voluminous history of the Second World War.[2] Up until the time Callaghan's book was published, *A House Divided* was the only memoir that was entirely based on events that still were among the most sensitive matters facing Her Majesty's government.

Meanwhile, the Cabinet secretary, Burke Trend, probably the most influential member of the Civil Service, had been briefed on this same matter by Allen, who after having read several chapters was genuinely troubled by the tone of Callaghan's manuscript. Allen, who had told Callaghan that "although I can remember quite a lot, I can not clearly remember the chronology",[3] sent the Cabinet Office a draft of a personal letter that he wrote in March 1973 as a response to Callaghan. That letter was distributed to and commented upon by senior civil servants in several departments who were apprehensive about directly confronting Callaghan. That suggests that the Cabinet Office was building its strategy in dealing with their concerns about the book at least in part around following up on Allen's private correspondence with the former Home Secretary. To a man, they were strongly critical of the project and doubtful about its purpose amid a general feeling that it might well inflame the situation in Northern Ireland "which [was] already sufficiently delicate".[4] Trend believed the events of 1969

---

[1] PRO, CAB 164/1204, Folio 12. Draft letter to Callaghan from Sir Philip Allen, March 1973.

[2] PRO, PREM 15/427. Memo on ministerial memoirs prepared for Prime Minister Edward Heath by Sir Burke Trend, September 1971.

[3] PRO, CAB 164/1204, Folio 12. Draft letter to Callaghan from Sir Philip Allen, March 1973.

[4] PRO, CAB 164/1204, Folio 17. Draft letter to Callaghan from Sir Burke Trend, 26 April 1973. A notation indicates the letter was not sent.

and 1970 were "inextricably linked" to the worsening Troubles in 1973 and that disclosures that Callaghan was making were "bound to have a direct bearing on what [would] happen in the immediate future".[5]

It was left up to Allen, at least initially, to deal with Callaghan. In what was a masterpiece of diplomatic writing, Allen drew attention to Callaghan's penchant for disclosing confidential information not by admonishing the practice, but by telling Callaghan that he, Allen, was "old-fashioned on these matters". Allen added, "I know that the conventions have been changing, and am well aware of what Harold Wilson for example put in his book."[6] The former permanent secretary, who had disclosed material in confidence to *The Times* on some of these same matters, although it is unlikely he had named names, told Callaghan, "I must clearly leave it to Burke [Trend] to raise any point about giving details of what civil servants, police officers and members of the Northern Ireland government said or advised from time to time, and what you thought about them". Allen added that "it is obviously not for me to comment on the political passages, including what you say about Reggie",[7] a reference to blistering comments made by Callaghan about the actions, or lack of action, of Reginald Maulding, Callaghan's successor as Home Secretary.[8]

Despite the pre-emptive warning from Allen, Callaghan resisted, in what another senior civil servant characterised as a "somewhat carefully worded reply",[9] several of the changes that were recommended by the Cabinet Office shortly thereafter. In that letter from 30 April 1973, Callaghan, citing pages and lines of text, responded to the concerns of Trend with comments such as "Yes, Harold Wilson certainly had this in mind", or "I prefer to leave it as it is", or "I see no reason to leave this out", or "I do not mind causing a little annoyance".[10]

---

[5] Ibid.

[6] Ibid. This refers to the recently published memoirs of Wilson entitled *A Personal Record: The Labour Government 1964–1970*.

[7] PRO, CAB 164/1204, Folio 12. Draft letter to Callaghan from Sir Philip Allen, March 1973.

[8] Ibid. In a self-deprecating moment, Allen wrote, "The only very minor point I would make is that if the references to me stay in, perhaps the 'Sir' could be left out after the first time!"

[9] PRO, CAB 164/1204, Folio 19M. Letter to M.A.Griffiths from Brian Norbury, 2 May 1973.

[10] PRO, CAB 164/1204, Folio 19. Letter to Sir Burke Trend from Callaghan, 30 April 1973.

Also, Callaghan, while allowing his material to be vetted by the Cabinet Office, as was required, seemed determined not to allow too much scrutiny – a disclosure that gives credence to the argument that the book was less a thoughtful discourse on how to resolve a terrible crisis than yet another move by Callaghan to cement the political gains that he had made on Northern Ireland. Trend had just begun to distribute the manuscript to the permanent secretaries, who like Allen were the civil servants who in effect ran the ministries, in May 1973, when he was told by Callaghan that he was "sending the book to press within 48 hours".[11]

Neil Cairncross, a deputy under-secretary of state in the Home Office, who is referred to in Callaghan's book as the "perfect civil servant",[12] was among those who were disdainful of Callaghan's manuscript. Cairncross, on whom Callaghan heaped praise for his role in Northern Ireland and who, in fact, helped Callaghan with the initial research of documents at the Home Office,[13] angrily told his colleagues that the book disclosed information that was supposed to have been kept sealed by the Official Secrets Act "until close to the end of the century".[14] Cairncross added that there was much that was "unfair" in the manuscript. "But it is natural, I suppose, that Mr. Callaghan should emerge from the book with more credit than Mr. Maudling."[15]

Cairncross had been at Callaghan's side during the triumphal tour in August 1969 when the much-publicised talks had taken place with the

---

[11] PRO, CAB 164/1204, Folio 19M. Letter to M.A. Griffiths from Brian Norbury, 2 May 1973.

[12] Callaghan, *A House Divided*, p. 89. But that may not have been as much of a compliment as it appeared to be. On p. 69, Callaghan lavished praise on his close adviser Tom McCaffrey, who was also a civil servant, for just the opposite characteristic, that is his "un-civil-service-like qualities" that made him able "to interpret the opinion of the man on the Clapham omnibus".

[13] PRO, CJ4/28. Letter to Callaghan from Sir Philip Allen, 12 August 1970. "We are getting out some material, and will be quick as we can – although as you will appreciate the boys in the Northern Ireland department are just a little pushed at this moment…"

[14] PRO, CAB 164/12.04, Folio 11. Note to Brian Norbury from Neil Cairncross, 26 March 1973.

[15] Ibid; PRO, CAB 164 /1204, Folio 31. Handwritten internal office memo which indicated that in June 1973 Neil Cairncross bumped into Callaghan's wife in the street. He told his colleagues that Audrey Callaghan mentioned that her husband was hoping the book would be out at the end of the summer. Apparently, there was such aversion to the book in Whitehall that another civil servant responded to that news by saying: "So be it. But I hope his conscience is clear!"

Cabinet in Northern Ireland. He had been deeply involved in the negotiations then and was troubled that the former Home Secretary was about
to "expose" the fact that ministers in Belfast were "effectively doing
Mr. Callaghan's bidding rather than acting as free agents". Cairncross
evidently could not understand why Callaghan would disclose that
information. After all, tensions on both sides were high. It had been
just over a year since Bloody Sunday and there had been a considerable
stepping up of attacks by the IRA against the British army and civilians
in Belfast. In addition, Cairncross, who had been asked to look at the
manuscript because he was "as well placed as anyone in the public service to pronounce upon some of the issues that Mr. Callaghan raises",[16]
felt that Callaghan's "tone of disparagement" towards officials who the
British government were still working with in Belfast, would make it difficult for Callaghan ever again to be a major player in Northern Ireland
"should the occasion arise".[17]

Callaghan, however, had no intention of ever revisiting that issue as
an insider for several reasons. First, he was too astute a politician to
ever allow himself to be dragged back into a battle that he had essentially won. Northern Ireland had been Callaghan's great victory and its
greatest value to him in opposition was not necessarily in how events
proceeded but in making dramatic gestures that would remind everyone
of how much better things had been when he was in charge. Secondly,
by being able to address the issue from either the opposition front bench
or as Labour Party spokesman, he was able to keep his hand in Northern Ireland affairs from a comfortable distance. Even though Wilson
stole some of his thunder by taking over shadowing Northern Ireland in
December 1971, Callaghan could still pick and choose if and when he
would respond to a particular event. Finally, Callaghan knew there was
no quick solution for the Troubles in the province. A memorandum that
he wrote three months before exiting office as Home Secretary touched
on his successes but was also frank in its discussion of the challenges
ahead.[18]

In other words, even though Callaghan was aware of the deterio-
rating situation as early as 1970, he was also aware of the continuing

[16] PRO, CAB 164/1204, Folio 2. Memo to Brian Norbury from C.J. Child, 27
February 1973.
[17] Ibid.
[18] PRO, CJ3/11, Folio 1. Draft paper to ministers from Callaghan assessing the
situation in Northern Ireland, 11 March 1970.

value that the issue provided for strengthening his political position and he was determined not to let Northern Ireland slip from his grasp. In August 1970, barely two months after leaving the Home Office, he began work on the book and asked Allen to inform Reginald Maudling of his intentions. That is just what Allen did and he told his new boss that he did not know of any way that he could deny Callaghan the documents he was requesting.[19] Callaghan's requests to Whitehall were sandwiched in between those of other memoir writers, including Harold Macmillan and Richard Crossman, whose works had raised concerns about shaking up the old conventions as well. In the case of Macmillan, the Cabinet Office expressed "considerable concern" about comments being made by the former Conservative Prime Minister about "personalities who are still alive".[20] In Callaghan's case, most of the people he referred to were not only still alive; they were still at their posts.

Also, a mere three weeks after Labour lost the general election, Callaghan tried to make another trip to Northern Ireland, this time as part of a delegation[21] of "observers" if the new Tory government allowed the Orange parades to take place as scheduled on 13 July 1970. Maudling's letter to Callaghan, which denied the request, cited the "very heavy burden"[22] such a visit would impose on the already taxed security forces. No doubt Callaghan would have given Maudling the same response if their roles had been reversed. The issue resurfaced again a month later, and Cairncross advised Maudling against an all-party fact-finding mission. He noted that "those who concern themselves with Northern Ireland do not on the whole make the claim that they are ill-informed; indeed their positions tend to be firmly entrenched."[23] When Cairncross's memo reached Maudling's desk, he approved it, and added the comment, "Let sleeping MPs lie."[24]

Ironically, at the same time that Callaghan was trying to jockey himself into the position of making a return visit to Northern Ireland, Dublin was acceding to the request of the new British government to "consciously avoid saying very much about the North so as to give

---

[19] PRO, CJ4/28. Handwritten note to Maudling from Neil Cairncross, undated.
[20] PRO, PREM 15/1552. Note to Prime Minister Heath from Sir Burke Trend, 2 July 1970.
[21] PRO, CJ 4/23. Letter to Callaghan from Maudling, 8 July 1970.
[22] Ibid.
[23] PRO, CJ 4/23. Memo to G. Angel from Neil Cairncross, 28 July 1970.
[24] Ibid. Maudling's handwritten comment is dated 29 July 1970.

time for progress to be made quietly in the direction of reform".[25] But Callaghan was determined to keep the spotlight focused on himself. Not long after – only five weeks into the Tory government's handling of the crisis – Callaghan appealed to his old friend Harry Nicholas, the general secretary of the Labour Party, to try and get the British trade unions and the party more involved in Northern Ireland politics. Callaghan proposed the idea of getting Labour's National Executive Committee (NEC) behind an "organisational effort" to affiliate the British Labour Party with the Northern Ireland Labour Party (NILP)[26] and thereby, with the help of the Northern Ireland trade unions, attempt to dislodge the Ulster Unionists from power.[27]

Callaghan's thought was to develop a working-class party of Catholics and Protestants that "[would] be capable of fighting all the 52 Stormont seats...which has never been done before".[28] It was an initiative that Callaghan persisted with until the debate was gradually overtaken by another political crisis in early 1971, over the Tory government's determination to take Britain into the EEC. Callaghan's idea of deepening the involvement of the trade unions and the British Labour Party in the widening Northern Irish crisis was a dramatic gesture, but it threatened to cause a major rift in the party and raised grave concerns in the Irish Republic as well. Ireland's ambassador to Britain told Callaghan prior to a visit that Callaghan made to Northern Ireland in March 1971 that any such move would be viewed by the Republic as a "further recognition of the continuing existence of the Border". The same "strong objections" were made to Callaghan when he visited Dublin as well.[29]

A regional group of the Parliamentary Labour Party, which included the shadow minister for parliamentary affairs, Fred Peart, was favourably disposed towards Callaghan's idea,[30] but support for his proposal was not broad. Although Callaghan was convinced that the hold on power of the Ulster Unionists was "feebler than it has been at any time since

---

[25] NAI, TAOIS 2001/8/10. Also, at that point Dublin seems to have felt that banning marches might have led to even more violence.

[26] At this point the Northern Ireland Labour Party had only a single MP at Stormont.

[27] Oxford, Wilson c.908, Folios 475–477. Letter to Harry Nicholas from James Callaghan, 22 July 1970.

[28] Ibid.

[29] NAI, DFA 2001/23/508. Discussion at the Irish Embassy in London between the Irish ambassador and a regional delegation of the British Parliamentary Labour Party, 30 March 1971.

[30] Ibid.

1921",[31] there was concern that this undertaking could "weaken" the new Social Democratic and Labour Party (SDLP), which had its roots in the civil rights campaign and had just begun to make some inroads into Northern Ireland politics.[32] Even Callaghan's protégé Merlyn Rees, who was appointed Secretary of State for Northern Ireland when Labour returned to power in February 1974, admits Callaghan's approach was flawed. Rees says that where Callaghan "was wrong in the early days was that [he thought] you could reform Stormont and carry on as before and that the Northern Ireland Labour Party led by the trade unions would play their part". Rees adds that the reality was that "the trade unions were split, [and many of] their members were voting for Paisley".[33]

It was about the time that Callaghan made an effort to promote his plan among shop stewards in Belfast that he decided to seek out help on his book project. Callaghan had not made much progress with the writing,[34] and contacted John Clare, the reporter who had covered Northern Ireland for *The Times* and was then working as a reporter at ITN. Clare says Callaghan offered him a flat fee to be his ghostwriter. Callaghan handed him half of the payment initially with the understanding that the balance would be paid upon the book's completion. Clare's agreement was strictly with Callaghan and Clare has no idea how much Callaghan was paid by Collins, the publisher. For the better part of a year, Clare met with Callaghan twice a week at 9 a.m. for an hour or two at a small flat that Callaghan and his wife occupied across the river from the Houses of Parliament, meeting Audrey Callaghan just as she was going out the door to do her charitable work. The tapes that were made of those conversations were transcribed by Callaghan's secretary Ruth Sharpe and given to Clare who worked on the material at home at night and weekends.[35]

As the months passed, the former reporter for *The Times* became so disenchanted with Callaghan's unwillingness to grasp the bigger picture

---

[31] Oxford, Wilson c.908, Folios 475–477. Letter to Harry Nicholas from James Callaghan, 22 July 1970.
[32] NAI, DFA 2001/23/508. Discussion at the Irish Embassy in London between the Irish ambassador and a regional delegation of the British Parliamentary Labour Party, 30 March 1971.
[33] Interview with Lord Merlyn-Rees, 1 July 2003.
[34] *Guardian*, 20 February 1971, p. 11. The columnist William Davis said that Callaghan was "still struggling to get past the first 5000 words of his memoirs" and might abandon the effort.
[35] Interview with John Clare, 19 April 2004.

that he refused to take the remainder of the payment at the conclusion of the project. Clare, who had been an eyewitness to the unfolding crisis in 1968 and 1969, felt the book was not making any contribution to advancing the understanding of the Troubles, but rather was a book that was all about Callaghan and his political ambitions. "There were bits that [Callaghan] was interested in either because he remembered them vividly or he thought they presented him in a particularly good light. And what seemed to him the boring bits in between he wasn't really concerned about." Clare agrees that Callaghan saw the book as a way of keeping himself at the forefront of the debate on Northern Ireland, a crisis that, up until that point, had been the biggest success of his political career.[36]

A review of the lengthy exchanges about Callaghan's book that took place in the spring of 1973 between numerous senior civil servants, who were prohibited from discussing Callaghan's manuscript with their ministers given the strict division between politics and the Civil Service, reflects a general belief that the book was an ill-timed project that could undermine the work of those individuals facing an increasingly dangerous environment in Northern Ireland and possibly "might even expose them to some degree of personal risk".[37] In the case of the former Prime Minister of Northern Ireland, Major James Chichester-Clark, who by that time had retired to his estate outside Londonderry, Cairncross concluded that not only would it "embarrass him personally; I suppose it is not beyond possibility that [the disclosures] might indeed endanger him". If one reads between the lines, there was a feeling that the book would further no cause except possibly the future political aspirations of the former Home Secretary.[38] When the Ministry of Defence first alerted the Cabinet Office in May 1972 that Callaghan was seeking material about troop movements for his book, a civil servant noted at the top of

---

[36] Ibid.

[37] PRO, CAB 164/1204, Folio 17. Draft letter to Callaghan from Sir Burke Trend, 26 April 1973. A notation indicates the letter was not sent.

[38] Ibid; PRO, PREM 15/902. Memo to R.J. Armstrong from W. Armstrong, 22 October 1971. At about this time, Callaghan and his book were briefly caught in the crossfire of a contentious debate between Crossman, who was preparing his diaries for publication, and senior civil servants over Crossman's unsuccessful attempt to gain access to ministerial papers for his research assistant, Janet Morgan. A Whitehall exchange drags Callaghan into the melee by saying that the former Home Secretary was recently denied such an arrangement for his book "and that there seem to be no special circumstances that would justify making an exception to the general principle in favour of Mr. Crossman".

the memorandum: "Trouble ahead? Do we say anything to Mr. C now or wait?"[39]

Arthur Peterson, who had replaced Allen as permanent secretary at the Home Office, told Trend, police forces are often reliant on each other and "if the disclosures in this book led to a feeling that advice given would be at any time regarded as less than strictly confidential, I can foresee a great deal of difficulty".[40] Cairncross was upset as well, viewing the disclosures of confidential material as a "breach" of principle,[41] while Trend wondered if some of Callaghan's harsh comments about the Royal Ulster Constabulary might call into "question the traditional – and constitutionally very important – relationship which since Peel's time has existed between the Home Office and the police".[42] Trend also asked rhetorically if such comments would bring the United Kingdom any closer to a settlement in Northern Ireland.[43] But that was not the purpose of Callaghan's book. His objective in selectively naming names and detailing how he had micro-managed the situation was to provide the evidence, while it could still further his ambitions, of just how he had succeeded where so many others had failed. Apparently, Callaghan felt the book was so important to burnishing his political reputation that he was willing to imperil the close relationship he had had with the police, one which went back to the late 1950s when he was the chief negotiator for the Police Federation and had helped to secure higher wages and better working conditions for the union.

The political inappropriateness of the project was also evident in Callaghan's hesitancy to give the current Secretary of State for Northern Ireland, William Whitelaw, any more than a general idea of what the book was about – indeed, he only promised to discuss it further with Whitelaw on the prompting of Trend, who suggested to Callaghan at the end of April 1973 that he "ought perhaps to tell Mr. Whitelaw that [he]

---

[39] PRO, CAB 164/1204, Folio 1K. Handwritten note to the Cabinet Office from the Ministry of Defence from May 1972. The reference to Mr. C could be Callaghan or Peter Carrington, the Secretary of Defence in the Heath government.

[40] PRO, CAB 164/1204, Folio 22. Letter to Sir Burke Trend from A.W. Peterson, 7 May 1973.

[41] PRO, CAB 164/1204, Folio 11. Note to Brian Norbury from Neil Cairncross, 26 March 1973.

[42] PRO, CAB 164/1204, Folio 17. Draft letter to Callaghan from Sir Burke Trend, 26 April 1973. A notation indicates the letter was not sent. The mention of Peel refers to Sir Robert Peel, the Home Secretary who established the Metropolitan Police in the early nineteenth century. Peel later became Prime Minister.

[43] Ibid.

was publishing a book about Northern Ireland and to give him some idea of its scope and nature". Callaghan responded to Trend by saying that he planned to talk to Whitelaw "about it more fully" and to "pay tribute" to him in the final chapter of the book.[44] Callaghan was good to his word at least on the point of homage. He referred to Whitelaw as someone "who from the start injected into his task new energy, imagination and considerable political flair".[45] Whether Callaghan went beyond the kind words, which immediately drew a comparison to Maudling, by letting Whitelaw know what he was actually up to is uncertain, but the first chapters of the book were sent off to the publisher within days of Trend's suggestion.[46]

Moreover, the documents show that at times Whitehall was less concerned with the content of the manuscript, given "strictly speaking, no breaches of the normal conventions",[47] than with the fact that Callaghan had had the audacity to write the book in the first place. The problem was rooted in a concern Trend had that memoirs from former ministers "usually [dealt] with events which [were] safely 'over and done with' ",[48] but Callaghan's book was not in that category. Howard Smith, who had been the last man to hold the post of UK government representative to Northern Ireland before the job was abolished with the advent of direct rule in 1972, joined the internal chorus of those in the Cabinet Office who felt "it was regrettable" that Callaghan was delving into this topic at all. Smith, who was later head of the counter-espionage agency MI5, added "that it used to be the convention that ministers... did not distinguish publicly between the views of officials and the views of ministers. This did not stop Lord George Brown; but there are one or two places in Mr. Callaghan's book where he, a *properer* man, might wish to think again."[49]

Anthony Howard, then editor of the *New Statesman*, says that when Callaghan signed the book contract with Collins "fairly shortly" after

[44] PRO, CAB 164/1204, Folio 18. Letter to Callaghan from Sir Burke Trend, 26 April 1973.

[45] Callaghan, *A House Divided*, p. 178.

[46] PRO, CAB 164/1204, Folio 19M. Letter to M.A. Griffiths from Brian Norbury, 2 May 1973.

[47] PRO, CAB 164/1204, Folio 14. Memo to C.J. Child from Brian Norbury, 5 April 1973.

[48] PRO, CAB 164/1204, Folio 17. Draft letter to Callaghan from Sir Burke Trend, 26 April 1973. A notation indicates the letter was not sent.

[49] PRO, CAB 164/1204, Folio 10. Memo to Brian Norbury from Howard Smith, 20 March 1973.

Labour was defeated in the 1970 general election: "Northern Ireland had been a success story as far as Callaghan was concerned. The problem was that when the book came out [in 1973], Northern Ireland was no longer a success story as far as anyone was concerned. We had abolished Stormont, there had been Bloody Sunday, Whitelaw, Maudling, it was a mess." Howard says Callaghan no doubt "was conscious of the fact that it was part of his record and [felt] it would do no harm to burnish and polish it a bit.... I don't think in fact it did any good because as I say by the time the book came out the situation was totally transformed."[50] The release of the book in September 1973 was also overshadowed by the announcement that same week that Prime Minister Heath would be making the first official visit to Ireland by a British head of government since the founding of the Republic.[51]

Nevertheless, Callaghan's first serious, lengthy writing project, while not entirely successful, was yet another attempt by him to use Northern Ireland to further his own political ends. That is evident for several reasons. First, the book was one more way, although a less helpful one, for Callaghan to maintain an indirect role, along with his official duties, in what had been his most successful accomplishment to date. As *The Sunday Times* Insight Team noted: "Callaghan defied history; [at that time] he was the only British politician ever to improve his reputation by dealing with Ireland."[52] He maintained an indirect role as well by seeing to it that Merlyn Rees eventually took over shadowing Northern Ireland. Rees, who later became Secretary of State for Northern Ireland and then succeeded Jenkins as Home Secretary shortly after Callaghan became Prime Minister, was so devoted to Callaghan that insiders at No. 10 Downing Street say he often hesitated to make major decisions on Ulster without first getting Callaghan's consent. Bernard Donoughue agrees: "Merlyn was Jim's man. I mean Merlyn would do what Jim told him."[53]

Secondly, the book was perfectly timed, at least from Callaghan's point of view, which might explain why he was so resistant to changes

---

[50] Interview with Anthony Howard, 12 March 2004.
[51] *Financial Times*, 4 September 1973, p. 1. That was also the week that workers at Labour Party headquarters won a pay package that reflected the spirit of the times. It included "the right to a free cup of coffee in the morning and a cup of tea in the afternoon – all backdated to May 1".
[52] *Northern Ireland: A Report on the Conflict* by the London *Sunday Times* Insight Team (New York, 1972), p. 148.
[53] Interview with Lord Donoughue, 9 July 2003.

suggested by the Cabinet Office that invariably would have delayed publication. In the British political system, the Prime Minister must call a general election within five years of taking office; rather than waiting to the last possible moment, most modern-day premiers set a date when their fortunes look bright, often in their penultimate year in office. Had Callaghan waited six months or a year any advantage the book, which was published only months before the February 1974 general election, gave him in furthering the notion that he was a kind of expert on Northern Ireland would have been lost. Callaghan characteristically played his cards close to his chest. Clare does not recall that Callaghan was eager to circulate chapters for comment beforehand: "It was just the two of us and Ruth [Sharpe] typing it up. No, really that's all there was. And again that tells you a lot about the book, doesn't it? The book wasn't about Northern Ireland, it was about Callaghan."[54]

Thirdly, the book allowed Callaghan once again to advance the argument, a misconception that persisted for years, that he had somehow got it right in comparison with the mayhem that erupted after he had left office. As Clare says, Callaghan could point to the book and say it is all in there.[55] Allen, who as permanent secretary worked for both Callaghan and Maudling, has repeatedly expressed the view that Callaghan had a handle on the problem and had he remained in office the Troubles might have been solved once and for all.[56] It is a "theory" that has been espoused time and again by Callaghan's surrogates, among them his parliamentary private secretary Roland Moyle[57] and his press secretary Tom McCaffrey.[58] But there are few detached observers of Northern Ireland who ascribe to that view; the journalist John Cole[59] on being interviewed, also discards that theory as unsustainable.[60]

---

[54] Interview with John Clare, 19 April 2004.
[55] Ibid.
[56] Interview with Lord Allen, 19 May 2003.
[57] Interview with Roland Moyle, 6 May 2004.
[58] Interview with Sir Tom McCaffrey, 3 July 2003.
[59] Interview with John Cole, 25 February 2004.
[60] Interview with Sir Brian Cubbon, 19 June 2003. Cubbon finds that hypothesis difficult to imagine as well. Cubbon concedes in those early days, "I don't think that we'd really read our history sufficiently closely to realise what the difference was between Republicanism and Nationalism. I once asked a schoolmaster down in Neury what the difference was, and he said, 'Well I'm a Nationalist – Gaelic football, Irish culture, Gaelic language' and he went on and on. I said, 'What's a Republican?' And he looked me straight in the eye and he said, 'It's very simple, a Republican is anti-British.' "

Finally, the book was an effort on Callaghan's part to enhance his image far beyond the shores of the United Kingdom. By publishing a book on this particular issue, with all its international ramifications, it allowed Callaghan to remind a small circle of influential international players just how significant a part he did play in the unfolding drama in Northern Ireland.[61] Until British troops were sent into Northern Ireland in 1969, Callaghan was best remembered in most foreign capitals for his failed Chancellorship two years earlier. Callaghan's book sold few copies, but, at least at one level, it did not need to be a bestseller as long as it showed up on the shelves of libraries at great universities. Its purpose was served by giving the former Home Secretary, who was sensitive about his lack of a university education, gravitas – at least in some quarters – and presented him as an expert in at least one significant area of "foreign" policy. This was important to Callaghan because in the shuffle that ensued after Jenkins left the post of deputy party leader in April 1972, Callaghan was within reach of his goal of becoming Foreign Secretary.[62]

Callaghan's book project was in a category of its own. The historian Kenneth Morgan notes that Callaghan was a traditionalist and as such was displeased by the diaries being kept of conversations in Cabinet by Crossman and Castle.[63] Yet Callaghan's book on Northern Ireland, while not revelatory on matters of Cabinet, was in the alarming pattern of ministerial memoirs that were becoming "more uninhibited".[64] Not only that, it was published a mere three years after Callaghan left office, appearing at a time when the Tory government was struggling to keep at least some control over the ever-expanding crisis.[65] By comparison the first diaries of Crossman, as revelatory as they were, were

---

[61] Martin Holmes, *The Labour Government, 1974–79: Political Aims and Economic Reality* (New York, 1985), p. 79. Although Callaghan was certainly an influential figure at one level, Holmes argues that before he became Prime Minister "his fame was limited outside the establishment and the labour movement."

[62] Interview with John Clare, 19 April 2004. Clare adds that, "In all the time I spent with him . . . . I detected absolutely no kind of sense of (the) history of this ghastly struggle between the British and the Irish, no kind of intellectual analysis."

[63] Interview with Lord Morgan, 30 March 2004.

[64] PRO, PREM 15/427. Memo on ministerial memoirs prepared for Prime Minister Heath by Sir Burke Trend, September 1971.

[65] That also contrasts with Callaghan's autobiography, which was not published until eight years after he was defeated as Prime Minister in 1979.

not made public until 1975, nearly ten years after they were written,[66] while Castle's diaries covering the period from 1964 to 1970 were not published until 1984.[67] Although Callaghan portrayed a statesman-like image on Northern Ireland, the facts indicate that he exploited officials and access to official information with one overwhelming goal in mind, namely to further his own political recovery.

Allen, moreover, possibly anticipating the strong criticism of Callaghan's project among his fellow civil servants, was uneasy about Callaghan's insistence in wanting to single him out in the book's preface. Allen discussed this concern with Trend, and a note for the record mentions not once but twice that Callaghan was "pressing" Allen to be cited as one of the people who had gone over the manuscript and that Allen did not know how to get around Callaghan's request.[68] The sense of urgency in those comments raise questions about whether Callaghan years earlier might have put undue pressure on Allen to act as his surrogate by supplying unsolicited material on the Northern Ireland crisis to *The Times*. Callaghan was not always the easiest person for civil servants to deal with. Both Allen and Brian Cubbon, who was Callaghan's private secretary and later served as permanent secretary at the Home Office, acknowledged as much in separate interviews.[69]

While both men are admirers of Callaghan, they both have been on the wrong end of Callaghan's occasional but volatile temper. In a telling example, Allen recalls that on one occasion he and Cubbon visited Callaghan in his suite at a Labour Party conference when Callaghan was in a "foul mood". In the midst of this, Allen remembers there was "a knock on the door and the waitress came in and wheeled a trolley with coffee and biscuits and things. And, of course, Jim was as nice, 'Oh hello Annie. How nice to see you. How is little Tommy' and all the rest of it. And away she went, and the bad temper came back again.... I don't know, it was partly contrived, but he could be very bad tempered. It wasn't always sunny Jim."[70]

---

[66] The Labour government tried to block publication of the first volume, which slightly delayed its appearance in bookstores.

[67] Castle's diaries for her later less-influential period in office (1974–76) were published in 1980, four years after she was sacked by Callaghan and a year after Callaghan was replaced as Prime Minister by Margaret Thatcher.

[68] PRO, CAB 164/1204, Folio 23. Note for the record, 8 May 1973.

[69] Interviews with Lord Allen, 19 May 2003, Sir Brian Cubbon, 19 June 2003.

[70] Interview with Lord Allen, 19 May 2003.

Regardless, Allen and Trend agreed among themselves that any such notation in the preface to Callaghan's book would be "inappropriate" no matter how "carefully worded" it might be.[71] They were both concerned that it would leave the reader with the impression that a senior civil servant was giving his imprimatur to Callaghan's work. It was awkward for Allen who had recently left his post at the Home Office where he had been working under Maudling, Callaghan's successor and someone whom Callaghan was sharply at odds with over the direction that the Tory government was taking in dealing with the worsening Troubles in Northern Ireland. Allen left it with Trend that "he would resist Mr. Callaghan's approaches".[72] However, Allen was unsuccessful. He was cited in the preface[73] along with Callaghan's friend Merlyn Rees – who was, of course, a Labour politician, not an impartial civil servant – as the two individuals "who read the manuscript and made many suggestions for improvement".

Morgan, Callaghan's biographer, believes that part of the reason that Callaghan wrote that book was that Callaghan felt that Maudling was somehow undermining Callaghan's great legacy in Northern Ireland: "Most people – including myself – think [Callaghan] handled it pretty well, and [there was] the feeling of course that it had not been [handled] very well afterward, which it most certainly hadn't." Morgan believes that Callaghan's role in Ulster greatly enhanced his political standing and "the book kind of reinforced that, but I don't think it made the most enormous stir really".[74] Apparently, it sold only a few thousand copies and was remaindered within a matter of months.[75]

Howard, the editor of the *New Statesman*, was astonished to learn, when it was brought to his attention, that a check of back issues indicated that his publication – which had reviewed over 250 books in the last six months of 1973, among them titles by Harold Macmillan, Michael Foot and Leo Abse – did not bother to even mention Callaghan's

---

[71] PRO, CAB 164/1204, Folio 23. Note for the record, 8 May 1973.

[72] Ibid.

[73] The usual disclaimer was added.

[74] Interview with Lord Morgan, 30 March 2004.

[75] Publishers do not disclose sales figures, but the general consensus among journalists and bookshop owners interviewed is that few copies were sold; Clare remembers it being remaindered after a few months.

book[76] and said he was surprised that Callaghan did not get after him about that.[77] But Callaghan was more determined that a review would appear on the pages of the *Guardian*, the newspaper that was playing such a vital role in his political rehabilitation. Correspondence between Alastair Hetherington, the *Guardian's* editor, and Cole shows Callaghan did call the newspaper's offices seeking just such a review in August 1973. Callaghan took the time to bring particular attention to the final chapter where he actually tried to stir the waters by making the case for a possible reunification of Ireland.[78] That suggests that he was far more spirited on the issue in opposition than he ever was in government before or after 1969. But the fact that Callaghan had felt it necessary to put in a bid for the *Guardian* to review the book is an indication of how the Troubles by 1973 were passing Callaghan by and how through the book he was trying to hold on to what had been his biggest political success.

Once again, the *Guardian* was more than generous in the coverage it provided Callaghan. The review of *A House Divided* dominated the entire top half of the opposite editorial page on 3 September 1973, the date of the book's publication.[79] The review was done by none other than Callaghan's friend Cole, the *Guardian's* expert on Northern Ireland. But the mood had changed; what had begun as a civil rights struggle in a distant province was now hitting home with the first signs of terrorism in England, and Cole's assessment was harsh. The review said Callaghan's "deficiency is that he does not listen well enough to what he does not

---

[76] Interview with Anthony Howard, 12 March 2004. But this was surprising as well because the previous editor of the *New Statesman* was Crossman. Crossman, who had grown to admire Callaghan and was close to Howard, took the editorship after the Labour government was defeated in 1970, but was dismissed in March 1972 ostensibly because of his too strong ties to Labour Party politics.

[77] Ibid. *New Statesman*, 21 September 1973, p. 1. The publication also ignored the book in an editorial on Northern Ireland that same month. It said that "for the presence of these troops to be vindicated, they must be seen to be contributing towards a lasting settlement." It added that "Labour's stance expresses ... the timidity of men only too happy, for once, that as they do not have power they cannot be charged with responsibility."

[78] (Manchester) *Guardian* Archive, C1/C1/3. Memo to John Cole from Hetherington, 3 August 1973.

[79] This is in comparison to a lengthy but much more modest review of the book on the Arts pages of *The Times*.

want to hear".[80] Cole did acknowledge that Callaghan "did a lot for Northern Ireland" in the early days of the Troubles and Northern Ireland "did much for Callaghan", but he said Callaghan is deluding himself if he thinks the IRA violence would have somehow never materialised if he had remained in charge. Cole said Callaghan was "a jollier-along, a man with the will to right a chronic wrong on civil rights", but at the same time Callaghan's book unfairly "heaps an appalling burden of guilt on his successor", Maudling.

As Cole aptly put it "there is no single set of villains". The review's headline, "Bargains Built on Shifting Sands", seemed to sum up a policy that had somehow lost its lustre. It appeared in large type under two large photographs – one a picture of Callaghan speaking, the other a photograph of a mother and her young children in tears at the funeral of a Catholic victim of the struggle. Callaghan's book, however, was certainly not ignored by the *Guardian*, which gave it by far the most extensive review of any newspaper.[81] Cole's criticism in that review of the former Home Secretary's constantly changing views on Northern Ireland – "everything is up for grabs"[82] – reflected less on Callaghan's initial decisions in 1969 and 1970 and more on troubling comments that Callaghan made in the book and in opposition.

Finally, there is one misconception tied to *A House Divided* that probably made many of Callaghan's colleagues take the book less seriously than they should have, namely the belief that Callaghan did not write the book himself. Unlike Jenkins or Denis Healey or Tony Crosland, Callaghan was not a natural writer and his colleagues in the Cabinet, as well as his fellow MPs knew that, but they were mistaken if they had assumed that Callaghan had not written it himself.[83] While it is true that John Clare was hired to be the ghost writer, Callaghan, a great orator in his own right, essentially spoke the book into a tape recorder and Clare simply straightened up his prose. Clare left Callaghan's comments the way Callaghan delivered them, and while they might have had little interest to the general public, since events essentially overtook the

---

[80] *Guardian*, 3 September 1973, p. 11. Robert Fisk made much the same point in his review of the book in *The Times* on the same day, saying "there are times when his lack of self-criticism becomes embarrassing ...."

[81] *Guardian*, 3 September 1973, p. 11.

[82] Ibid.

[83] Interview with John Clare, 19 April 2004.

story, the book was not given proper consideration by those who might have gained a great deal more knowledge of their adversary if they had studied it.

Brian Faulkner, the former Prime Minister of Northern Ireland, was one of the few politicians who evidently did read it closely.[84] In his memoirs, the Ulster Unionist leader is critical of what he referred to as Callaghan's "superficial circuses and messianic visits".[85] Faulkner took umbrage with Callaghan's portrayal in the book of the Cabinet meeting in Belfast that concluded Callaghan's August 1969 tour. Faulkner wrote there was nothing about the discussions "to justify the subsequent building up of the melodrama of a 'dramatic watershed' in Stormont/Westminster relations such as Callaghan later described in his book".[86] Faulkner, whom former Irish Prime Minister Liam Cosgrave describes as a "practical" man,[87] chided Callaghan's preoccupation with image, citing the reference in the book – one that Faulkner quotes word for word – to Callaghan's determination to stage "a cocked hat affair" upon his arrival in Ulster in the aftermath of the troop deployment.[88]

But Callaghan's colleagues and adversaries in that Labour government make no reference to *A House Divided* in their memoirs and historians of the early period of the Troubles rarely analyse it. William Rodgers, who at one point had been considered for the post of Northern Ireland secretary and later served in Callaghan's Cabinet, was astounded to learn that Callaghan had written a book on the subject: "Good God, how extraordinary!"[89] It is not indexed in the memoirs of Wilson, Jenkins,[90] Castle,[91] or Healey even though it is quite revealing of

---

[84] PRO, CAB 164/1204. Memo to T.C. Platt from G.W. Roberts, 3 September 1973. This was in addition to Prime Minister Heath, who in early September 1973 asked the Northern Ireland Office if there was any truth to Callaghan's assessment that the Tory government's failures in their first month in office led to the increasing Troubles. The Northern Ireland Office's conclusion was that "the IRA was already beginning to show its hand."
[85] Brian Faulkner, *Memoirs of a Statesman* (London, 1978), pp. 90–91.
[86] Ibid., p. 68.
[87] Interview with Liam Cosgrave, 1 October 2004.
[88] Faulkner, *Memoirs*, p. 67.
[89] Interview with Lord Rodgers, 23 March 2004.
[90] Interview with Lady Jenkins, 21 April 2004. She was unaware of the book and when asked if her husband had ever discussed it with her, she responded, "Absolutely not."
[91] Barbara Castle, *Fighting All the Way* (London, 1993), p. 393. Castle's memoirs do not even mention the Troubles in Northern Ireland. The only reference to Ireland in the entire book is of fond memories of a holiday there in 1967.

Callaghan's duplicitous nature. In fact, Healey did not remember at first that Callaghan had written such a book when a question was posed to him about it. Nor does the former Defence Secretary have a copy of the book in his vast home library, even though Healey's name appears nine times in the index and Healey, along with Callaghan, was one of the major players in Northern Ireland during the period the book covers, 1969 and early 1970.[92]

Shortly after *A House Divided* was released in September 1973, the *Irish News*, a Belfast daily with Nationalist sympathies, editorialised that Callaghan had used the book to "set himself up as an authority on the North". The newspaper was critical of the fact that despite his attention to the issue, and Wilson's "several schemes for settling the 'Irish Question'", there was not a single resolution on Northern Ireland before the annual Labour Party conference that October. It asked rhetorically, "What [was] the reason for this quite extraordinary omission...?"[93] No doubt, there were many but at least two reasons stand out: one being that with the escalating Troubles, along with the advent of direct rule and the opening of talks with Dublin, the party leadership had felt it would be better to remain safely on the sidelines; the other was that there was another parallel issue that Callaghan had found far easier to manipulate to his political advantage, namely the controversy over Britain's recent entry into the EEC. As the book project showed, Ulster became an increasingly difficult crisis for Callaghan to exploit in opposition. Events were moving too fast, the nature of the Troubles had changed and Wilson, as party leader, was more determined than ever to play a bigger part in resolving the crisis. Therefore, as the debate over EEC membership intensified, Callaghan latched onto that problem, which would gradually replace Northern Ireland as the issue that would complete his political recovery.

The Debate over Europe

The EEC debate was a political sleight of hand and like Northern Ireland had all the hallmarks of an issue ideally suited to someone of Callaghan's temperament. Although Callaghan would emerge in the spring of 1971 as a critic of Europe, he had backed Wilson in the then Prime Minister's spirited bid to join the EEC in 1967. In fact, in July 1966,

---

[92] Interview with Lord Healey, 22 March 2004.
[93] *Irish News & Belfast Morning News*, 22 September 1973, lead editorial.

Wilson told the *Guardian's* Hetherington that Callaghan, who was then Chancellor, "wanted passionately to get into Europe [and in so doing] he had been injudicious in his dealings with the French", in particular Premier Georges Pompidou and Foreign Minister Maurice Couve de Murville. Wilson said Callaghan "had listened to them too much" but had "learned from the experience" after Pompidou and Couve de Murville "had used his words against Britain immediately afterwards".[94] Later that year, Callaghan, although still supportive of the bid, was more tepid in his enthusiasm,[95] possibly because it had become apparent to him that Britain would have to devalue the pound if it were to join. In the end, the effort came to nought when President Charles de Gaulle, in May 1967, effectively vetoed Britain's application after having suggested that its economic affairs were not yet in order. De Gaulle, who was sceptical of the depth of Britain's commitment to Europe and uncomfortable with its special relationship with the United States, had in 1963 stood in the way of an earlier British bid for membership under the Conservative government of Macmillan for some of the same reasons.

After de Gaulle left public life in 1969, the British bid was once again pursued[96] – most intently on 12 February 1971, when the Heath government made a major effort to push the latest round of negotiations forward. But it was Crossman, a Labour MP and then editor of the *New Statesman*, who initially emerged as the chief critic of the move within the Labour Party, not Callaghan. Crossman made a blistering attack on the EEC in a signed editorial in the *New Statesman*, which also suggested that Wilson was "once again 'leaving his options open' ".[97] Just prior to a major speech that same day that was to be Wilson's response to Heath's initiative on the talks – which were being conducted by a negotiating team that had been "brought back to full strength" under the previous Labour government[98] – rumours circulated that, indeed, Wilson might equivocate on his earlier long-standing support for EEC membership.

The speculation so troubled George Brown, his former Foreign Secretary, that Brown met with Wilson before he was to deliver that speech

---

[94] BLPES, Hetherington 12. Notes from a meeting with the Prime Minister from 8 August 1966.

[95] Crossman, *Diaries*, Vol. II, p. 116.

[96] The EEC agreed to reopen the negotiations in December 1969, and talks got underway the following year.

[97] *New Statesman*, 12 February 1971, p. 1.

[98] NAI, DFA 2003/1/323. Internal report by Kevin Rush of the Irish Embassy in London, 1 May 1970.

to get his assurances that that was not the case.[99] Wilson repeatedly told Brown, with Joe Haines present, that he would "stand by the statement [they] agreed to make at [the 1970 Labour Party conference in] Blackpool and on our tour round Europe", in early 1967 when both men were promoting British membership. But Wilson added a troubling comment: "Of course, it is not quite like we thought it was." Brown then asked Haines to show him the part of the speech that confirmed that Wilson would remain a supporter of the Common Market, but Wilson interjected that Haines had not seen those comments. Brown, who had been, along with Wilson, the chief promoter of the Labour government's bid to restart negotiations in 1966, recalled that "Haines didn't know what to say". Brown angrily warned Wilson that if he switched sides, "I will anchor you to what you said" when Labour was in office.[100]

In the end, Wilson, possibly in deference to Brown's still considerable influence in the party, did not deviate greatly from his earlier pro-EEC stance and his remarks in that speech, while cautious, still reflected a willingness to take a bipartisan position. On the other hand, Callaghan in the early months of 1971 had not taken a strong policy position on the issue, one way or the other.[101] But that changed on 25 May, just one day after the *Guardian* in its lead editorial had complained that "no one seems capable of initiating" what it called the "Great Debate" on Europe.[102] As evidence of how Callaghan had remained in the shadows up until that point, there was no mention in the *Guardian*'s editorial of Callaghan, a man whom the *Guardian* in its news pages would refer to a day later as "probably the most significant alternative leader of the Labour Party to Mr. Wilson".[103] Instead, the *Guardian* editorial in its discussion of the issue had cited everyone but Callaghan – from Wilson to Healey to Jack Jones and even Douglas Jay and Jeremy Thorpe, the leader of the Liberal Party.[104]

---

[99] Oxford, Brown 5102, Folios 152 and 153. Internal memorandum dated 12 February 1971.
[100] Ibid.
[101] *Daily Mail*, 18 February 1971, p. 1. Callaghan had actually first raised questions about the Heath initiative earlier, but the *Daily Mail* felt it was less a challenge to Wilson than a "sign that the Labour Party is now rapidly scrambling back on to the fence in an effort to snatch popularity".
[102] *Guardian*, 25 May 1971, p. 10.
[103] *Guardian*, 26 May 1971, p. 1.
[104] *Guardian*, 25 May 1971, p. 10. However, it was widely known that Callaghan was planning a major speech for the following day.

Callaghan launched his attack at a by-election meeting in Southampton while Wilson was far from London, attending the Socialist International Conference in Helsinki. As the *Daily Mail*'s political editor Walter Terry noted "almost everything was thrown in – Chaucer, Shakespeare, Napoleon and the prospect of the innocent British being tricked".[105] But Callaghan's address on 25 May was not simply a case of his stating his position on Europe. Instead, it had all the hallmarks of yet another move on Callaghan's part to carefully reposition himself within the party.[106] That said, it must be stressed that given the complexity of politics the move more than likely was not part of any grand scheme. Nevertheless, it was strangely reminiscent of the strategy that he had taken on *In Place of Strife* for several reasons.

First, although Callaghan had had ample opportunity over the previous three months to raise the point that "the people of Britain are entitled to know where *we* stand"[107] on the Common Market, he waited until Wilson had left the country to do so. As the *Daily Mail* reported, it was a case of Callaghan "barging in fast while Mr. Wilson was away".[108] Also, Callaghan delivered his challenge on the very day that Wilson was set to give his own response to critical talks between Heath and Pompidou that were thought to have ironed out many of the differences between the two sides. It was similar to what Callaghan had done two years earlier, when he had thrown the Labour government into disarray with his opposition to *In Place of Strife* on the eve of Wilson's departure for Nigeria. Callaghan had struck out on his own and embraced a populist approach that gave only superficial attention to legitimate questions over the Common Agricultural Policy and monetary union and focused instead on stirring up old hostilities between the English and the French. Callaghan gravely warned of "the French dominated EEC" that would threaten "a complete rupture with our identity".[109]

Secondly, Callaghan's speech was aimed at an important segment of Wilson's support, namely the left-wing of the Labour Party, which was

---

[105] *Daily Mail*, 26 May 1971, p. 1.

[106] Peter Kellner and Christopher Hitchens, *Callaghan: The Road to Number 10* (London, 1976), p. 116. The authors believed that Callaghan "achieved the calculated effect of defining both the tone and the parameters of the debate to come".

[107] Text of Callaghan's speech, *Guardian*, 26 May 1971, p. 6.

[108] *Daily Mail*, 26 May 1971, p. 1.

[109] Ibid.

strongly opposed to British entry. Callaghan cleverly repositioned himself as the centre-right figure most sympathetic to the left on this single issue in much the same way that he had done with the anti-war protests in Grosvenor Square and in the fight over *In Place of Strife*. He also took advantage of the fact that the debate over Europe looked likely to bring together the old left–right alliance within the trade union movement that had defeated the Industrial Relations Bill.[110] Callaghan was quick to join the chorus of objections, as he had done two years earlier, to any fast-track approach on the measure. He warned the Tories against trying to push the bill through "on a hot afternoon early in August", and in remarks reminiscent of those made at the joint NEC-Cabinet meeting in May 1969 demanded that there be plenty of time for debate not only in Parliament but before the party conferences in the autumn.[111]

Thirdly, Callaghan's manoeuvre was reminiscent of his earlier attack on trade union reform in that he had used the issue not only to delineate himself from Wilson, but from his other chief adversary Jenkins, who unlike Castle was still in contention to succeed Wilson and in that sense was still standing in Callaghan's way. Jenkins, who would later become President of the European Commission, was one of the strongest supporters of a united Europe. His position on the EEC was deeply embedded in principle, as had been the case for his support for an early short bill on industrial relations. Callaghan's remarks about how in the face of French dominance of the EEC "the language of Chaucer, Shakespeare and Milton must in [the] future be regarded as an American import from which we must protect ourselves"[112] had to be directed as much at Jenkins's Continental sophistication as they were at the EEC or Wilson.

Finally, as had been the case in the great battle over industrial relations, Callaghan had a stealth ally in the *Guardian*. The predicament Wilson found himself in was illustrated by a political cartoon by Les Gibbard that accompanied the *Guardian*'s extensive page-one coverage of the two men's speeches the following morning. It showed a pipe-smoking Wilson sitting on the fence while two gladiators, Callaghan

---

[110] *Guardian*, 27 May 1971, p. 13. But Miscellany noted that the left "is still hedging its bets" on Callaghan, saying that Hugh Scanlon, the leader of the Amalgamated Union of Engineering Workers, planned to put up a candidate to challenge Callaghan for party treasurer.

[111] Text of Callaghan's speech, *Guardian*, 26 May 1971, p. 6.

[112] Ibid.

and Jenkins, charged towards him in opposite directions. The Callaghan story was correctly given the greater prominence by being featured above the fold, whereas the coverage of Wilson's speech, which suggested that Heath and Pompidou had struck "a private nuclear deal", was at the bottom of the page. That story, however, carried an unflattering headline: "Mr. Wilson Decides to Play the Nuclear Card."[113] The *Guardian*'s coverage of Wilson's "nuclear" remarks, which were elaborated upon in a follow-up story the next day, contrasted with that of the *Telegraph*, the *Financial Times*, the *Daily Mail*, the *Daily Express* and the *Evening Standard*, none of which gave great weight to those comments or for that matter any other aspects of the Helsinki address. As the *Financial Times* said "the really significant speech was Mr. Callaghan's".[114]

Regardless, the *Guardian*, whose pro-Market editorials had been among the most comprehensive of any national newspaper, failed to critique Callaghan's speech in its editorial columns even though the address had been referred to in its news coverage as a "political watershed for the party".[115] The omission is all the more conspicuous given the lengthy lead editorial that appeared the following morning in *The Times*, which warned that the speech might signal a strategy that would "destroy the unity of the Labour Party and leave a legacy of bitterness comparable to that of the original Bevanite split".[116] Even after several other newspapers, including the *Financial Times*, the *Daily Express* and the *Evening Standard*, added their editorial comments[117] on Callaghan's remarks – in some cases at length – the *Guardian* remained silent. Over the next few days, it gave its opinion of the prices and incomes policy, housing and homelessness and even ran a long excerpt in its editorial columns from Wilson's forthcoming memoirs.[118] But not a word appeared about Callaghan's landmark address, even though the

---

[113] *Guardian*, 26 May 1971, p. 1.

[114] *Financial Times*, 26 May 1971, p. 1.

[115] *Guardian*, 26 May 1971, p. 1.

[116] *The Times*, 27 May 1971, p. 17.

[117] David Owen, *Time to Declare* (London, 1991), p. 176. Owen, whom Callaghan as Prime Minister elevated to the post of Foreign Secretary, wrote that "the impact of the speech on Harold Wilson and its effect within the Labour Party was tremendous."

[118] The *Guardian* even wrote two editorials on EEC-related matters in the week after Callaghan's address, one on the dispute over fishing rights, on 28 May 1971, and the other on sugar, on 2 June 1971.

Guardian had been the newspaper that had just called for someone to reinvigorate the EEC debate.[119] No doubt the *Guardian*, given its strong support for the EEC application,[120] would have had to have been sharply critical of Callaghan's posturing if it had ventured an opinion. The fact that it did not was particularly helpful to him, and suggests there was a conscious decision on the *Guardian*'s part not to attack Callaghan, whom Hetherington was indebted to for having "materially helped to secure the paper's survival".[121] The *Guardian* had certainly not been silent when Crossman delivered his broadside against the EEC the previous February. It had called Crossman's approach "disingenuous" and said that what he wanted was to "push Labour into stating conditions that [would] make British entry totally impossible".[122] But Callaghan, who pushed Wilson into a difficult corner and triggered a whole chain of events with his May 1971 remarks, delivering what Peter Jay concedes was the "Eurosceptics speech of the decade",[123] escaped unscathed. In addition, despite the *Guardian*'s pro-European stance, its chief editorial writer Mark Arnold-Forster, whether on his own or with Hetherington's knowledge, moonlighted for Callaghan. Sometime that year, he wrote a speech for the former Chancellor to deliver in Newcastle that was critical of Britain joining the EEC, saying "we all know, more or less, how the capitalist system works in Britain, and it's not the way it works in Europe... "[124]

What happened two months later makes it clear just how big an impact Callaghan did have on the turn of events. On 17 July 1971, Wilson delivered his most critical statement yet on Europe at a special Labour Party conference. The Irish government, which was trying to secure its own membership of the Common Market at the same time and feared that Britain might pose obstacles to its entry,[125] had monitored

---

[119] *Guardian*, 29 May 1971, p. 10. The only mention of Callaghan in its editorials over several days was an innocuous comment about how he had "judiciously" noted that the nation's economic troubles had worsened under the Tories.

[120] David Butler and Uwe Kitzinger, *The 1975 Referendum* (London, 1996), p. 230. Indeed when it came to the referendum a few years later, the authors say "the fullest and most imaginative coverage was the *Guardian*'s."

[121] BLPES, Hetherington 14/6. Letter to Callaghan from Hetherington, 10 April 1968.

[122] *Guardian*, 12 February 1971, p. 10.

[123] Interview with Peter Jay, 11 December 2003.

[124] Oxford, Callaghan 42. Draft of speech (undated, but clearly from 1972).

[125] When Ireland put the matter to a referendum in May 1972 more than 83 per cent favoured joining.

the emerging internal party debate. A senior Irish diplomat, who was among the 1000 delegates who attended the conference at Central Hall in Westminster, noted an important "shift in emphasis" in Wilson's approach to the EEC. He said that while Wilson's attack on the terms being discussed by the Heath government was expected,[126] "more significant was the fact that he moved on from this criticism to a more general attack on the EEC itself".[127] That speech did not go unnoticed on the editorial page of the *Guardian* the following Monday. The headline on its lead editorial minced no words; it simply read, "Mr. Wilson Deserts Europe". The editorial was followed up a few days later with another editorial with an equally blunt headline that asked, in a reference to the failed 1967 bid, "Why Ever Did He Apply?"[128]

But the report by the Irish diplomat at the special Labour Party conference also noted that Callaghan, speaking for the National Executive, had resisted the call for a "hastily prepared resolution" opposing British entry and instead urged the party to come to a position "after due deliberation and adequate analysis".[129] Now that Callaghan had exacerbated the situation and pushed Wilson further into the anti-EEC column – a position that would in the weeks and months ahead make the breach between Wilson and his deputy leader Jenkins nearly unbridgeable – he shifted himself back towards the centre. He was the voice of moderation within the party and was determined not to let the anti-Marketeers rule the day. Callaghan's move to delay a vote amid the demand for an "anti-EEC vote there and then" was presented to the conference as simply a procedural matter. But Callaghan, a few weeks earlier, had actually asked Jones and Hugh Scanlon to intercede with their supporters to head off a definitive vote by the anti-Marketeers. Callaghan, citing "our credibility in the country" and "the need to maximise party unity", had begun to work behind the scenes to restore calm and keep the issue in flux until the Labour Party conference in the autumn. He told Jones and Scanlon that he had "reason to believe that Harold Wilson agrees

---

[126] Alan Sked and Chris Cook, *Post-War Britain, A Political History* (Middlesex, 1984), p. 264. On 9 July 1971, Wilson established specific criteria upon which the Labour Party would back the Heath initiative, dealing with everything from sugar quotas to the balance of payments.

[127] NAI, DFA 2001/23/880. Report to the Irish ambassador in London from P. Cradock, 20 July 1971.

[128] *Guardian*, 19 July 1971, p. 10; 22 July 1971, p. 10.

[129] NAI, DFA 2001/23/880. Report to the Irish ambassador in London from P. Cradock, 20 July 1971.

with [that idea] and accepts it".[130] That would seem to be indicative of an improvement in the relationship between the two men, now that Jenkins had been marginalised.

Callaghan's restraint in dealing with Wilson was evident, as well, when he uncharacteristically came to Wilson's defence a few days later after Jenkins had attacked Wilson's shifting position on the EEC before a meeting of the Parliamentary Labour Party.[131] The *Guardian* columnist Peter Jenkins wrote that Jenkins, as the deputy leader of the Labour Party, "had been given no fore notice on Saturday that Mr. Wilson intended to mount a frontal attack on the terms of Common Market entry and repudiate the Labour government's and his own commitment to Europe". On the other hand, the columnist added that Wilson had been "given no warning that he would be devastatingly refuted in the presence of the whole party on Monday night". The columnist concluded that it might be "one of those moments in politics when something quite suddenly happens to change things".[132] Something had happened but, as is so often the case, so much of the attention had shifted to the widening gulf between Wilson and Roy Jenkins that Callaghan's role in promulgating the divide – and in the process moving closer to Wilson – had gone unnoticed.

After Roy Jenkins's speech, a conciliatory Callaghan, while refraining from taking on Jenkins directly, urged "support and understanding" for of all people, Wilson. Callaghan said that the wait-and-see attitude that Wilson was endorsing on Europe was a sure way for a politician to make himself unpopular with the press. He said that Wilson was "voicing the disquiet of millions of people in this country who have not yet spoken and who are deeply concerned about the Common Market gamble".[133] Callaghan's words of praise for the opposition leader demonstrated a warming of the relationship between the two men. But the shifting positions of Wilson and others in the party leadership so frustrated Prime Minister Heath that at one point he had actually commissioned an

---

[130] Oxford, Callaghan 42. Letter to Jack Jones from Callaghan, 29 June 1971.

[131] Bernard Donoughue, "Harold Wilson: the Life and Legacy of a Labour Prime Minister", *Labour History: The Journal of the Labour History Group* (Spring, 2004), p. 13. Donoughue believed that during this period Wilson "clung on to the leadership, mainly because the supporters of Callaghan and Jenkins each reluctantly preferred to stay with the apparently doomed incumbent rather than to risk precipitating the accession of the other".

[132] *Guardian*, 21 July 1971, p. 11.

[133] *Guardian*, 24 July 1971, p. 18.

internal government report "of all the different postures taken up by the opposition since the conclusion of the European negotiations". He was particularly annoyed with those "who are repeatedly changing their minds, such as Denis Healey". Heath told his advisers that "it may never be necessary to use this but I would like to have it handy at the earliest possible moment".[134]

Wilson and Callaghan eventually teamed up to tackle the problem, which like the issue of trade union reform two years earlier, threatened to seriously divide the Labour Party. In early October 1971, the Labour Party conference formally backed the idea of offering the nation, if the Labour Party was returned to power, a renegotiation of the terms. Three weeks later, Parliament, with the support of Roy Jenkins and a third of Labour MPs, enacted legislation by a majority of 112 votes that would begin the long legislative process of bringing Britain into the Common Market on 1 January 1973. Callaghan had forced Wilson to retreat from Europe,[135] the very thing that Brown had tried to prevent, and by so doing had put Jenkins into an impossible position in the spring of 1972 as bill after bill dealing with all facets of the EEC bid proceeded to work their way through Parliament.[136]

Jenkins was not close to Hetherington,[137] nor would Jenkins have been aware of the close relationship that Callaghan had enjoyed with the editor of the *Guardian*. Nevertheless, Jenkins had a surprisingly frank discussion with Hetherington on 9 March 1972, which might have been rooted in the fact that the two men were both strong supporters of Britain joining the EEC. At a private meeting in the House of Commons, Jenkins acknowledged his frustration with Wilson, who "was allowing

---

[134] PRO, PREM 15/511. Minute from the Prime Minister to Donald Maitland, Michael Wolff, Peter Moon and Douglas Hurd. Memo is undated, but it appears to be from August 1971 given the other documents in the file and handwritten notations on the document.

[135] NAI, DFA 2003/17/391. Memo on Wilson's visit with Ireland's Prime Minister, 18 November 1971. Wilson's view on the EEC had shifted so much by mid-November 1971 that he had referred to the EEC as "that capitalist club" in a meeting with Jack Lynch. Wilson also "demurred from the notion that mutual entry into the European Communities would solve anything" in regards to the Irish Troubles.

[136] Sked and Cook, *Post-War Britain*, p. 265. There were 104 separate votes on legislation involving the EEC application.

[137] Interview with Lady Jenkins, 21 April 2004. Jennifer Jenkins says there was no special relationship between her husband and Hetherington. He "was never an intimate friend. He used to see him from time to time. But I wouldn't have said he was close to him."

himself to be pushed further and further away from a consistent stand" on Europe. More importantly, he sought out Hetherington's advice on a matter that would have a profound impact not only on his own career but on the future leadership of the Labour Party, namely whether or not he should resign as the party's deputy leader. Hetherington acknowledged that Jenkins faced "an interminable dilemma" and said that he could see no way that Jenkins could remain true to his principles in the current circumstances.[138]

Hetherington told Jenkins that when it came to Europe you could vote against your conscience "once to keep yourself straight with the party and to compensate for the resentment stirred up by the October vote [in which he had supported the bill in Parliament that would begin the process of taking Britain into the EEC]. You couldn't do it a second time."[139] Although Jenkins says he was still undecided about resignation as late as 28 March 1972,[140] Hetherington's notes indicate that Jenkins initially had agreed with Hetherington's assessment, more than two weeks earlier, that there was no other way for him to get out from under the difficulty that he had found himself in but to resign.[141] On 13 March, only a few days after their meeting, the *Guardian* published an editorial saying Jenkins's "position has been damaged by the European controversy".[142] But the more radical view that Hetherington expressed to Jenkins privately was not put forward in its editorial columns, suggesting that Hetherington was more concerned with quietly shaping the future direction of the Labour Party's leadership than fostering a debate on the issue. In addition, it would have been difficult for the *Guardian* to publicly call for Jenkins's resignation after it had suggested no such course of action when Callaghan repeatedly defied the leadership over *In Place of Strife*.

Over the next few weeks, Jenkins pondered his position and felt that he had no choice but to resign after the shadow Cabinet, in the wake of a French plan to put the expansion of the EEC to a national referendum, reversed its earlier position and backed a rebel-Tory initiative calling for the question of EEC membership to be placed before the

---

[138] BLPES, Hetherington 19/22. Notes from a discussion between Hetherington and Jenkins, 9 March 1972.

[139] Ibid.

[140] Roy Jenkins, *A Life at the Center* (New York, 1991), pp. 321–328.

[141] BLPES, Hetherington 19/22. Notes from a discussion between Hetherington and Jenkins, 9 March 1972.

[142] *Guardian*, 13 March 1972, p. 10.

voters.[143] The *Guardian* said, "it was not a good issue on which to resign" but said "resignations of principle, if based on a sound assessment of events, almost always pay in the end".[144] Jennifer Jenkins says, however, that although her husband "continued to try to re-establish himself, it was not actually possible after that".[145] Within days of Jenkins's departure from the Labour opposition's front bench, the shadow Cabinet was reshuffled and Callaghan emerged as shadow Foreign Secretary. He was now one step closer to the prize that he had so long craved, the very position that Jenkins had been promised by Wilson if Labour had won in 1970.[146]

Conclusion

When the long process of Callaghan's political recovery began, after he was forced to resign from the Treasury, three obstacles in particular stood in the way of his recovery: the ascendancy of Castle, the considerable strength of Jenkins within the Labour Party, and the lack of a strong issue on which to rebuild his reputation. With Jenkins's resignation on 10 April 1972, the second of the three obstacles was removed, and the final obstacle, the lack of a compelling issue – which had been made more arduous by Wilson's expanded interest in Irish affairs – became easier for Callaghan to overcome. Although Jenkins would return to the shadow Cabinet and re-emerge as Home Secretary in the first Labour government of 1974, he would never again be viewed as seriously as an alternative to Wilson for the party's leadership. As had been the case at the time of *In Place of Strife*, Jenkins's political ambition was restrained by a matter of principle.[147] In Callaghan's case, there were no such inhibitions. His position on Europe was not rooted in principle but rather was part of a calculated strategy to use the issue to his political advantage. That was evident for several reasons.

---

[143] There were fears that by allowing a referendum on the EEC it would open the way for other contentious issues, such as capital punishment, being put to the voters. In actuality, the referendum that eventually did take place in May 1975 was the only national referendum in Britain's history.

[144] *Guardian*, 11 April 1972, p. 12.

[145] Interview with Lady Jenkins, 21 April 2004.

[146] BLPES, Crosland M3/234. Entry in Susan Crosland's diary from 3 April 1970. Crosland told his wife that Jenkins told him that he had been "virtually promised" the job by Wilson if Labour was returned to power in June 1970.

[147] Gallup Public Opinion Polls, April 1972. In a poll, 57 per cent of those surveyed said they thought that Jenkins had done the "right" thing by resigning.

First, he left just enough room for manoeuvre in that May speech so as to be able to move comfortably back into the centre of the debate once he had accomplished his longer-term objective, which was to lay the groundwork for a showdown between Wilson and Jenkins. The malleability of his position is apparent from looking at the coverage of that speech by two of the most skilful political correspondents in Fleet Street, Ian Aitken of the *Guardian* and John Bourne of the *Financial Times*. The two reporters often shared information "for instance, Bourne passing on material from his excellent Conservative sources to Aitken and Aitken reciprocating on the Labour side",[148] but that did not prevent them from drawing different conclusions about where Callaghan had placed himself in the great debate over Europe. On the same day, Aitken wrote that Callaghan had "ostensibly climbed down on the anti-Common Market side",[149] while Bourne said Callaghan "still technically sat on the fence...a well padded one which he seems to enjoy occupying".[150]

Secondly, Callaghan, unlike Jenkins, had no disciples on the issue, which would give credence to the argument that he never cared passionately about the EEC.[151] Rather, the EEC was an issue, like Northern Ireland, that Callaghan knew he could manipulate for his own political purposes. Although Peter Jay is correct in saying that "alliances which had been held together for convenience in relation to one controversy ceased to apply in relation to another",[152] few of those who had been closely identified with Callaghan on other major concerns followed his lead on Europe.[153] For example, although Douglas Houghton and Callaghan had grown closer than ever over *In Place of Strife*, Houghton was solidly in the pro-EEC camp right from the start and remained there. Within the Cabinet, Callaghan and Crosland often had been

---

[148] NAI, TAOIS/2004/21/470. Briefing paper ahead of a luncheon for British parliamentary correspondents given by Irish Prime Minister Liam Cosgrave, September 1973.

[149] *Guardian*, 26 May 1971, p. 1.

[150] *Financial Times*, 26 May 1971, p. 1.

[151] Gallup Public Opinion Polls, October 1971. The public was not entirely clear on Callaghan's position. Of those surveyed, 23 per cent thought he was in favour of joining on the current terms, 36 per cent thought he was against and 41 per cent did not know his view.

[152] Interview with Peter Jay, 11 December 2003.

[153] BLPES, Dalton I/52, Folio 7. Dalton wrote in his diary in July 1960 that Callaghan has "promise and poise. But too obviously a trimmer. And doesn't seem to have any deep convictions."

philosophically close, but on Europe Crosland was apathetic, arguing that it just was not that important of an issue.[154]

Thirdly, once again, Callaghan's speech was impeccably timed to tap into public uncertainty over a major policy decision; as had been the case with the publication date of his book, he had an uncanny ability to seize the moment. In early 1971, less than a quarter of the British electorate agreed with the Heath government's plans to join the EEC.[155] In addition, Europe had begun to overtake Northern Ireland as the issue of most importance to voters after the usual economic concerns, such as joblessness and rising consumer prices.[156] That would change when the Irish Troubles intensified over the summer, but it was clear that both Northern Ireland and the EEC were issues that increasingly concerned a significant part of the electorate. Callaghan capitalised on that fact and carved out a place for himself in the acrimonious debate over Europe while he had kept his hand in Northern Ireland as much as he could.[157]

Finally, Callaghan's thrusting himself into the European debate was prompted by his need to latch on to another issue when his efforts to cement his reputation on Northern Ireland fell short. Callaghan's position was complicated by the fact that Wilson had made inroads in the debate on Northern Ireland while Callaghan's plan to broaden ties between the British Labour Party and the Northern Ireland Labour Party had faced obstacles that at times were difficult to overcome. For example, in March 1971, Callaghan made a walking tour through some of Belfast's "worst riot-scarred areas"[158] and, along with Nicholas, met with shop stewards and party officials to try to "breathe new life"[159] into the NILP. But he did it on the day that the NILP had accepted a ministerial post in the Faulkner government and in so doing

---

[154] Roy Jenkins, *A Life at the Center* (New York, 1991), p. 296.

[155] NOP Bulletin, March 1972. In March 1971 only 22 per cent of those polled favoured entry into the EEC. A year later that figure jumped to 40 per cent.

[156] Callaghan would never have wanted to take a lead in the debate on the economy, given his less-than-successful stint at the Treasury.

[157] NOP Bulletin, February 1972. In September 1971, 13 per cent of those surveyed thought Ulster was the "single most important problem" facing Great Britain, up from less than 3 per cent in June. In the case of the EEC, the figure was also 13 per cent, but up from 11 per cent. Therefore the two issues Callaghan embraced were the ones that over a quarter of those surveyed thought most pressing.

[158] *Irish News & Belfast Morning News*, 26 March 1971, p. 1.

[159] *The Sunday Times*, 28 March 1971, p. 4.

alienated themselves from the Catholics. The astounding thing was that Callaghan continued to pursue that strategy long after it was clear that it was unworkable. Then in November 1971, Callaghan was part of the Labour Party delegation that visited Belfast and upon completion of talks with officials from the SDLP and NILP, voiced support for a strong Stormont, arguing that the Republic of Ireland would play only a "minor role" in any future settlement.[160]

Less than a week later, however, Wilson made his own trip to Belfast with a follow-up visit to Dublin, where he met with Irish Prime Minister Jack Lynch.[161] Wilson's eagerness for an all-party conference was seen by the Irish as rooted in his desire to secure "a place for himself" at the negotiating table, but it was deeper than that. It was one more indication that he had no intention of ceding any more ground to Callaghan on the issue.[162] Many of the points that Callaghan had put forward in Belfast earlier that month would be negated when Wilson delivered his own major address on Northern Ireland not long after his return from Dublin.[163] In that speech, one the *Guardian* called "brilliantly" executed,[164] Wilson became the first major political figure in Britain to put forth a specific plan to unite Ireland. In a complete reversal of what Callaghan had said about the Republic of Ireland only days earlier, Wilson called for the parliaments of Britain, Northern Ireland and the Republic of Ireland to draw up a new constitution to put the unification plan into effect. It had gone far beyond Callaghan's idea of "a limited programme [of change] over two years",[165] but what had most annoyed the shadow Home Secretary was that Wilson had not even bothered to consult him.[166]

---

[160] *Guardian*, 12 November 1971, p. 1.

[161] NAI, DFA 2003/17/391. Briefing prepared in advance of Wilson's visit with the Irish Prime Minister, 16 November 1971. Irish officials felt that much of the "do nothing" attitude of the Tory government on Northern Ireland was most likely the result of Heath not wanting to further "antagonise" the right wing of his party amid its displeasure with Britain's EEC bid.

[162] NAI, DFA 2003/17/391. Internal memo detailing dinner given for Wilson by the Irish Prime Minister at Iveagh House, Dublin, 18 November 1971.

[163] *Cork Examiner*, 20 November 1971. The Irish newspaper's lead editorial said, "the crisis simply can not be solved by one man" but added that "at this juncture [Wilson] must be among the best-informed of the British politicians" on the issue.

[164] *Guardian*, 26 November 1971, p. 14.

[165] *Guardian*, 12 November 1971, p. 1.

[166] Tony Benn, *Office Without Power, Diaries 1968–72* (London, 1988), p. 387. Callaghan "was cross to have been upstaged by Harold on Ireland".

During the years in opposition, Europe gradually began to overtake Northern Ireland as the compelling issue that would allow Callaghan to complete his political recovery. Callaghan and Wilson, particularly after Jenkins's resignation as deputy leader, would eventually become inseparable not only in their policy towards Europe but later on Northern Ireland as well. In an insightful editorial, published three months before Jenkins's resignation, the *Guardian* noted the first signs of a sea change in the relationship between the two men. It editorialised that their "style of politics [had] become remarkably similar".[167] Tom McNally, who was a Labour Party official at the time and later became a senior adviser to Callaghan at the Foreign Office and at No. 10, agrees that it was during this period that Callaghan and Wilson grew closer than ever "partly because they were two well-travelled pragmatists who knew if they didn't hang together they certainly would hang separately".[168]

---

[167] *Guardian*, 31 December 1971, p. 10.
[168] Interview with Lord McNally, 17 July 2003.

8
Conclusion

Callaghan finally made it to No. 10 Downing Street in April 1976, after Harold Wilson unexpectedly resigned from office three weeks earlier, less than a year and a half after leading the Labour Party to victory in yet another general election in October 1974. Why, though, had Wilson quit? Was there another economic crisis on the horizon? Was the government's majority so small that it would be impossible to govern? There were rumours that he was facing health problems or an unfolding scandal. As time passed it became increasingly clear that Wilson, by then the longest-serving Labour Prime Minister in history, was simply tired; he had had enough and wanted to retire. He had even given his old rival Callaghan advance notice of his intentions. Callaghan, though, knowing Wilson, could never be certain that the resignation would actually happen, until it did.

Although Callaghan was four years older than Wilson, he was Wilson's preferred candidate when the Parliamentary Labour Party voted to elect its new leader, who would, of course, become Prime Minister on Wilson's departure from office. Roy Jenkins, who Callaghan had upstaged on the European issue, joined the leadership fight but received only 56 votes on the first ballot; that was less than Callaghan's 84 votes. Tony Benn received 37 votes, Denis Healey 30 votes and Tony Crosland 17. The stalwart of the left, Michael Foot, led them all on the first ballot with 90 votes. But it was obvious to Jenkins that as soon as the centre and centre-right coalesced, Callaghan would be the winner and the next Prime Minister. Jenkins pulled out of the race, clearing the way for Callaghan to be elected on the third ballot.

Jenkins's less than impressive showing in the leadership contest was not surprising; after he had resigned as deputy leader in 1972, he had never really regained his momentum in the party. The resignation that

Callaghan had indirectly fostered did great long-term damage to the Labour Party. Jenkins's departure over the European question and the fact that "the party [seemed] to have no desire to use his talents"[1] was one of the factors that led him eventually to quit the party altogether in 1981. Jenkins would become one of the founders of a new party, the Social Democrats, which would be a thorn in the side of Labour and contribute to its 18-year hiatus from governing after the 1979 defeat. Yet that was still far in the future; in 1973 and 1974, Europe, which had caused so much division within the Labour Party, became the issue that finally brought Callaghan and Wilson together. During the campaign for the February 1974 general election, which would return Labour to power within a minority government, Wilson and Callaghan were inseparable in their determination to do two things: to renegotiate the terms of entry into the European Economic Community (EEC) and then, once that was done, to give the electorate a chance to decide whether or not to remain in Europe.[2]

When Labour went back to the country in October 1974, its victory in that year's second general election slightly expanded its position by giving it an overall majority of three seats. By that time, Jenkins, as Home Secretary, "entirely" agreed with Foreign Secretary Callaghan's proposal to establish "a small working party" within the government that would report to the leader of the House of Commons, the Foreign Secretary and the Home Secretary on matters involving what was still being referred to as a "possible referendum",[3] even though by then it was inevitable that such a referendum would be held. Jenkins's agreement to that proposal was indicative of the change that had occurred.

In the new Wilson government, Callaghan was no longer the outsider. Years earlier, at the time of the great debate over trade union reform, Richard Marsh, the young up-and-coming Transport Minister who was sacked by Wilson over his opposition to *In Place of Strife*,

---

[1] Cambridge, Stewart 8/1/7. Entry in personal diary, 9 September 1972.

[2] PRO, FCO 30/2216, Folio 58. Letter to the Prime Minister from Frank Allaun, 29 September 1974. Allaun seemed to be concerned with a shift in the outlook of Callaghan and Wilson on the EEC in the run up to the October 1974 general election. Allaun told Wilson that "on Friday night when you answered questions on TV and much more so on Saturday night, when Jim talked about the way the EEC was improving under our influence, millions of viewers must have thought you were equivocating. People have since told me on the doorstep that they fear you have no intention of coming out."

[3] PRO, PREM 16/87. Letter to Antony Acland of the Foreign Office from S.G. Norris of the Home Office, 25 October 1974.

recalls that Callaghan "wasn't part of the group", most of whom were Oxford-educated and of similar class backgrounds.[4] By January 1975, Callaghan, Wilson, Jenkins and Barbara Castle, who was then Health Secretary, were operating in a different environment. Eric Varley, the Energy Secretary, told Alastair Hetherington that "Callaghan was very much more effective than he seemed to have been in the early days of the first Wilson government". In Varley's opinion, Callaghan was now the most influential member of the Cabinet, followed by Healey, who was then Chancellor, Jenkins and Crosland, who was Environment Secretary.[5] No longer was there the acrimony that had marked Callaghan's dealings with Jenkins and Castle over *In Place of Strife*.[6] Now that he was at the epicentre of the negotiations over Europe and Jenkins was neutralised, Callaghan no longer felt the compelling need, as he had on Northern Ireland, to have total command over all aspects of the debate.

Jenkins, among others in the party, had opposed the idea of having a referendum on Europe, hence the compromised wording during the two general election campaigns of 1974 that called for the matter to be put before the electorate but which failed to be specific about just how that would be done. Jenkins's initial opposition to such a move was not without merit. After all, there was no precedent in the British model for putting any issue, not even the premiership, directly to the voters. In the case of the referendum, however, the electorate was being asked not only to approve or disapprove of a major constitutional question, but to pass judgement on a matter that already had been decided in the Houses of Parliament. Only the thin smokescreen of Foreign Secretary Callaghan's renegotiation of the terms and the consultative nature of the 1975 referendum stood in the way of what would have been an unprecedented undermining of the sovereignty of Parliament had the electorate opted to withdraw from Europe.[7] That might explain why Callaghan resisted the idea of the Foreign Office playing the lead role

---

[4] Interview with Lord Marsh, 15 July 2003.
[5] BLPES, Hetherington 22/15. Notes from a meeting with Eric Varley, 27 January 1975.
[6] John Cole, *As It Seemed to Me: Political Memoirs* (London, 1996), p. 68. Cole implied that after 1974, Wilson no longer saw Callaghan "as a possible threat to his leadership".
[7] PRO, FCO 30/2117. Memo to Mr. Butler from I.F. Parker, Research Dept., 13 November 1974. It might not have been as risky a ploy as it seemed on the part of Callaghan and Wilson. An internal study of similar efforts by other nations revealed that if a government has "a clear idea of what they want and are ready to make the effort, the government calling the referendum are in a strong position also to call the tune".

in addressing any "constitutional" questions that might arise about the referendum in Parliament.[8]

The arrangement was not only awkward constitutionally, but "awkward" politically, as well, a point that George Thomson, one of the UK's two commissioners to the European Community, made to Hetherington in September 1974.[9] It was not inconsistent, however, with Callaghan's behaviour towards the institutions of government during the time of his political rehabilitation. In case after case, Callaghan took full advantage of the unique flexibility of the British model, at times stretching the system to its limits, to achieve his political goals. In June 1975 when voters overwhelmingly backed the government's renegotiated terms and voted to remain in Europe,[10] Wilson told Kenneth Stowe, the Cabinet secretary, that he had planned such a scenario all along.[11] Stowe says, "That was characteristically Wilson, working out how to undermine, outflank, outwit, overcome what he saw as a totally misplaced opposition."[12] But Benn wrote in November 1970, six months before Callaghan made his landmark speech on Europe, that among his colleagues in the shadow Cabinet only Callaghan had appreciated the political possibilities that Benn's idea of a referendum might provide. Benn quoted Callaghan as saying, "Tony may be launching a little rubber life raft which we will all be glad of in a year's time."[13]

The way Callaghan orchestrated the renegotiation of the terms of entry into the EEC and the subsequent referendum was the convergence of his efforts to rebuild his reputation. It was typical Callaghan. Despite all of the meetings and speeches, in the end the renegotiation "proved to be a perfunctory affair. The original terms of entry were modified in no substantial respect ... "[14] In an ironic twist, once

---

[8] PRO, PREM 16/87. Letter to N. Stuart, private secretary, from P.J. Weston, Foreign Office, 1 November 1974.

[9] BLPES, Hetherington 22/28. Notes from a discussion between Hetherington and George Thomson, 13 September 1974. Thomson feared that if Labour "won an outright majority (in the October 1974 election) some of the unions and the anti-marketeers would be trying to pin Harold down on points on which they were suspicious".

[10] Callaghan and Wilson forged a powerful leadership alliance by endorsing the re-negotiation. Over 68 per cent of British voters favoured remaining in the EEC.

[11] Interview with Sir Kenneth Stowe, 12 May 2004.

[12] Ibid.

[13] Benn, *Office Without Power, Diaries 1968–72*, p. 316.

[14] F.S. Northedge, "Britain and the EEC: Past and Present" in *Britain and the EEC: Proceedings of Section F (Economics) of the British Association for the Advancement of Science, Liverpool 1982*, edited by Roy Jenkins (London, 1983), p. 26.

the renegotiation was completed, it was Callaghan who Wilson marshalled to oversee the implementation of the extraordinary strategy that would allow ministers to – on this one occasion – abstain from collective Cabinet responsibility and campaign for or against the initiative over whether to remain in the EEC.[15] While Grosvenor Square proved Callaghan's rehabilitation was possible and the opposition to *In Place of Strife* reasserted his dominant role in the Cabinet, paving the way for his great public successes in Northern Ireland, the way he manipulated the European question made him the only logical successor to Wilson.

Kenneth Morgan argues that Callaghan "felt thoroughly at home with the comfortable conventions of an unwritten constitution".[16] But it was more than that. Callaghan's manoeuvring showed how the unique flexibility of the British political system, with its lack of a formal written constitution and its dependence on convention, is especially reliant on the goodwill of those in power. Although historians often comment on Callaghan's breach of collective Cabinet responsibility over the reform of industrial relations, there were numerous occasions when he violated that principle, directly or indirectly, in the determination to rebuild his political reputation after he had been forced to resign from the Treasury. That had certainly been the case when his remarks outside Cabinet led to an internal crisis in December 1967 over whether or not to supply arms to South Africa. It was true as well when in May 1968, as Home Secretary, he had broken with official Cabinet policy and, in a speech before the Fire Brigades Union, called for an end to the prices and incomes policy, which oversaw trade union wage settlements. It was the case a year later, in May 1969, when he suddenly changed the position that he had agreed to within Cabinet and denounced the interim Industrial Relations Bill before the joint NEC-Cabinet meeting at Downing Street.

Even Callaghan's behaviour in dealing with the crisis over Northern Ireland demonstrated a willingness to violate if not the letter, then certainly the spirit of that convention. Although the Cabinet was on holiday in August 1969 and had handed emergency powers to Callaghan, Wilson, Healey and if available, Michael Stewart, the Foreign Secretary, to deal with any crisis in their wake, that still does not fully explain why a senior minister like Castle, then First Secretary, should learn

---

[15] BLPES, Orme 1/4. Note from the Prime Minister on Cabinet Procedure on Membership of the EC, 3 April 1975.
[16] Morgan, *Callaghan: A Life*, p. 760.

of the commitment of British troops to Northern Ireland through the newspapers. It demonstrates, as did Callaghan's repeated clashes with Healey on Northern Ireland, a willingness to undermine the principle of collective responsibility to satisfy one man's appetite to advance his own political ambitions.

If there had been any doubt about Callaghan's determination to use Northern Ireland to rehabilitate himself, it was allayed by the highly political nature of his book on the subject, which was published less than six months before the February 1974 general election. Here as well, Callaghan strained the conventions governing ministerial disclosures, which contributed to the frustration and indignation of a cadre of senior civil servants. Unlike Jenkins, who had testified before the Franks Commission in February 1972 calling for a less restrictive approach to the rules on ministerial memoirs,[17] Callaghan urged the perpetuation of the status quo. Yet while he was testifying that "the law must apply to all",[18] he was preparing to make disclosures in his book on Northern Ireland that would teeter on the edge of acceptability within the established conventions.

In addition, the disclosures in that book raise questions about just how committed Callaghan was to finding a solution in Northern Ireland. Bernard Donoughue, the head of the Policy Unit at Downing Street, says that when Callaghan was Prime Minister he "didn't want any clever initiatives or things like that.... He decided [the Northern Irish question] was insoluble".[19] But it would seem that Callaghan of all modern-day Prime Ministers would have been especially well suited for the challenge. So why was so little progress made during his premiership? Also, political considerations aside, how could an individual who had presented himself as passionate about solving the crisis in Northern Ireland, endorse an initiative to sharply increase the representation of the Ulster Unionists in the British Parliament?[20] It was a decision that even his friend Merlyn Rees found distasteful. Rees wrote that taking

---

[17] PRO, HO 292/26. Minutes from a meeting of the Departmental Committee on Section 2 of the Official Secrets Act of 1911, 15 February 1972.

[18] PRO, HO 292/26. Minutes from a meeting of the Departmental Committee on Section 2 of the Official Secrets Act of 1911, 7 December 1971. Callaghan testified that "it does not matter whether they are ministers or whether they are civil servants or members of the press".

[19] Interview with Lord Donoughue, 9 July 2003.

[20] The Ulster Unionists expanded their representation to 18 seats from 12 seats, a move that was orchestrated to ensure the Callaghan government's survival in 1977.

such a move at a time "when power sharing in the province was the main issue [of contention with the Catholics] was to show a lack of understanding of the split nature of society in Northern Ireland".[21]

Yet the constant strain Callaghan put on the internal workings of Cabinet government in his long journey to Downing Street was in stark contrast to the reverent way that he dealt with the Labour Party. Throughout the entire time of his political rehabilitation, Callaghan never positioned himself ahead of what the party would tolerate on any given issue.[22] While Attlee had kept the party's National Executive Committee (NEC) from involvement in the day-to-day implementation of policy, he had recognised the NEC's "constitutional" role to set the agenda within a Labour government. Therefore when the party presented its manifestos at the annual conferences, they were not simply a loosely constructed list of future aspirations. Instead, they represented the guidelines within which a Labour government would function. It was within those parameters that Callaghan operated as well, and that is confirmed by his unwillingness to deviate too much from the party line.[23] The response that Callaghan gave to a BBC interviewer in October 1973, when asked for his opinion about the public financing of campaigns, was typical of his response to so many other issues over the course of his career: "I wouldn't want to go ahead of public opinion on the matter, and public opinion isn't ripe for it yet."[24]

Despite Callaghan's bluff manner in the Cabinet, the truth is that Castle and Jenkins were actually more authoritarian than Callaghan in their approach towards governance vis-à-vis the Labour Party. They were less impeded by the special relationship that existed between the Labour

---

[21] Merlyn Rees, *Northern Ireland: A Personal Perspective* (London, 1985), p. 322.

[22] Interview with Lord Brooks, 16 July 2003. Callaghan reverence for the party extended from the National Executive right down to the meetings of the constituency in Wales. He was constantly juggling his appointments when he was a Cabinet minister to avoid missing Labour party events in his constituency. The constituency provided the lifeblood for his political survival and Callaghan had a great appreciation for that fact, even scheduling his overseas travels as Foreign Secretary to avoid missing a key event in the constituency. That contrasts with the much more casual attitude towards constituency matters taken by Jenkins. (Giles Radice, *Friends and Rivals*, p. 81.)

[23] Mikardo, *Back-Bencher*, p. 183. However, the Labour MP Mikardo, who was part of the party's left wing, felt that Wilson and Callaghan, particularly in opposition, were "shifting decision-making from annual conference and the NEC to the shadow Cabinet, or even the Leader's office".

[24] British Library, Sound Archive, T635WC1, BBC Radio 4 programme. A conversation with the new chairman of the Labour party, 4 October 1973.

Party and a Labour government; hence Castle moved too far ahead of the party on trade union reform, and Jenkins jumped ahead of the party in the debate over Europe.[25] Callaghan took great liberties as Home Secretary, particularly in blocking the entry of Kenyan Asians into the country and in committing troops to Northern Ireland. In both cases he was operating on questionable constitutional grounds at least initially, but in neither case had he challenged the position of the National Executive or the party conference.

To demonstrate just how important the party was to Callaghan, he had been in utter despair after he briefly lost his seat on the National Executive to Benn in 1962.[26] Not only that, but apparently his bid for the treasurer's job in 1967 was propelled by his fear that he was in danger of not being re-elected from the constituency section.[27] One of the great political differences between Callaghan and Jenkins was their approach to the Labour Party. Jenkins did not have that same deference for the powerful parallel role of the NEC. If he had, he never would have given up his seat and resigned as deputy leader over Europe.[28] Even George Brown, who eventually left the party,[29] was determined to remain on the National Executive after he broke with Wilson and angrily quit as Foreign Secretary in March 1968. The same was true of Ray Gunter when he resigned from the Cabinet a few months later. In fact, Brown and Gunter were able to harness their antagonism

---

[25] Harry Harmer, *The Longman Companion to the Labour Party 1900–1998* (London, 1999), p. 25. At the Labour Party conference in Blackpool in October 1968, Chancellor Jenkins and First Secretary Castle defied the wishes of conference, which had voted overwhelming in favour of eliminating a statutory incomes policy.

[26] Interview with John Cole, 25 February 2004.

[27] Interview with Lord Healey, 22 March 2004. Healey adds that at that time the party treasurer was a "tool" of the trade union leaders.

[28] BLPES, Dalton I/52, Folio 7. Callaghan's reluctance to enter the race for deputy leader in 1960 was tied to the fear that if he lost, he would lose his seat on the NEC.

[29] Brown lost his seat in Parliament in the 1970 general election. Brown, therefore, was forced to give up his position as deputy leader of the Labour Party and chairman of the party's powerful Home Policy Committee. Jenkins won the deputy leadership post, which Callaghan did not contest. Instead, Callaghan got himself elected chairman of the Home Policy Committee. Patrick Bell in the *Labour Party in Opposition, 1970–1974* (London, 2004), p. 98, says "Jenkins took the headlines the following morning, but it was Callaghan who, having chosen not to contest the deputy leadership, demonstrated a greater appreciation of where power was located in the Labour Party in opposition."

towards Wilson and, along with Callaghan, demonstrate the powerful parallel role of the NEC by defeating the Prime Minister's handpicked candidate for Labour Party general secretary in July 1968. That was a move that turned out to be especially helpful in Callaghan's bid to use the fight over *In Place of Strife* to set the stage for his political recovery.[30]

The fact that Callaghan's political rehabilitation was so deeply rooted in the intricacies of the constitutional relationship between the Labour Party and a Labour government had its effect on Wilson's dealings with the Labour Party as well. It gradually brought Wilson back into line on Labour Party matters. In the early days of the 1964 Labour government, the Prime Minister kept his distance from Labour Party headquarters and as a result the National Executive lost influence. In fact, the balance of power shifted so considerably that Ian Aitken of the *Guardian* wrote in 1966 that "the NEC, once the battlefield over which some of the most dramatic controversies in Labour Party history were fought, is now no more than a minor offshoot of the Downing Street command post".[31] That is confirmed by the tone of a memo that Marcia Williams sent to Wilson in June 1965 urging the Prime Minister to agree to do an extensive interview with Kenneth Harris of the *Observer*. She told Wilson it was "an excellent idea, particularly as the emphasis again will be on your own personality rather than the Labour Party". Wilson responded: "I [very] much agree".[32]

It was only after Callaghan, in the bid to regain a more prominent role for himself, helped to orchestrate the coup against Wilson's candidate for Labour Party general secretary that the tide began to change. In November 1968, Wilson and Harry Nicholas were at odds over the constitutional issue of whether ministers of the Crown could be brought before NEC subcommittees "and called to account on particular issues, e.g. those which form the subject of [Labour Party] conference decisions".[33] Nicholas's less-than-co-operative attitude so

---

[30] But Callaghan might have been less than generous towards Brown than his public persona revealed. In a review of Brown's memoirs, which appeared in *The Sunday Times* (28 March 1971, p. 38), John Grigg wrote that Brown had apparently lost his seat in Parliament as a result of Callaghan's "'gerrymander' over Parliamentary boundaries".

[31] Ian Aitken, "The Structure of the Labour Party", from *The Left, A Symposium Edited by Gerald Kaufman* (London, 1966), pp. 22–23.

[32] Oxford, Wilson c.1067. Memo to the Prime Minister from Marcia Williams, 24 June 1965.

[33] PRO, PREM 13/2474. Letter to the general secretary of the Labour party from the Prime Minister, 11 December 1968.

angered Wilson that he threatened to prohibit ministers from addressing the subcommittees.[34] The difficult relations between the Prime Minister and the National Executive deteriorated even further when the industrial relations plan was put to a vote on the eve of Wilson's peace mission to Africa, despite the Prime Minister's request for a postponement. Callaghan's vote against *In Place of Strife*, without a doubt, strengthened the hand of the NEC. After the joint NEC-Cabinet meeting at Downing Street, in which Callaghan denounced the short bill on industrial relations, Wilson and Castle not only missed the next NEC meeting, they failed to send the customary notes of regret.[35] Yet by the time the controversy erupted over Europe, Wilson fell into line with Callaghan's attitude of deference towards the National Executive.[36]

This change is evident from a conversation that Wilson had with Hetherington in December 1972, less than seven months after Jenkins's resignation and amid the escalating anti-EEC rhetoric on the eve of Britain's entry into the European Community. Wilson confided to Hetherington that there would be a better than 60 per cent chance of Britain remaining in the Common Market if a new Labour government had the opportunity to renegotiate the terms. Hetherington could not believe what he had just heard[37] because the tone of Wilson's public statements at the Labour Party conference in Blackpool had convinced him and others at the *Guardian* that Wilson was turning his back on Europe". In other words, the Callaghan-inspired anti-EEC rhetoric had reached such a crescendo that they thought that any ploy on Wilson's part about renegotiating the terms was really being sought not to keep Britain in the EEC but as "the most expedient way of getting us out of Europe".[38]

What is noteworthy about Callaghan's political rehabilitation is how limited a role Parliament played in it, particularly given that Callaghan was a gifted orator and had extraordinary command of the House.[39] He understood that great speeches were only one dimension in the

---

[34] PRO, PREM 13/2747. Letter to the general secretary of the Labour party from the Prime Minister, 15 February 1969.

[35] Minutes of a meeting of the Labour Party's National Executive Committee, 21 May 1969.

[36] However, by that time Wilson was no longer Prime Minister.

[37] BLPES, Hetherington 20/34. Notes from a meeting between Hetherington and Wilson, 11 December 1972.

[38] Ibid.

[39] Interview with Leo Abse, 20 May 2003.

leadership struggle;[40] in that sense he recognised both the power and limitations of Parliament. Although a British government with a clear majority can make sweeping changes in governance, which would be nearly impossible in the systems of other Western democracies, the ability to manoeuvre within the House of Commons itself was constrained for someone like Callaghan. On the front bench, Wilson, Callaghan, Jenkins, Castle and Healey had to be part of a team. As we have seen, the Cabinet, however, was a much more private affair and a far more effective venue for undermining one's political rivals. There, messy deeds could be done without doing irreparable harm to one's public image. Callaghan's appreciation of that fact might explain his determination, when he finally became Prime Minister, to rid his Cabinet of undesirables.

One of Callaghan's first acts as Prime Minister was to call Castle into No. 10 and request her resignation from the Cabinet. He told her that she, although nearly the same age as he, needed to make way for a younger person. He also cleverly eliminated Jenkins, not by requesting his resignation, which would have been unthinkable, but by passing over Jenkins for the vacancy created at the Foreign Office by his own elevation to the premiership. Instead of appointing Jenkins, the logical successor given that he had held two of the other great offices of state and had broad interest in Europe, Callaghan named Crosland. Crosland was indifferent on Europe, had had little knowledge of foreign affairs and had fared far worse than Jenkins in the leadership contest. It was a decision that must have been particularly galling to Jenkins and must have seemed like the settling of old scores. Not long after, Jenkins left the government to become President of the European Commission. With Wilson, Jenkins and Castle gone, would Callaghan's final arrival at No. 10 Downing Street now merely represent a pyrrhic victory for Labour?

Looking back, it is amazing how Callaghan's conformity in one area of public life – the Labour Party – permitted his lack of conformity in another, namely the Cabinet. It is amazing, too, how many misconceptions exist about Callaghan's political career, misconceptions that Callaghan and those around him fostered. He was thought to be a man who took political risks, whether it be in dealing with the student protesters in London or the Troubles in Northern Ireland, yet every

---

[40] Interview with Lord Hattersley, 1 March 2004. Roy Hattersley feels that one of Jenkins's mistakes was that he had felt that he could make his way to No. 10 on the back of his impressive oratory in Parliament.

one of his political moves was carefully calculated.[41] He was thought to be a man who had no strong identification with the press, yet the relationship he had with the *Guardian* had considerable impact in re-establishing his reputation. He was thought *not* to be a deep thinker, yet he had a more profound understanding of the political system in which he was operating than most of his rivals. None of his rivals, not even Wilson, who was a more popular figure within the party, used the intricacies of the system to their political advantage as well as Callaghan had. That might explain why Crosland felt in 1972 that the only person who would be able to successfully lead a badly needed reform of the Labour Party's constitution was Callaghan.[42]

Callaghan was a man who held all four of the great offices of state. But he failed at one, the chancellorship, and used every opportunity in the second, the Home Office, and in his quest for the third, the Foreign Office, to undermine his rivals in the journey that eventually led him to the premiership. Callaghan's political recovery became the purpose of much of his career in public service and at times his allegiance to the Labour Party tested his loyalty to the government. Callaghan was a great political tactician, but more than likely only within the crises in which he found himself, whether it be the anti-Vietnam war protests at Grosvenor Square, *In Place of Strife*, the Troubles in Northern Ireland or the battle over Britain's entry into the EEC. While Callaghan always had an eye on No. 10, and there is always the possibility that he plotted and planned within a grand strategy, politics is so complex that one cannot ignore the other, far more likely possibility: that the pattern of his behaviour only revealed itself in hindsight, and that Callaghan – the great opportunist that he was – might never have seen the pattern himself.

---

[41] That aversion to risk was evident years later when he failed to call a general election upon his elevation to the premiership in 1976 or in the fall of 1978 when the Labour Party was particularly well suited to go to the country.

[42] BLPES, Hetherington 20/38. Notes from a luncheon meeting between Hetherington, Cole and Crosland, 4 December 1972.

Epilogue

It took many years, but Callaghan finally admitted that Britain might have been better off had the industrial relations reforms proposed by Wilson, Castle and, to a lesser extent, Jenkins been enacted in 1969. Callaghan's admission came after he had been Prime Minister and had experienced his own troubles with the trade unions. While he was out of the country, a wave of strikes in the winter of 1978–1979 intensified. With mountains of rubbish uncollected in city streets, hospitals understaffed and graves undug, the "Winter of Discontent" was a public relations disaster that signalled the beginning of the end of Callaghan's political career.

That spring Callaghan faced a vote of confidence in Parliament. He lost by a single vote that forced him to call a general election at a particularly inopportune time. It was that election in May 1979 that heralded the start of the Thatcher revolution. Ironically, the man who had been a hero to the Irish Catholic population of Northern Ireland in the summer of 1969 might not have lost that vote of confidence – and his ability to remain at Downing Street – had two Irish Catholic Members of Parliament joined in support of his government. Instead, they chose to abstain.

Appendix

10 April 1968

Dear Jim,

To your parting comments of yesterday, can I add one thing. We may disagree about the Immigrants Bill – and I sympathise with Audrey's action, for no doubt Miranda would do the same in similar circumstances – but I am far from unmindful of the debt the "Guardian" owes you from fifteen months ago. Not many people know of it, but it is a real one: you materially helped to secure the paper's survival. It's something that I shall never forget.

Yours,

ALASTAIR[1]

---

[1] BLPES, Hetherington 14/6. Copy of letter to Callaghan from Hetherington, 10 April 1968.

Glossary

Backbencher: A Member of Parliament who does not hold a post in the government and thus sits on the back benches in the House of Commons.

Buckingham Palace: The royal residence that all future and soon-to-be past prime ministers visit before moving in or out of No. 10 Downing Street, which is located a mile away. The role of the British monarch, while limited, is still an essential part of the transition of power and governance in general in the United Kingdom.

Cabinet: The executive body that emanates from Parliament and runs the country. It meets regularly at No. 10 Downing Street. Its members are usually from the majority party and hold seats in either the House of Commons, which is typical, or the House of Lords, which is less typical. Most ministers, except for the Prime Minister, are Secretaries of State responsible for administering departments of government. The size of the Cabinet, sometimes as many as two dozen members, is at the Prime Minister's discretion.

Chief Whip: The MP from the governing party who keeps the rest of the party in line in Parliament, and whose office is at No. 12 Downing Street. The proximity of the Chief Whip's office to that of the Prime Minister and the Chancellor of the Exchequer says a great deal about the importance of the post.

Downing Street: The small cul-de-sac, home to the Prime Minister and the Chancellor, that is located off Whitehall, a main street lined with government buildings that extends from Trafalgar Square to the Houses of Parliament. The term Whitehall is synonymous with the administration of government, just as Westminster is synonymous with Parliament.

House of Commons: The only democratically elected legislative body that represents the whole of the United Kingdom, with members from the nations of England, Scotland and Wales and the province of Northern Ireland. The Prime Minister has an office in the Commons as well as in Downing Street.

House of Lords: While the Lords can review and delay bills, it is less likely to initiate legislation. Its members are appointed by the sovereign on the recommendation of the Prime Minister. Members of the Lords are either hereditary peers, whose seats are passed down from their heirs, or life peers, whose seats are fixed for a single life term. Peers, unlike MPs, do not represent a constituency.

Member of Parliament: The term refers only to the 650 or so individuals elected to the House of Commons, not to members of the House of Lords, who are ennobled. The length of a member's term of office coincides with that of a Prime Minister, which can be as long as five years. An MP need not live in the constituency from which he or she is elected.

Palace of Westminster: The formal name for the Houses of Parliament, which include the House of Commons and the House of Lords. The gothic structure with its famous clock tower at one end is located on the embankment of the Thames, a five-minute walk from Downing Street.

Parliamentary Secretary: One of dozens of government jobs that a Prime Minister hands out to the party's MPs, some at the junior ministerial level. It can be a first step to a Cabinet appointment. More often than not it is a reward for good behaviour and helps to ensure the Prime Minister has a solid block of support in Parliament.

Permanent Secretary: Senior civil servants who head various departments and are responsible for the day-to-day operations of government, hence the "permanent", non-political nature of the post. Since the Prime Minister does not have a department, there is no permanent secretary assigned to Downing Street. But the mandarin who is – the Cabinet secretary – is more often than not the most influential civil servant of all.

Shadow Cabinet: A group of the most influential members of Her Majesty's Loyal Opposition, the largest opposition party in Parliament. The shadow Cabinet sits on the Front Bench, opposite the government in the House of Commons. Shadow ministers are briefed in preparation for the moment when the government loses office and vacates No. 10 Downing Street. There is a shadow Chancellor, a shadow Home Secretary, etc., but no shadow Prime Minister. That individual is referred to as the Leader of the Opposition.

Smith Square: The location at one time or another of the central offices of Britain's main political parties – the Conservatives, Labour and the Liberals. The square near Parliament and less than a mile from Downing Street was also home to the Transport and General Workers Union for much of the twentieth century and, for a shorter time, the Trades Union Congress.

Bibliography

I. Primary sources

1. Public papers

British Parliamentary Papers, 1966–1975 (Institute of Historical Research).

Public Records of the United Kingdom, Public Records Office at Kew, Surrey. *(The documents most often cited include those from the Cabinet Office [CAB], the Prime Minister's Office [PREM], the Home Office [HO], the Foreign and Commonwealth Office [FCO], the Ministry of Employment and Productivity [LAB] and the Northern Ireland Office [CJ], although the papers of the Treasury, the Ministry of Defence and other ministries were consulted as well.)*

Public Records of the Republic of Ireland, National Archives in Dublin. *(The series most often cited include the records of the Department of Foreign Affairs [DFA], the Department of the Taoiseach [TAOIS], and papers from overseas embassies [EMB], notably London, Brussels and Lagos.)*

Minutes of the British Labour Party's National Executive Committee.

Transcripts and other written documentation of radio and television programming, BBC Written Archives at Caversham, near Reading, UK.

2. Private collections, manuscripts

Lord Brown papers (Special Collections and Western Manuscripts, Bodleian Library at Oxford University).

Lord Callaghan papers (Special Collections and Western Manuscripts, Bodleian Library at Oxford University).

Anthony Crosland diaries and papers (British Library of Political & Economic Science).

Hugh Dalton papers (British Library of Political & Economic Science).

Michael Foot papers (Labour History Archive & Study Centre, Manchester).

Guardian Collection (John Rylands Library, Manchester). *Note: Some of the material in this collection, which is referred to in the footnotes as (Manchester) Guardian Archive, is typed carbon copies of notes, the originals of which are in the Hetherington papers referred to below. However, some hand-written notations appear in one collection that do not appear in the other.*

Guardian News & Media Archive (London). *Note: This collection includes information on the business side of the newspapers' operations.*

Judith Hart papers (Labour History Archive & Study Centre, Manchester).

Eric Heffer papers (Labour History Archive & Study Centre, Manchester).

Alastair Hetherington papers (British Library of Political & Economic Science).

Gerald Kaufman papers (Churchill College, Cambridge University).

Jack Lynch papers (National Archives, Dublin).

Lord Merlyn-Rees papers (British Library of Political & Economic Science).

LSE Oral History Series (British Library of Political & Economic Science).
Lord Orme of Salford papers (British Library of Political & Economic Science).
Peter Shore papers (British Library of Political & Economic Science).
John Silkin papers (Churchill College, Cambridge University).
Jean Stead papers (Guardian News & Media Archive).
Lord Stewart papers (Churchill College, Cambridge University).
Lord Wigg papers (British Library of Political & Economic Science).
Harold Wilson papers (Special Collections and Western Manuscripts, Bodleian Library at Oxford University).

3. Interviews with author

Leo Abse, 20 May 2003 (London).
Lord Allen of Abbeydale, 19 May 2003 30 July 2003 (Englefield Green, Surrey).
Tony Benn, 21 July 2003 (London).
Lord Brooks, 16 July 2003 (House of Lords).
Lord Christopher, 2 March 2004 (House of Lords).
John Clare, 19 April 2004 (Lobby of the *Daily Telegraph*).
John Cole, 25 February 2004 (London School of Economics).
Liam Cosgrave, 1 October 2004 (Royal Dublin Society, Dublin).
Lord Croham, 3 May 2004 (South Croydon, Surrey).
Susan Crosland, 13 November 2004 (London).
Sir Brian Cubbon, 19 June 2003 (London School of Economics).
Lord Donoughue, 9 July 2003 (House of Lords).
Paul Foot, 23 April 2004 (Offices of the *Private Eye* in London).
Geoffrey Goodman, 23 February 2004 (London School of Economics).
Joe Haines, 25 March 2004 (Tunbridge Wells, Kent).
Lord Hattersley, 1 March 2004 (London).
Lord Healey, 22 March 2004 (Alfriston, East Sussex).
Anthony Howard, 12 March 2004 (London).
Lord Hunt, 16 March 2004 (London).
Lady Jay, 3 March 2004 (Westminster).
Peter Jay, 11 December 2003 (London).
Lady Jenkins, 21 April 2004 (London).
Jack Jones, 18 June 2003, 10 December 2003, 5 May 2004 (Transport House).
Gerald Kaufman, MP, 18 December 2003 (House of Commons).
Sir Tom McCaffrey, 3 July 2003 (Great Bookham, Surrey).
Lord McNally, 17 July 2003 (House of Lords).
Lord Marsh, 15 July 2003 (House of Lords).
Lord Morgan, 30 March 2004 (House of Lords).
Roland Moyle, 6 May 2004 (London School of Economics).
Lord Murray, 20 April 2004 (House of Lords).
Sir Michael Palliser, 31 July 2003 (London).
Lord Merlyn-Rees, 1 July 2003 (House of Lords).
Lord Rodgers, 23 March 2004 (House of Lords).
Sir Kenneth Stowe, 12 May 2004 (London).
Lord Taverne, 1 April 2004 (House of Lords).
Alan Watkins, 6 November 2003 (London).

II. Primary published sources

1. Newspapers, periodicals, broadcasts and polling data

Selected editions of *The Times, Guardian, Daily Mirror, Daily Telegraph, Daily Mail, Daily Express, Sun, Evening News, Evening Standard, Financial Times, The Sunday Times, Observer* and other British newspapers. (From collections held at the Library of Congress, Senate House in London and the British Library of Political & Economic Science.)

Selected editions of the *Irish Times, Irish Independent, Irish Press, Belfast Telegraph, Irish News & Belfast Morning News* as well as other newspapers from the Republic of Ireland and Northern Ireland (From collections held in the archives of the Dublin City Library and at the Library of Congress).

Tribune, The Economist, Listener, Spectator, Private Eye, the *New Statesman* (British Library of Political & Economic Science and the Library of Congress).

Selected recordings of Callaghan's speeches and broadcasts. (Sound Archives at the British Library.)

National Opinion Polls and Gallup Public Opinion Polls covering the public's reaction to major events during the years of Callaghan's political rehabilitation.

2. Diaries and memoirs

Abse, Leo, *Private Member* (London, 1973); *Margaret*: Daughter of Beatrice (London, 1989).

Benn, Tony, *Out of the Wilderness: Diaries 1963–67* (London 1987); *Office Without Power: Diaries 1968–72* (London, 1988); *Against the Tide: Diaries 1973–1977* (London, 1989); *Conflicts of Interest, Diaries 1977–1980* (London, 1990).

Brown, George, *In My Way* (London, 1971).

Callaghan, James, *Time and Chance* (London, 1987); *A House Divided: The Dilemma of Northern Ireland* (London, 1973).

Cairncross, Alec, *The Wilson Years: A Treasury Diary, 1964–1969* (London, 1997).

Castle, Barbara, *The Castle Diaries, 1964–70* (London, 1984); *The Castle Diaries, 1974–76* (London, 1980); *Fighting All the Way* (London, 1993).

Cole, John, *As It Seemed to Me: Political Memoirs* (London, 1996).

Crosland, Susan, *Tony Crosland* (London, 1982).

Crossman, Richard, *The Diaries of a Cabinet Minister*, Vol. I 1964–1966 (London, 1975); *The Diaries of a Cabinet Minister*, Vol. II 1966–1968 (London, 1976); *The Diaries of a Cabinet Minister*, Vol. III 1968–1970 (London, 1977); *The Backbench Diaries of Richard Crossman*, edited by Janet Morgan (London, 1981).

Donoughue, Bernard, *Prime Minister: The Conduct of Policy Under Harold Wilson and James Callaghan* (London, 1987); *The Heat of the Kitchen* (London, 2002).

Driberg, Tom, *Ruling Passions* (London, 1977).

Evans, Harold, *Good Times, Bad Times* (New York, 1984).

Faulkner, Brian, *Memoirs of a Statesman* (London, 1978).

Goodman, Geoffrey, *From Bevan to Blair* (London, 2003).

Gormley, Joe, *Battered Cherub: the Autobiography of Joe Gormley* (London, 1982).

Haines, Joe, *The Politics of Power* (London, 1977); *Glimmers of Twilight: Murder, Intrigue and Passion in the Court of Harold Wilson* (London, 2003).

Hastings, Max, *Barricades in Belfast: The Fight for Civil Rights in Northern Ireland* (New York, 1970).

Hattersley, Roy, *Who Goes Home? Scenes From a Political Life* (London, 1995).

Healey, Denis, *The Time of My Life* (London, 1989).

Heffer, Eric, *Never a Yes Man* (London, 1991).

Hetherington, Alastair, *Guardian Years* (London, 1981).

Ingham, Bernard, *Kill the Messenger* (London, 1991).

Jay, Douglas, *Change and Fortune* (London, 1980).

Jenkins, Roy, *A Life at the Centre* (London, 1991). Note: The U.S. edition, *A Life at the Center* (New York, 1991), has some different material from the London edition and was also used as a source.

Jones, Jack, *Union Man* (London, 1986).

King, Cecil, *The Cecil King Diary* (London, 1972); *The Cecil King Diary, 1970–1974* (London, 1975); *Strictly Personal* (London, 1969).

Longford, Frank, *The Grain of Wheat* (London, 1974).

Margach, James, *The Abuse of Power: The War Between Downing Street and the Media From Lloyd George to Callaghan* (London, 1978).

Marsh, Richard, *Off the Rails* (London, 1978).

Mason, Roy, *Paying the Price* (London, 1999).

Maudling, Reginald, *Memoirs* (London, 1978).

Mikardo, Ian, *Back-Bencher* (London, 1988).

Owen, David, *Time to Declare* (London, 1991).

Rees, Merlyn, *Northern Ireland: A Personal Perspective* (London, 1985).

Shinwell, Emanuel, *I've Lived Through It All* (London, 1973).

Short, Edward, *Whip to Wilson* (London, 1988).

Steel, David, *Against Goliath* (London, 1989).

Stewart, Michael, *Life and Labour* (London, 1980).

Thatcher, Margaret, *The Path to Power* (London, 1995).

Thomas, George, *Mr. Speaker: The Memoirs of the Viscount Tonypandy* (London, 1985).

Wigg, George, *George Wigg* (London 1972).

Williams, Marcia, *Inside No. 10* (London, 1972); as Marcia Falkender, *Downing Street in Perspective* (1983).

Wilson, Harold, *A Personal Record: The Labour Government, 1964–1970* (Boston, 1971); *Final Term: The Labour Government 1974–1976* (London, 1979).

Wyatt, Woodrow, *Turn Again, Westminster* (London, 1973).

III. Secondary sources

1. Books

Adonis, Andrew, and Thomas, Keith (eds.), *Roy Jenkins: A Retrospective* (Oxford, 2004).

Amis, Kingsley (ed.), *Harold's Years: Impressions from the New Statesman and the Spectator* (London, 1977).

Arthur, Paul, and Jeffrey, Keith, *Northern Ireland Since 1968* (Oxford, 1996).

Beckerman, Wilfred (ed.), *The Labour Government's Economic Record: 1964–1970* (London, 1972).

Bell, Patrick, *The Labour Party in Opposition, 1970–1974* (London, 2004).

Bew, Paul, and Patterson, Henry, *The British State and the Ulster Crisis, From Wilson to Thatcher* (London, 1985).

Buckland, Patrick, *A History of Northern Ireland* (New York, 1981).

Butler, David, and Kavanagh, Dennis, *The British General Election of February 1974* (New York, 1974).

Butler, David, and Kitzinger, Uwe, *The 1975 Referendum* (London, 1996).

Butler, David, and Pinto-Duschinsky, Michael, *The British General Election of 1970* (London, 1971).

Campbell, John, *Roy Jenkins: A Biography* (London, 1983).

Catterall, Peter (ed.), *The Northern Ireland Question in British Politics* (London, 1996).

Conroy, Harry, *Callaghan* (London, 2006).

Crosland, Anthony, *The Future of Socialism* (London, 1964).

Crossman, Richard, *Inside View: Three Lectures on Prime Ministerial Government* (London, 1972).

Dalyell, Tam, *Dick Crossman: A Portrait* (London, 1989).

Darby, John (ed.), *Northern Ireland: The Background to the Conflict* (Belfast, 1983).

Davies, Norman, *The Isles: A History* (Oxford, 1999).

Davis, William, *Three Years Hard Labour: The Road to Devaluation* (London, 1968).

Day, Robin, *But With Respect: Memorable Television Interviews with Statesmen and Parliamentarians* (London, 1993).

Dell, Edmund, *The Chancellors, A History of the Chancellors of the Exchequer, 1945–90* (London, 1996).

Derbyshire, J. Denis, and Derbyshire, Ian, *Politics in Britain From Callaghan to Thatcher* (Cambridge, 1988).

Ekwe-Ekwe, Herbert, *Conflict and Intervention in Africa: Nigeria, Angola, Zaire* (New York, 1990).

Ekwe-Ekwe, Herbert, *The Biafra War: Nigeria and the Aftermath* (New York, 1990).

Falola, Toyin, and Heaton, Matthew M., *A History of Nigeria* (Cambridge, 2008).

Feather, Victor, *The Essence of Trade Unionism* (London, 1963).

Foot, Paul, *The Politics of Harold Wilson* (London, 1968); *The Rise of Enoch Powell: An Examination of Enoch Powell's attitude on Immigration and Race* (London 1969).

Goodman, Geoffrey, *The Awkward Warrior: Frank Cousins, His Life and Times* (London, 1979); *Brother Frank: The Man and the Union* (London, 1969).

Harmer, Harry, *The Longman Companion to the Labour Party, 1900–1998* (London, 1999).

Harris, Kenneth, *The Prime Minister Talks to the Observer* (London, 1979).

Hetherington, Alastair, *News, Newspapers and Television* (Basingstoke, 1985).

Hoggart, Simon, and Leigh, David, *Michael Foot: A Portrait* (London, 1981).

Hollingsworth, Mark, *MPs for Hire: The Secret World of Political Lobbying* (London, 1991).

Hollowell, Jonathan (ed.), *Britain Since 1945* (Oxford, 2003).

Holmes, Martin, *The Labour Government, 1974–79: Political Aims and Economic Reality* (New York, 1985).

Howard, Anthony, *Crossman: The Pursuit of Power* (London, 1990).

Howard, Anthony, and West, Richard, *The Making of the Prime Minister* (London, 1965).

Jefferys, Kevin (ed.), *Labour Forces: From Ernest Bevin to Gordon Brown* (New York, 2002).

Jenkins, Peter, *The Battle of Downing Street* (London, 1970).

Jenkins, Roy, *Pursuit of Progress: A Critical Analysis of the Achievement and Prospect of the Labour Party* (London, 1953).

Jenkins, Roy (ed.), *Britain and the EEC: Proceedings of Section F (Economics) of the British Association for the Advancement of Science, Liverpool 1982* (London, 1983).

Jones, Bill, and Robins, Lynton (eds.), *Two Decades in British Politics, Essays to Mark 21 Years of the Politics Association, 1969–1990* (Manchester, 1992).

Kaufman, Gerald (ed.), *The Left: A Symposium Edited by Gerald Kaufman* (London, 1966).

Kavanagh, Dennis, and Seldon, Anthony, *Powers Behind the Prime Minister: The Hidden Influence of No. 10* (London, 1999).

Kellner, Peter, and Hitchens, Christopher, *Callaghan: The Road to Number 10* (London, 1976).

Loughlin, James, *The Ulster Question Since 1945* (New York, 2004).

Marshall, Geoffrey (ed.), *Ministerial Responsibility* (Oxford, 1989).

Morgan, Kenneth, *Callaghan: A Life* (Oxford, 1997); *Labour People* (Oxford, 1992).

Murphy, John A., *Ireland in the Twentieth Century* (Dublin, 1975).

Norton, Philip, *The British Polity* (New York, 1991).

O'Leary, Brendan, and McGarry, John, *The Politics of Antagonism: Understanding Northern Ireland* (London, 1993).

Palliser, Michael, *Britain and British Diplomacy in a World of Change* (London, 1975).

Pelling, Henry Mathison, *A Short History of the Labour Party* (London, 1978).

Perkins, Anne, *Red Queen: The Authorised Biography of Barbara Castle* (London, 2003).

Pilkington, Colin, *Issues in British Politics* (London, 1998).

Pimlott, Ben, *Harold Wilson* (London, 1992).

Radice, Giles, *Friends and Rivals: Crosland, Jenkins and Healey* (London, 2002).

Ramsden, John (ed.), *The Oxford Companion to Twentieth-Century British Politics* (Oxford, 2002).

Richards, S.G., *Introduction to British Government* (London, 1978).

Rose, Peter, *How the Troubles Came to Northern Ireland* (London, 2000).

Seldon, Anthony, *New Labour, Old Labour: the Wilson and Callaghan Governments, 1974–79* (London, 2004).

Sked, Alan, and Cook, Chris, *Post-War Britain: A Political History* (Middlesex, 1984).

Solomon, Robert, *The International Monetary System 1945–1976, an Insider's View* (New York, 1977).

Stremlau, John J., *The International Politics of the Nigerian Civil War 1967–1970* (Princeton, 1977).

Taylor, A.J.P., *British Prime Ministers and Other Essays* (London, 2000); *English History 1914–1945* (Oxford, 1966).

Watkins, Alan, and Alexander, Andrew, *The Making of the Prime Minister, 1970* (London, 1970).

Wilson, Trevor (ed.), *The Political Diaries of C.P. Scott 1911–1928* (Ithaca, 1970).

Winchester, Simon, *In Holy Terror: Reporting the Ulster Troubles* (London, 1974).

Young, John, W. *Britain and European Unity, 1945–1999* (New York, 2000); *The Labour Governments 1964–70, Vol. II, International Policy* (Manchester, 2003).

2. Journal articles

Alexander, Alan, "People, Polls and Parties: the British General Election of 1970", *Queen's Quarterly* (Canada), Vol. LXXVII, No. 3 (Autumn 1970), pp. 356–367.

Akinyemi, A.B., "The British Press and the Nigerian Civil War", *African Affairs*, Vol. 71, No. 285 (October 1972), pp. 408–426.

Bale, Tim, "Dynamics of a Non-Decision: The Failure to Devalue the Pound, 1964–70", *20th Century British History*, Vol. 10, No. 2 (1999), pp. 192–217.

Dell, Edmund, and Hunt, Lord, of Tanworth, "The Failings of Cabinet Government in Mid to Late 1970s", *Contemporary Record: The Journal of the Institute of Contemporary British History*, Vol. 8, No. 3 (Winter 1994), pp. 453–472.

Donoughue, Bernard, "Harold Wilson; the Life and Legacy of a Labour Prime Minister", *Labour History; the Journal of the Labour History Group* (Spring 2004), pp. 10–16; "The Prime Minister's Day: The Daily Diary of Wilson and Callaghan, 1974–79", *Contemporary Record: The Journal of the Institute of Contemporary British History*, Vol. 2, No. 2 (Summer 1988), pp. 16–19.

Fyvel, T.R., "The Dismissal of British Labour: A Political Letter", *Dissent* (November–December 1970), pp. 550–557.

Haines, Joe, "Wilson and the Press", *Labour History; the Journal of the Labour History Group* (Spring 2004), pp. 17–19.

Hansen, Randall, "The Kenyan Asians, British Politics and the Commonwealth Immigrants Act, 1968", *The Historical Journal*, Vol. 42, No. 3 (September 1999), pp. 809–834.

Morgan, Kenneth, "Labour Since 1945", *Contemporary Record: The Journal of the Institute of Contemporary British History*, Vol. 1, No. 4 (Winter 1988), pp. 5–10.

Newsinger, John, "Ulster and the Downfall of the Labour Government 1974–79", *Race and Class*, Vol. 33, No. 2 (October–December 1991), pp. 45–57.

Saggar, Shamit, "Re-Examining the 1964–70 Labour Government's Race Relations Strategy", *Contemporary Record: The Journal of the Institute of Contemporary British History*, Vol. 7, No. 2 (Autumn 1993), pp. 253–281.

Index

on (July 1971), 181–3; and
Jenkins, 183, 184–6; public's view
of, 188, 194; UK referendum on,
192, 194–5
Evening Standard, 27, 28, 43, 46 n., 81,
180

Faulkner, Brian, 174, 188
Fearless, HMS, 45, 49–50, 49 n., 64
Feather, Victor, 30, 75
Financial Times, 16, 119, 167 n., 180,
187
Fire Brigades Union, 19 n., 195
Fisk, Robert, 173 n.
Fleet Street, 7, 82, 112; preponderance
of titles, 7; press reaction to
Callaghan NEC vote, 57;
description of, 93; demand for
"exclusives", 115; and Northern
Ireland, 134; reporters collaborate
on sources, 187
Foot, Michael, 6, 11, 13, 77 n., 171,
191
Foot, Paul, 7 n.
Fowler, Norman, 25, 132
Franks Commission (1972), 196
Frost, David, 10–11, 12
Frost Programme, 10–11
Future of Socialism, 35

Gaitskell, Hugh, 3, 47 n., 99, 100, 122
Gardiner, Gerald, 24
general elections, 1964 (*Labour wins 4
seat overall majority*), 9; 1966
(*Labour's majority increases to 98
seats*), 97; 1970 (*Conservatives win
30 seat majority*), 27 n., 137, 150,
150 n., 156, 186, 186 n., 198 n.;
February 1974 (*hung parliament;
Labour forms government*), 168,
192; October 1974 (*Labour returns
with 3 seat majority*), 191, 192,
192 n., 194 n.; 1979 (*Conservatives
win 43 seat majority*), 192, 203
Ghana, 56
Gibbard, Les, 133, 179
Glasgow Herald, 69 n.
Goodman, Geoffrey, 43, 83, 93; letter
to Callaghan on industrial

relations, 83 n.; *Guardian*, assesses
influence of, 99, 143–4
Gormley, Joe, 60–1, 75
Gowon, Yakubu, 40 n., 41, 44, 53
Great Ormond Street Hospital for
Children, 105
Greenwood, Anthony, 29–30, 30 n.,
91
Grigg, John, 199 n.
Grosvenor Square (1968), 24–9; seen
as turning point for Callaghan,
24, 26; "startling" plot, *The
Times* warns of, 24, 26–7;
Callaghan's even-handed
approach praised, 25–6; civil
unrest, concerns over, 25; police
role, 25; press coverage criticised,
26–8; *Tribune* on, 26; Callaghan
cites "semi-hysteria", 27
Guardian, 93–123; Biafra talks, reports
breakthrough on, 47; only
national newspaper to oppose *In
Place of Strife*, 93–6; appeals to
younger readers, 98; circulation,
99; rejects merger with *The Times*,
99 n.; editorial independence of,
101–2; financial troubles of,
101–2, 107; moves news
operation from Manchester to
London, 101; earlier influence of,
102–3, 144–5; Kenyan Asians
crisis, seeks resignations over,
104–5; on Race Relations Bill,
105–7, 108–9; must not fail,
Wilson says, 108; breaks sexual
taboos, 118; opposes sending
troops to Northern Ireland, 124
see also Cole, Hetherington, Peter
Jenkins
Gunter, Ray, 42, 43, 75, 107; conspires
with Callaghan on Nicholas
appointment, 29–31, 198–9; on
Castle, 32; resigns, 33

Haile Selassie, 52
Haines, Joe, 70, 177; Callaghan
challenge, advises Wilson on,
41–4; and *Guardian*, 53–4, 116 n.;
Callaghan, describes approach of,

Stonham, Victor, 132
Stormont, 128, 133, 136, 140 n., 152
Stowe, Kenneth, 39 n., 194
Sun, 7, 41, 44, 77, 99
The Sunday Times, 7, 14, 62 n., 74
Sunningdale agreement (1973), 153–4, 154 n.

Tanzania, 40 n., 50
Taverne, Dick, 6
Tebbit, D.C., 55
television, impact of, 27, 41, 118, 133–4, 136
Terry, Walter, 46 n., 93, 178
Thatcher, Margaret, 1, 4, 94 n.
That Was The Week That Was (BBC), 68, 74
Thomas, George, 31 n.
Thomas, Hartford, 94 n.
Thomson, George, 43, 194
Thorpe, Jeremy, 177
The Times, 10–12, 15, 24–7, 47, 82, 99 n., 119, 122, 146, 170, 180
Torode, John, 94 n.
trade unions, 30 n.; sponsoring of MPs by, 84; historic role of, 88, 89; public support for, 89; Callaghan and, 90–1
Trade Unions Congress (TUC), 30, 74, 75, 90, 111 n.
Transport & General Workers Union (TGWU), 24, 32, 33, 37, 89, 90
Transport House, 7, 37
Trend, Burke, 138, 165–6; troop deployment, questions Callaghan view of, 148; Callaghan memoir, upset by, 157–9, 170–1
Tribune, 7 n., 11, 26–7, 31
Tubman, William, 56 n.

Ulster, *see* Northern Ireland
Ulster Unionists, 128, 162, 196
US Embassy (London), 25, 136

Varley, Eric, 193
Vietnam, 28, 28 n.
Vietnam war protests, *see* Grosvenor Square

Wadsworth, A.P., 102
Walker, David, 16
Watkins, Alan, 22, 29, 31, 112
Whitelaw, William, 144, 165–6, 167
Williams, Len, 30
Williams, Marcia, 69–71, 119 n.; Wilson, influence on, 30, 69–70, 199; Callaghan, warns of threat from, 50–3; Nigeria, asks Wilson to return early from, 50–1; Healey's assessment of, 52; Callaghan, opinion of, 65; Haines's assessment of, 65
Wilson, Harold, 18, 19, 58–61, 199; rejects devaluation (1964), 9; target of Peter Jay's column, 10–11, 13; "Pound in Your Pocket" speech, 12; and Chief Whip, 20, 85–6; public support for, 22 n.; Vietnam policy, 28; fight over party general secretary (1968), 30–1; promotes Castle to "super ministry", 31; Callaghan "grateful" to, 35; Callaghan disrupts Nigerian peace mission of, 38–9, 40–4, 48–56; joined Bevan in resigning from Attlee government (1951), 47 n.; and Marcia Williams, 65, 69; and interim Industrial Relations Bill, 67, 73, 75, 86–7, 91; seeks Callaghan pledge on collective Cabinet responsibility, 74; removes Callaghan from Inner Cabinet, 79–82; and Lords Reform Bill, 84–6; and *Guardian*, 96, 97, 99–100, 100 n., 103, 108, 109–10, 115, 119–20, 121, 122, 133; election as party leader (1963), 99–100; and *Daily Mirror*, 102 n.; Northern Ireland, meets Callaghan to discuss troop deployment to, 126; Northern Ireland, defers to Callaghan on, 131–2, 134–5, 136, 141–2; and Philip Allen, 146; Northern Ireland, assesses Maudling on, 149 n.; tea with Callaghan, 151; loses 1970 general election,